AF605978

BLACK THEOLOGY AND THE MENACE OF RACIAL APOCALYPSE

CYRIL ORJI

Black Theology and the Menace of Racial Apocalypse

Lonergan and Racial Reconciliation

UNIVERSITY OF TORONTO PRESS
Toronto Buffalo London

Toronto Buffalo London
utppublishing.com
Printed in the USA

ISBN 978-1-4875-5801-7 (cloth)
ISBN 978-1-4875-5804-8 (EPUB)
ISBN 978-1-4875-5803-1 (PDF)

Lonergan Studies

Library and Archives Canada Cataloguing in Publication

Title: Black theology and the menace of racial apocalypse : Lonergan and racial reconciliation / Cyril Orji.
Other titles: Lonergan and racial reconciliation
Names: Orji, Cyril, author
Series: Lonergan studies.
Description: Series statement: Lonergan studies | Includes bibliographical references and index.
Identifiers: Canadiana (print) 20250130939 | Canadiana (ebook) 2025013103X | ISBN 9781487558017 (cloth) | ISBN 9781487558048 (EPUB) | ISBN 9781487558031 (PDF)
Subjects: LCSH: Black theology – History. | LCSH: Racism. | LCSH: Lonergan, Bernard J.F. | LCSH: Theology.
Classification: LCC BT82.7 .O75 2025 | DDC 202.089/96–dc23

Cover design: Kristjan Buckingham
Cover images: Kristjan Buckingham

We wish to acknowledge the land on which the University of Toronto Press operates. This land is the traditional territory of the Wendat, the Anishnaabeg, the Haudenosaunee, the Métis, and the Mississaugas of the Credit First Nation.

University of Toronto Press acknowledges the financial support of the Government of Canada, the Canada Council for the Arts, and the Ontario Arts Council, an agency of the Government of Ontario, for its publishing activities.

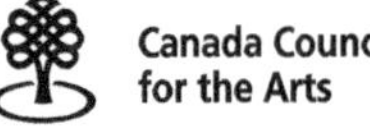

Funded by the Government of Canada | Financé par le gouvernement du Canada | Canada

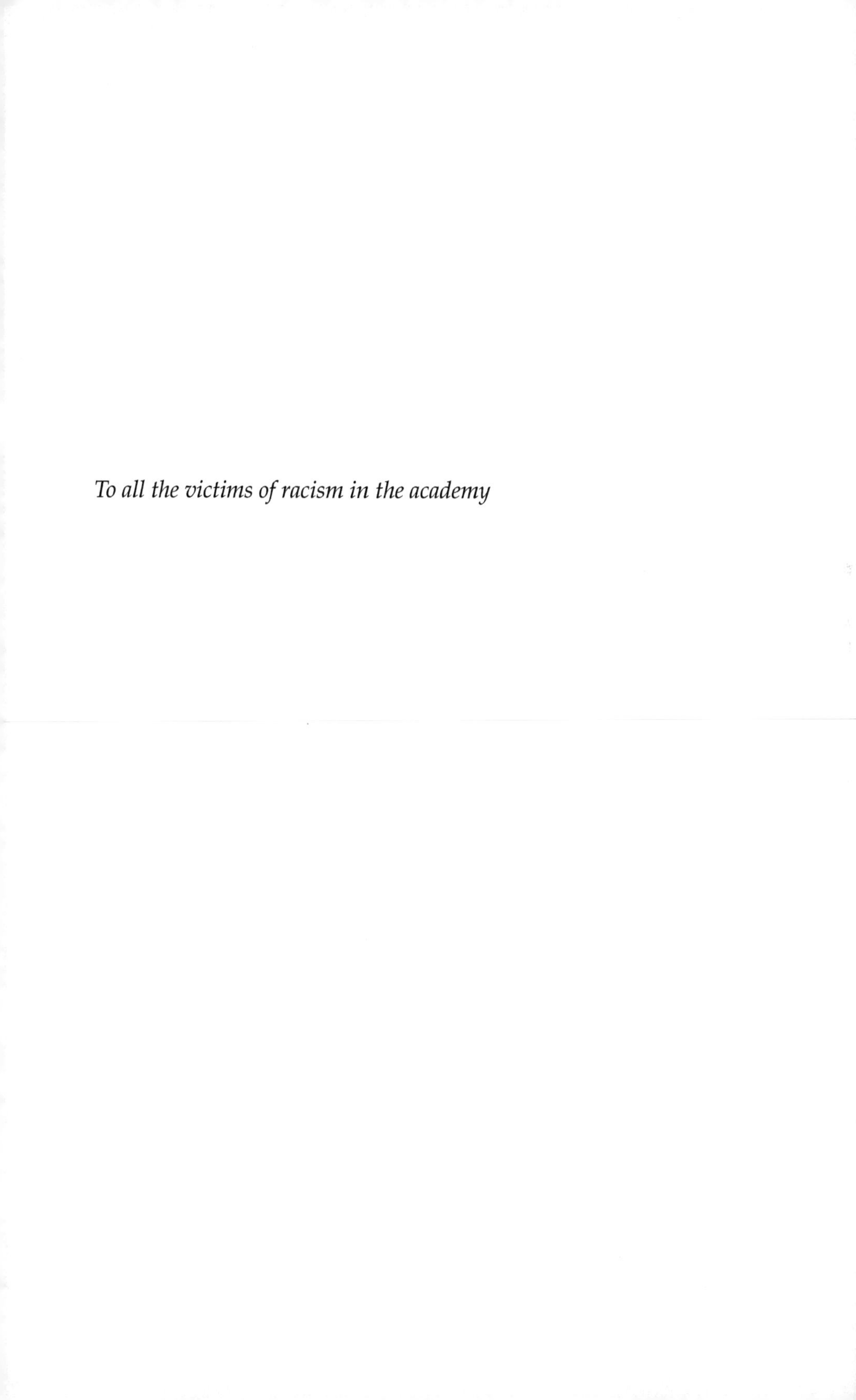

To all the victims of racism in the academy

Contents

Acknowledgments

"I sit on a man's back, choking him and making him carry me, and yet assure myself and others that I am sorry for him and wish to lighten his load by all means ... except by getting off his back."

– Leo Tolstoy

Racism feeds on a system that enables it. This book about racism and its various avatars is also about how God is in the story. The fine points are about the grace that God gives to undo evil and the good that God brings out of evil because that is the nature of our omnipotent God. The academy, at least in the United States, was never designed with Black people in mind. Many fine professors of colour are quitting, for reasons that border on what Leo Tolstoy described so well in the quotation above. These professionals are frustrated because they do not see a future for themselves in the academy. It is to these people I have dedicated this book. James Baldwin's insights and ideas shape aspects of this book. He alluded to the problems people of colour face on a daily basis. The academy historically has never been a friendly landscape for Black people. It takes faith to understand that when you are Black and successful in the academy, God must be at the root of it. It is God who alone arrests the terrors of the night and the arrows that fly by day (Ps.91:5), who provides the moral authority and the prophetic vision of this work.

On the human side, I could not have written this book without the support of many colleagues and their encouragement. Any time an author writes a book, there are people behind the scenes who contribute in various ways to the finished product. Some of my chapters were written during my fellowship year at Boston College in 2020. My friends at the Lonergan Center at Boston College have always been rock solid in their support – Pat Byrne, Fred Lawrence, and Mary Elliot and all the good people there. My thanks also to the 2020 class of fellows whose critique and valuable feedback were indeed helpful when I presented the chapters at weekly seminars.

My thanks to the University of Toronto Press (UTP), especially Stephen Shapiro. When I proposed the idea of the book Mr. Shapiro was enthusiastic and supportive and remained so throughout the entire process. His support and encouragement have been invaluable. How can I forget the anonymous reviewers of the manuscript? Although they remain anonymous, without them the book would never be what it is. They pushed and challenged me and led me to sources that otherwise would never have been within my reach. The present ordering of the chapters is slightly different from the original arrangement – again, thanks to the suggestions of the reviewers. In my letter to UTP during the review process, I noted my heartfelt thanks for the thoughtfulness UTP put into choosing the reviewers of my manuscript. If I may quote from my letter, "They have indeed enriched my manuscript. If there's a time one can call a peer-review process 'successful,' this is one good instance. Although they remain anonymous, I will forever be indebted to them because they provided useful insights and pushed and challenged me in positive ways." There are many other creative, like-minded people at UTP who worked tirelessly behind the scenes to bring this manuscript to completion. I cannot thank them enough for their dedication to the project. One name I cannot omit is UTP's copy editor, Evelyn Mackie. Her professionalism and eagle-eyed vision is indeed first class.

Lastly, but not least, thanks to another kind-hearted person the good Lord directed my way during the writing process, Heather Jannetta. It was a moment of epiphany when I discovered the passion for racial reconciliation of this Baldwin-enthusiast. I was fine-tuning the manuscript when Eddie Glaude's *Begin Again: James Baldwin's America and Its Urgent Lessons for Our Own* (2020) came out. She thought engaging with Glaude's work would help me make some fine connections and hurriedly sent me a copy. She was absolutely right. While the labours of these good people have enriched my manuscript, I remain solely responsible for any shortcomings.

Preface

Racism takes centerstage in Black Theology because racism is an existential reality that inevitably confronts the Black person in their existential situation. This book is my own modest attempt to wrestle with the new forms of racism that have come to light in the wake of the coronavirus pandemic of 2020. The pandemic was coterminous with the death of George Floyd, the unarmed Black man killed in police custody in Minneapolis, Minnesota (25 May 2020). It was not by happy accident that a public health issue and racial discourse collided in these events. For Black people in America, the two have always been intertwined. The National Advisory Commission of Civil Disorders, known as the Kerner Commission, pointed out in 1968 that the reason our nation was moving toward two societies, one Black, one white – separate and unequal, was due to a conglomeration of events, including "poor health and sanitation conditions in the ghetto" and a culture of prejudice or racism.[1] Racism is part of the grand ideology of the classical control of meaning. Black Theology is a Christian protest against racism in Church and society and is part of the modern mediation of meaning. The kind of meaning Black Theology mediates runs counter to classical expectations.[2] Unfortunately, Black Theology has far too often been misunderstood. There would be as many white people who would be upset with me for choosing to write about racism as there would be Black people upset with me for intruding or bringing, in their words, "a white theologian" (Bernard Lonergan) into Black Theology. I will address this matter squarely in the introduction. But it is enough to say here that the conundrum itself speaks to the larger matter of misunderstanding the act of insight. The act of insight is about understanding correctly what is there to be understood. Half measures are of no use. Therefore, I urge such critics to suspend judgment until they have read to the last line of the last page of the last chapter of this book. They will discover that

Black Theology is a locus of encounter, dialogue, and insight. We need not be reminded that the occurrence of insight, as Lonergan carefully pointed out, is not restricted to the minds of mathematicians and the mind of physicists alone. And I add that the occurrence of insight is not restricted to the minds of mainstream theologians or Black theologians with sympathetic ties to the Black power movement of the civil rights era either. On the contrary, "one meets intelligence in every walk of life."[3] Intelligence, whenever or wherever it occurs, Lonergan writes, "is marked by a greater readiness in catching on, in getting the point, in seeing the issue, in grasping implications, in acquiring knowhow."[4]

I write primarily for Black people and ethnic minorities who have been stigmatized as coloured. As victims, they understand racism far better than those who benefit from it or who study it for intellectual satisfaction. Oppression is best grasped from the vantage point of the oppressed. This is not necessarily because the oppressed possess the truest understanding of racial oppression, but because when you are born Black and by this accident of birth (to employ a baseball metaphor) have three strikes against you even before you discover who you are, racial discourse for you cannot just be academic. In her well-researched work, *Biased: Uncovering the Hidden Prejudice That Shapes What We See, Think, and Do* (2019), the Harvard-educated African American professor of psychology at Princeton, Jennifer Eberhardt, tells the story of how she walked into an auditorium filled with Oakland Police officers. At the time, she was working as the chair of the federal oversight team investigating civil rights violations by members of the Oakland Police Department. She was trying to share her team's findings with the officers and "to help the officers understand the insidious ways in which implicit bias could act on human decision making."[5] Not only was her message met with an instant resistance, she soon realized that the same officers she was about to train have been conditioned by racial images to perceive a Black man on the street as dangerous and a threat and also conditioned to think of a Black woman as incapable of being an expert in her field. Realizing how racialized and gendered implicit bias is, Eberhardt recounts how she soon came to the realization that she was facing a hostile crowd at every step of the way and how the realization made her shift her teaching from the data she was collecting in her research to her everyday life experience. Critical analysis of race must begin from the objective experiences of the oppressed and racialized people of colour in order to understand the dynamics of structural power relations.[6] I write secondarily for those who may be motivated to support racial justice and racial reconciliation. I do that only for consciousness raising. I place my bet on the new generation of American youth. The way they rallied, organized marches, protested, and more importantly, the way they expressed outrage at the killing of George Floyd shows that transformation of consciousness is still a real possibility. It is crucial that white subjects buy into racial justice and racial reconciliation, since they possess arguably the greatest form of investment in race. The dilemma, however, is that they have the most to give up in terms of material resources.[7] Not everyone understands racism, including those motivated to support racial justice. This can make the discourse on racial analysis very difficult and uneasy. There is no denying that whites, as a social group, maintain supremacy in almost all facets of social life.[8] But equally true is the fact that "Whiteness, as a set of normative cultural practices, is visible most clearly to those it definitively excludes and those to whom it does violence."[9] A major problem in discourse on racial analysis is navigating the thin line between tapping into a white subject's desire for racial justice and the psychological dissonance it produces in not being able to accept the about-face that comes from giving up certain privileges that have long been taken for granted. This is the double bind at work in racial discourse.[10] It is not easy to let go of the defensiveness, of what has been termed "white fragility," and face up to the truth of the experiences of those who have been disadvantaged and hurt.[11] But my belief that divine grace is still at work in the face of human obtuseness remains unshaken.

BLACK THEOLOGY AND THE MENACE OF RACIAL APOCALYPSE

Lonergan and Racial Reconciliation

Introduction

The aim of this work is to engage in conversation two different kinds of discourse, Black Theology and the theology of Bernard Lonergan, in an attempt to further contemporary global discourse on racism. Lonergan's philosophical notion of bias (a catchword for demeaning ideologies that include bigotry, alienation, and prejudice) and its theological antidote, conversion (a technical term for how to foster reconciliation and ecclesial repentance, among others), are a goldmine waiting to be tapped by Black Theology. It is becoming trite to have to address why one would employ theological categories derived from a so-called "white Western thinker" in Black Theology. Not only is the question badly framed, its suppositions are absurd. The question is reminiscent of the kind of questions James Cone was forced to confront in the early days of his own experiment with Black Theology. He was asked whether his sources were Black enough and whether he had relied too much on "white thinkers," like Karl Barth and Paul Tillich. This old question sometimes resurfaces and is posed anew because of some confusion regarding the proper cultural hermeneutic or theological methodology for Black Theology. Black Theology is a theology that must be done in a context of race, sex, gender, and class oppression.[1] But it is also a theology that must be done in the context of the World Church. While it is true that Black Theology must opt for a theological anthropology that pays attention to culture vis-à-vis race, class, and gender, and that any methodology that does not pay attention to these matters is deficient,[2] it is equally not true that such a methodology can be located only in African understandings of what it means to be human or only in African American folklore and spirituality. The foundation for Black Theology did not begin with Cone or the revolutionary movements in South Africa that sought the liberation of Africans and by extension all Black people in the world. The foundation for Black Theology "has always existed whenever and wherever God has chosen to collaborate with the poor for justice."[3]

The method that Lonergan introduced to theology is no ordinary method. It is not your everyday method, like the ones used in the sciences that merely provide a description of a hypothesis and are meant to be copied or imitated.[4] His method is an intelligible, interlocking set of terms and relations that helps a person set forth "what they can discover in themselves as the dynamic structure of their own cognitional and moral being."[5] Built into this method is the activity of divine grace that is active in the world and a recognition that human reception of this grace can at times be perverted by human sinfulness, such as oppression, alienation, and all kinds of ideologies like slavery, racism, sexism, and classism. In a nutshell, this nuanced method is a theological anthropology that speaks to the issues at the heart of Black Theology – the reality of race, sex, gender, and class oppression. Appropriating this method in Black Theology will in fact enrich many of the African and African American derived paradigms, folklores, and spirituality, and will help bring Black Theology to a new stage of meaning. Lonergan may not have spoken of race as "the superlative overarching mark of what a human being is,"[6] but he addresses the same issues at the heart of racial justice, particularly the bias that underpins modern construction of race, class, and gender oppression. Unlike many Western-derived paradigms that try to locate the essence of humanity in Western philosophical thoughts and systems, Lonergan's method is transcultural because it speaks to our shared common humanity. His analysis of culture is not based on assumptions about European Enlightenment and its idea of the ideal person; it is in actual fact a critique of these. He chastises and denounces them as part of that long process of classical control of meaning that overlooks significant differences in meanings and values of human life. Lonergan is clear that for every people, including Africans and African Americans, there is some apprehension of meaning and value in their way of life.[7] He replaces the classicists' deficient assumptions with a critical control of meaning that attends to human beings "in their concrete living"[8] and asks that we endeavour to know people "in all their diversity and mutability."[9] Furthermore, he warned people of every culture to be careful of "the vertical invasion of the Barbarians."[10] The phrase "vertical invasion of the Barbarians" was an expression that goes back to the German industrialist and politician, Walter Rathenau (1867–1922). It is a term now used to denote the cultural invasion of a people. The invasion of a people can occur not only horizontally through incursion of their territory by pacific or violent means, but also vertically through culture. The latter undermines the foundation of that culture, corrupts it, sets the stage for its decline.

The starting point of Lonergan's discussion of meaning and values of human life is human interiority, something that Black Theology has all along taken for granted, albeit without much development. The emphasis Lonergan places on interiority is an invitation to pay as much attention to the interior motivations (inner word) of a speaker as we do to the outer word. This is because meaning "is embodied or carried in human intersubjectivity, in art, in symbols, in language, and in the lives and deeds of persons."[11] Black Theology must be willing to engage in a self-scrutiny, adapt, and reinvent itself or be saddled with stunted growth. Cone himself suggested that the time has come for Black Liberation Theology in the United States to listen to outside voices to see its own blind spots.[12] Some critics have taken to writing obituaries of Black Theology for continuing to repeat the mantras of previous generations, which these critics now find to be irrelevant and grossly misappropriated.[13] There are even some who think "that the tradition of black theology, originating in the mind of James Cone and defended" by generations after him, "is ineffective as a Christian system."[14] While I do not share this overly negative assessment, it is becoming obvious that in the new cultural matrix of a World Church, Black Theology can no longer limit itself to some narrow selected Christian themes and metaphors. Appropriating the theological method of Lonergan will help Black Theology bridge the divide between Black Theology and mainstream Christian theology because what "builds the bridges between the many expressions of the faith is a methodical theology."[15] Since Black Theology is a theology of the Christian church as a whole, i.e., a Christian theology that pays attention to the needs of the Black community, Black Theology needs to be more inclusive. Black Theology is not the only theology addressing the issues of identity and mission as it relates to God's predilection for the poor and the oppressed. These have always been a major issue in Christian theology as a whole. To be inclusive, Black Theology must be concerned with how to help Christian theology be faithful to this mission.

One of the objectives of this work is to delineate ways that can help move Black Theology to a new stage of meaning. It is in line with Cone's suggestion that the time has come for us to "pause for a moment to evaluate our past and present struggle for justice and the gospel's relation to it so that we can see more clearly what must be done to make it [a] humane future for our children."[16] This work is, therefore, a line of development in Black Theology. It arose out of the need for a self-scrutiny that seeks to avoid overlooking those issues not addressed by the forebears of Black Theology. Cone himself acknowledged later in life that there were some "glaring limitations" in his work and that one of these limitations is his "failure to incorporate a global analysis of oppression into *A Black Theology of Liberation*."[17] He also acknowledged later that his criticism of white theologians was meant to be prophetic, not cynical. Not only does Lonergan provide resources for many of the missing links, he also provides a way of engaging in self-scrutiny. His work provides in addition a vocabulary for conceptualizing "the disease of racism that perverts one's moral sensitivity and distorts the intellect,"[18] and how this disease adapts to reinvent itself in new forms in changing circumstances.

A society can only reckon with its negative past if certain groups, especially the oppressed and marginalized, keep the memories alive. Contents of collective memories are unique to particular peoples, times, and places.[19] Although the memories of the injustices suffered by African Americans have been kept alive in many places, they are uniquely kept alive in the poetic imagination of James Baldwin (1924–87). Poets are those members of society best endowed to detect and preserve some deeply challenging truths, whether through fictions, binaries, or exposures of oppression in society. They are best equipped to capture and preserve in a unique way acts of insight that the ordinary person will either overlook or fail to grasp. Baldwin occupies a prophet-like position in African American culture. He saw it as his moral responsibility as a Black writer to excavate and tell the real history of America to his fellow Blacks.[20] In a profound way Baldwin's life and works anticipate some contemporary questions about racial justice that have yet to be answered. His poetic imagination can help Black Theology contextualize the memories and stories of prejudice and racial bias. His critique of racism can enrich and broaden Black Theology's own critique of racism and its own self-scrutiny.

Taken together, Lonergan and Baldwin offer resources, philosophical, doctrinal, and theological, for conceptualizing, understanding, and in some cases resolving some contested issues in racial justice. In the past, Black Theology may have been content with a method or a theological anthropology or even an analysis that presupposes a Marxist political and social theory. But not only are these inadequate for a world cultural matrix, entirely new categories are needed to move Black Theology forward. This work, therefore, transposes some of traditional Black Theology's categories of expressions into new categories of meaning, using a more historically-minded framework that speaks to the larger issues of the day as they bear on bias (prejudice) and racism. It is offered as part of the "conversation about the critical and self-reflective nature of Christian theology"[21] that will serve Black Theology in the future.

The book has six thematic chapters. Chapter 1 sets the context for the work. It uses theoretical concepts, some of which are drawn from Lonergan, to draw attention to what might be termed a racial apocalypse. There are, in all, seven horse riders of racial apocalypse to which Black Theology must be attentive. While Lonergan provides some of the theoretical concepts, Black writers and authors, especially Baldwin, provide insights that help situate them in the American context and expand our understanding of their practical application. The resurgence of Baldwin's work in the last decade is seen as a welcome development that can help Black Theology broaden and deepen its critique of racism.

Chapter 2 examines the meaning of Black Theology, especially as understood by some of the contemporary pioneers of the twentieth century. This is followed by a schematization of the stages of Black Theology as delineated by Cone and his protégé, Dwight Hopkins. The chapter suggests a new framework for schematizing Black Theology, especially in the light of the goodwill, symbolic or real, received by black people from all over the globe following the death of George Floyd in 2020. Using Lonergan's idea of stages of meaning, there is the suggestion that Black Theology, still in the first stage of meaning, may have received a catalyst to usher in a second stage with the death of Floyd. The first stage of Black Theology was dominated by the early pioneers of the movement, like Cone and Deotis Roberts. It received a boost with the refinement and development provided by Womanist theologians, like Katie Cannon and Delores Williams. The methodological approach adopted by the theologians of the early stage made them emphasize scripture and experience. Understandably, this could have been a critical methodological move at the time. But a movement from the first stage to a new stage of meaning will require a different methodological approach, which in turn requires a shift from the data of sense to the data of consciousness.

Chapter 3 deals with the issue of bias and shows the relevance of the work of Lonergan to Black Theology. It shows how Lonergan's understanding of bias can help Black Theology understand bias (prejudice) in all its forms, including those preconscious prejudices and ideologies that are meant to alienate and demean the other. The chapter also shows how the tools Lonergan provides can help Black Theology engage the new critical race theory. The conversations between Black Theology and the new critical race theory have been moving independently of each other. These two need to be harnessed and the chapter suggests a way of doing it. The chapter also engages emerging new studies in social psychology on the issue of bias and how it leads to forms of discrimination.

It ends with a mechanism for an action plan on what it means for Black Theology to appropriate Lonergan's notion of bias.

Chapter 4 gives an exposé of a new form of problem that was brought to light during the pandemic and lockdown of 2020 – the Karen phenomenon. Thoroughly analyzing it as part and parcel of a system of kyriarchy, the chapter places the phenomenon in its social and historical contexts, showing its ties to white privilege. Distinguishing between the phenomenon of white privilege, which is the other side of racism from the White Privilege discourse that attempts to address the matter, some key questions are raised: Is White Privilege discourse a problem of conceptualism and intellectualism that Lonergan says are incomplete forms of knowledge? What is Black Theology to do with White Privilege? How and in what ways is White Privilege a theological problem for Black Theology? In what ways might Black Theology offer resources to subjects of White Privilege so that they can overcome white privilege? While not pretending to offer an exhaustive solution, the chapter uses concepts and ideas from Lonergan to address these matters.

Chapter 5 takes a critical look at how the systems of racial and social control adapt, morph, and are re-imagined in the social context by the privileged and dominant group. It examines the variety of terms that are used to speak of the many manifestations of racism, including microaggressions. Recognizing that microaggression has become a substantive part of race discourse and has been used by professionals and educators in many campuses in the United States and beyond, the works of Derald Wing Sue and some other leading proponents of microaggression are examined, analyzed, and critiqued. Without diminishing the import of the concept and the psychological solutions proponents have suggested as remedies for microaggressions, the chapter also recognizes some of the problems that have trailed the concept – the misuses and misunderstandings – and makes philosophical and theological arguments regarding why Black Theology will be better served with the concept of dramatic bias.

Chapter 6 offers a Five-Dimensional Conversion Process (5D-C Process) derived from Lonergan as a schematic solution to the problem of racial bias. The biblical context of conversion is identified and analyzed using the grammar of conversion that is current within and outside of Catholicism – specifically Barth, Calvin, and the Reformed traditions. The questions of who needs to be converted, the conditions for conversion, and what true repentance entails are analyzed psychologically and theologically in their individual and communal contexts. By addressing these matters, the chapter shows how the perpetrators and victims can both benefit from the 5D-C process.

Chapter One

The Seven Horse Riders of Racial Apocalypse

In Bernard Lonergan's critical realist view of history, there is both the recognition and acceptance of such a thing as the spirit of an age. He reckons that there are indeed situations in which the spirit of an age might be an aberration or even a folly.[1] This recognition, albeit unexpressed, is the fundamental datum of experience of Black Theology. It is, however, the datum which contemporary Black Theology prescinds in the quest for racial justice and racial reconciliation.[2] Racism morphs, changes, and adapts. New forms of racism are emerging in the twenty-first century and finding expressions in two particular ways: in prejudices that follow individual actions, sometimes regardless of intent, and in the in-built prejudices in institutional and societal structures. These two forms of prejudices, which some behavioural scientists have taken to naming microaggressions (individual prejudices) and macroaggressions (societal expression of prejudices) because they exist in structural inequities, programs, policies, and practices,[3] are coalescing into racial apocalypse. They are the aberrations and folly of our age. They generate new wounds, open up old ones hitherto unhealed, and create in the minds of victims and perpetrators, who are both wounded in distinct and various ways, an aberrant consciousness. The wounds lead to a collective trauma that manifests intergenerationally.[4] The horror they induce is a horror of massive proportions. It is participated in and witnessed by many, bringing about a sense of collective guilt.[5] The multi-faced expressions of the horror are what have been summarized here as the seven horse riders of racial apocalypse – the same aberrant consciousness that Lonergan warns could lead a society to cataclysm.[6]

Drawing from the work of Lonergan helps us retrieve a theological legacy. He has a robust method of understanding and relating things to one another (cognitional method) that helps our effort to distinguish between the world of common sense and the world of facts (which he calls the world of science). To relate the one world to the other requires a shift to interiority – to understand why there are different cognitional procedures in the one and in the other.[7] This will help us understand, as well as address, some contested issues in human race relations in ways that are philosophically, psychologically, and theologically sound. The interdisciplinary nature of this procedure complements what some contemporary race theorists are already doing with the work of James Baldwin. One of the challenges of this chapter is to show how a fusion of these two imaginations (Lonergan and Baldwin) advances Black Theology's quest to grasp the aberrant consciousness, which has made the Black subject the virtual equivalent of "poor" and "lower class" of society,[8] whether in Africa, the United States, or elsewhere in the New World. In the United States, the latter years of Barack Obama's presidency witnessed an unprecedented resurgence in Baldwin's life and work, particularly among activists in the Black Lives Matter (BLM) movement.[9] In protesting on the streets and demanding political and social reforms, they appealed to Baldwin's critical insights and revelled in his sexuality as a way of disrupting older forms of politics that have done violence to Black bodies, especially the Black homosexual other.[10] More recently, the Public Broadcasting Service (PBS) in the United States has taken the lead in airing an Oscar-nominated documentary of Baldwin's life and work, under the title, "I Am Not Your Negro."[11] The documentary is an indictment of America's failure to rectify its perennial race problem. The present chapter validates this retrieval and provides justification for drawing from the poetic imagination of the man who understands the American riddle very well.[12] Baldwin's life embodies the dilemma of African American life in the drama of life in America that goes under the label "living while Black." Not only are there a plethora of lessons to be learned from Baldwin's treatment of race in his novels, it is also important to note how he anticipates contemporary questions about racial justice and racial reconciliation that have yet to be answered. Lonergan provides resources for responding to and addressing many of these questions, which have long been begging to be answered. Black Theology, after all, is not a rejection of Christianity, but an attempt to distinguish between "the spiritual heart of Christianity and the purely cultural western mores with which it has become associated."[13] Baldwin's poetic imagination, when combined with the theological astuteness of Lonergan, offers resources that can "imagine an answer to the moral reckoning that confronts us all."[14] Thus a fusion of these two horizons is needed to help Black Theology understand and respond adequately to these moral reckonings.

To be clear, there is no suggestion here that our foray into the work of Lonergan and Baldwin will help bring an end to racism. Far from it. The goal of this endeavour rather is to add to the resources from which Black Theology can draw in the endless battle against the lower viewpoint of racism. No psychologically sound person can think about a world without racism. The best one can hope for is a mitigation. Even eternal optimists know that racism will always be a fact of human life, precisely because of the seven horse riders of racial apocalypse discussed in this chapter. For this reason, the oppression to which Black Theology speaks must include the subjugation of people of all races. Black Theology must be a theology of hope that draws attention to the oppression of Black people. But this must not exclude the oppression of the poor non-raced white people, regardless of whether whites in general have been centred as the human norm by mainstream society.[15] Many poor whites still suffer oppression from the dominant class. One of the criticisms of Black Theology in the United States is "that it has fallen in behind the violence of Black Power and has failed to display the truly Christian insights of Martin Luther King."[16] Long before the new racial awakening that came to light in 2020 (see chapter 2), Black Theology had received a boost, albeit without much significance, from an unlikely source, i.e., from some white scholars who indicated their willingness to examine the location and power of whiteness in society.[17] The white self, until then, for many of these scholars at least, "was an invisible and non-researched category, even difficult to name and not perceived as a distinctive racial identity."[18] The American cultural critic, Michael Dyson, shedding light into this invisible non-researched category, has helpfully distinguished three key features of whiteness: whiteness as identity (i.e., white self-understanding that distinguishes it from Blackness), whiteness as ideology (i.e., understanding of whiteness as domination and enduring myth), and whiteness as institution (i.e., institutional expressions of whiteness in homes, schools, and churches).[19] The white self, however it is understood, has remained remarkably invisible. But the new racial awakening has helped to inoculate the distance that exists between Black Theology and the white self.[20] More than ever, the inoculation is helping Black Theology call attention to the power of whiteness, i.e., how it can be understood and interrupted, and where necessary, how it can be transformed.[21] But the goodwill does not come without difficulties. It makes addressing racism even more delicate. Where before one had to speak to the brutality of racism without offending the innocent white bystanders, it becomes even harder to do so now. The delicate balance remains how to enhance the discourse in ways that manage the discomfort of white audience.

The English novelist Henry Graham Greene (1904–91), who gained a reputation as an avowed Catholic writer following his conversion to Catholicism in 1926, once remarked that he was not a Catholic writer, but a writer who happened to be a Catholic.[22] In the same vein, I have written this work, not as a Black Catholic writer, but as a writer who happens to be by accident and circumstance Black and Catholic. I have written, not as part of an armchair détente, but from the experiences of being Black and Catholic in a Church community that has yet to fully understand how the two come together. As a Black man, I know a lot about racism. I also know the academy to be a place of ironies and binaries. I have deliberately refrained from using my own personal examples to talk about racism so the work does not usurp a memoir still to come. The shared experiences of many in this big pot of lower viewpoints called racism are enough to convey what needs to be conveyed about racism in the church, society, and the academy. On the one hand, the academy is thought to be the one place in society where the boundaries of knowledge and understanding are to be expanded.[23] It at times lives up to this expectation by generating fine theories, including theories on race and racism.[24] On the other hand, the academy remains a landfill of white privilege. Racism and white privilege are corollaries, but the academy does not get it. Racism and white privilege are two sides of the same coin, but the academy does not seem to care. A large part of this refusal to understand is because many do not understand dramatic bias (what psychologists call preconscious bias) and how it works without self-conscious reasoning. Behavioural and social psychologists have tried to shed light on some forms of oppression that ethnic minorities face minute by minute, hour to hour, and day to day. They tell us that the majority of this oppression is "'micro' (not immediately visible to the eye), insidious, psychologically and physically draining, and often not definable, illegal, or open to redress."[25] Some psychologists have even coined the terms *modern racism*, *aversive racism*, and *subtle racism*, "to capture and understand the essence of the many forms of non-blatant racism."[26] Lonergan's own preferred term for this preconscious racism is dramatic bias. It is a better term, philosophically and theologically at least, for conceptualizing how the unconscious mind works – how one "would continually interact with seemingly good people who would, nonetheless, demonstrate irrational behaviour that created disparities in the way they treated people and ran organizations."[27] If ever there was a sector of society that needed more education on racism, it is clearly the academy and the business world. Both sectors seem to have perfected the art of microinequities (a pattern of overlooking, under respecting, and devaluing a person because of their race).[28] Thankfully, there is some progress in this education effort, however miniscule.[29] But the education must lead to an appreciation and understanding of dramatic bias – an ideology of unconscious motivation. Studies in social psychology illuminate what Lonergan calls dramatic bias – that a large part of the behaviour that produces racial discrimination is influenced by unconscious racial motivation. There are several possible explanations for this. First, there is the Freudian theory that the human mind is quick to defend itself against the discomfort of guilt. It does so by denying or refusing to recognize those ideas and belief systems the individual has learned are good or right.[30] Second, cognitive psychology helps to explain how culture, such as media, family, and even institutional authorities, transmits certain beliefs and preferences that are considered very much part of the culture.[31] When these beliefs and preferences are taken to be a part of the culture, quite often they are not experienced as explicit lessons. "Instead, they seem part of the individual's rational ordering of her perceptions of the world. The individual is unaware, for example, that the ubiquitous presence of a cultural stereotype has influenced her perception that Blacks are lazy or unintelligent. Because racism is so deeply ingrained in our culture, it is likely to be transmitted by tacit understandings ... These tacit understandings, because they have never been articulated, are less likely to be experienced at a conscious level."[32] Understandably, the academy was not originally designed to be inclusive. The problem, however, is that it has intentionally remained so, even when the rest of society is evolving. It is in the academy where Dyson's three features of whiteness are fostered and incubated. The academy has chosen to remain a locus of identity politics by refusing to give adequate attention to this monster of preconscious prejudice Lonergan calls dramatic bias. By identity politics, I do not mean the strategic placements that benefit minority groups. By identity politics, I mean group distinctiveness that makes the racial minority know he or she is an outsider. Sadly, it is in the academy that the triads of identity, ideology, and institution are articulated and reinforced over space and time.[33] More sadly, it will remain so for a very long time because of this failure to grasp the intricacies of dramatic bias.

A Statement of the Problem

The year 2020 will forever be significant in the annals of racial discourse in the United States. It was a momentous year in people's awareness of some of the underlying currents of racism and their manifold expressions. Even some race-sceptics who usually dismiss race-talk as "playing the race-card" were awakened from their dogmatic slumber. Thus, for many outside of the Black community, 2020 was a year of a new racial awakening. This new racial awakening was precipitated by two main events that unfolded in the midst of a global pandemic. The first was the death of George Floyd in police custody in Minneapolis, Minnesota. Multiple incidents of bias that have sparked nationwide outrage led up to the killing of Floyd. There is Trayvon Martin, a seventeen-year-old African American who was fatally shot and killed by a neighbourhood watchman on 26 February 2012 in Sanford, Florida. There is Michael Brown, an eighteen-year-old Black man who was fatally shot on 9 August 2014 by a white police officer in Ferguson, Missouri. There is Ahmaud Arbery, a twenty-five-year-old Black man who was chased by three armed white residents of a South Georgia neighbourhood on 23 February 2020 and shot to death. The list goes on. All these incidents, different in some ways, bear some similarities. They all point to bias against African Americans. The second was the Karen phenomenon that exposed the hidden side of racism – entitled white subjects who use their privilege and force in a system that is tilted towards them to defame and brutalize Black subjects. The first, i.e., the death of George Floyd, was met with nationwide mass protests of unimaginable proportion. The second, i.e., the Karen phenomenon, became an internet sensation; it developed memes to shame and defame the entitled "superbrats" in a way no one could have imagined. But despite the role played by these two events in the new racial awakening, things have not really changed that much with respect to everyday racism in society. At the end of December 2020, there was the event that was dubbed the "SoHo Karen" – an entitled woman attacked and accused a fourteen-year-old African American boy of stealing her iPhone in a hotel in New York. It was later found that the woman had forgotten her iPhone in her Uber ride. But the damage had been done. The issue raised again the problem of racial profiling.[34] Then there was the ugly event of 6 January 2021 in which a mob, claiming to be supporters of then former President Donald Trump, invaded the U.S. capitol in Washington DC and unleashed death and destruction. The siege on the capitol, for many African Americans, brought to the fore the issue of double standards in policing in the United States. In June 2020, for example, a peaceful protest by members of the Black Lives Matter (BLM) movement in the same Washington DC was met with heavy police presence and teargas. The then-President Trump even threatened to call in the military on mostly innocent peaceful protestors. But in the case of the insurrection at the Capitol (predominantly white) that unleashed chaos, there was no show of force by police; no military presence.[35] They had near-uninhibited access to the Capitol. Michelle Obama could not but call out the gulf in differing responses to the BLM protest and the capitol riot. Not mincing words, she said: "Seeing the gulf between the responses to [the Capitol Hill riot] and this summer's peaceful protest [of BLM] and the larger movement for racial justice is so painful. It hurts. And I cannot think about moving on or turning the page until we reckon with the reality of what we saw yesterday. True progress will be possible only once we acknowledge that this disconnect exists and take steps to repair it."[36] If it is not the SoHo Karen, it is the office Karen, if it is not the office Karen, it is the double standard in policing or law enforcement that is so apparent for all to see. To evoke the words of Frederick Douglass, "It was not color but crime, not God but man, that afforded the true explanation of the existence of [a racial double standard]."[37]

The African American novelist, Ralph Waldo Ellison (1914–94), whose works Baldwin invokes brilliantly and at times weaves into his own work, could not have captured better the intellectual and social dilemma of Black life in the United States in his classic, *Invisible Man* (1952).[38] The setting of the classic novel was the deep south in the 1920s and Harlem, New York, in the 1930s. "Invisibility" was Ellison's metaphor for describing the web of racism in which the Black subject is trapped. In the novel, Ellison "wrestles with the cognitive dissonance of opportunity served up alongside indignity."[39] The Black subject, Ellison writes, is invisible, not because of some biochemical accident or supernatural conspiracy, but "simply because people refuse to see me." In what now seems like a prophetic allusion to the racial events of the 2020, Ellison ends his book with a police chase of a Black man during a riot in Harlem. During the chase, the Black man happened to trip and fall down a manhole in the middle of the street. Rather than try to rescue him, the police simply put the cover of the manhole back in place, trapping the Black man in the manhole and tucking him away for life. It was Ellison's way of showing how the invisible man can be easily tucked away without qualms or remorse. Black people are still forced today to be invisible because of the colour of their skin. Racism feeds on stereotypes and stereotypes lead to psychic distortion that makes the Black subject reluctantly accept his or her invisibility. It is psychic distortion that makes the Black subject visibly invisible, lose their individuality, and become what they are imagined to be by the larger society. Ellison's own moment of truth came, he tells us in an interview, when he realized he had lost his individuality because people saw him as a reflection of their preconceived ideas of who they thought he was. In that interview, Ellison warns the Black subject about the dangers of accepting an identity imposed on one from outside. Each individual has to discover "himself and the world himself. Usually this is done through some sort of pain."[40]

Recovering the Heroic Virtues and Poetical Imaginations of James Baldwin

Racism is a distortion and a corruption in the human capacity to love and act justly.[41] This is why theology needs, not only a method and a language, but also an imagination that does not collapse or erase differences. If imagination is "the power of giving form to human experience"[42] and if imagination implies operating not just in the realm of metaphysical abstraction, but in the realms of creativity, aesthetics, and experience,[43] then the imagination theology needs must be one that has the capacity to listen to the other receptively and contemplatively.[44] Pope Francis calls this theological imagination *ecclesia discerns* (a listening church).[45] An imagination, to be considered Christian or Catholic, must have the capacity to describe where God is to be encountered, as well as discern how and in what circumstances human acting is in accord with divine grace. Some theological imaginations, particularly the socially derived ones that are rooted in racism and prejudice are prone to division. They are also dehumanizing and tend to close the circle of mutual encounter, friendship, and grace.[46] Any imagination, theological or social, in which people pretend not to see colour, is biased and destructive. Such imagination needs to be tossed out and eradicated because it has no place in Christian theology. Rather, what Christian theology needs is a theological imagination that describes "how God interacts with the human on an emotional and embodied level, a space where the language of theology blends into lived experiences."[47] Black Theology can uncover from the poetic writings of Baldwin a creative, aesthetic, and experienced-based imagination that is a locus of encountering God for the oppressed and deprivileged.

Baldwin's biography matters, if we are to understand the arc of his thinking.[48] A recap of some salient features of the life of this brave man whose work was ignored in theological circles until most recently will help to steer us in the right direction. "His motivations across the globe, his personal relationships, his immediate family … his personal disasters and triumphs, his volatility and gentleness,"[49] all play a crucial role in helping us grasp what contemporary culture can learn from him. It is understandable, though not acceptable, if Baldwin's work was ignored for a long time. After all, even the revered Rev. Martin Luther King Jr. was a little sceptical of the man. In 1963 King was caught on an FBI secret tape expressing concerns about Baldwin. Many of those around King equally felt uncomfortable around Baldwin. Perhaps it was Baldwin's "queerness" that unsettled them.[50] In spite of their circumstantial and temperamental distance, Baldwin, like King, was convinced that the only way of resolving American racial impasse was through a coalition of conscience ready to do battle for the principles of justice, goodwill, and brotherhood. It was while in high school that Baldwin discovered that he might be gay. But he had to live on the down-low because of society's homophobic hegemony, closeting his sexuality from his family.[51] After graduation from high school, "He meandered between confused heterosexual attraction – nearly marrying – and chance queer encounters in public places, like movie theaters."[52] Later he tells us that his escape to Paris in 1948, in addition to escaping from his existential dread – racism in America, was an effort to reconcile the mystery of his sexuality. "I no longer felt who I really was, whether I was really black or really white, really male or really female."[53] Even when he returned to the United States during the civil rights era, the homophobia did not disappear. Accused of giving himself up to political sodomy of the white man, a civil rights era slur referred to him as "Martin Luther Queen."[54] He internalized the public homophobic acrimony against him, considering it a spiritual bankruptcy of a nation that would force others to forfeit their chance of living a normative life.[55] When he publicly came out as gay in the 1980s, Baldwin spent the rest of his life "challenging heteronormative black and white sexuality on its own terms, ridiculing the fetishizing of straight bodies and straight lives as part of a culture of reaction, repression, in gay panic in the United States."[56] In this courageous effort, he made his sexuality an integral aspect of his attack against racism, sexism, and homophobia. Baldwin embodies the virtues of courageous grace, resistance, and survival that Black Theology will need. Baldwin was never a conformist and his words and actions all point towards the prophetic.

The one time Baldwin recalls ever responding with violence to racism was when he threw a water mug full of water on a waitress who would not serve him because of the colour of his skin. Even in the midst of this ugly incident, Baldwin recalls having an epiphany from the encounter: "I could not get over two facts, both equally difficult for the imagination to grasp, and one was that I could have been murdered. But the other was that I had been ready to commit murder. I saw nothing very clearly but I did see this: that my life, my real life, was in danger, and not from anything other people might do but from the hatred I carried in my own heart."[57] It was this hatred for racism and fear that he might kill somebody in an act of rebellion or be killed that made him leave the United States for Paris. One of his close friends, Eugene Worth, had committed suicide in 1946 by jumping off the George Washington Bridge in New York. Baldwin thought he understood whatever must have driven his friend to commit suicide and felt that if he did not leave for Paris he too might have met the same fate.[58] In fact, Baldwin did go into deep depression and attempted suicide in 1969 after the assassination of Dr. Martin Luther King Jr. and what he saw as the failure of the civil rights movement.[59]

Baldwin recalls how Paris was "the best and the most important years" of his life because in Paris he was, at least, free of the most existential dread of his life – racism.[60] Baldwin knew that escaping Harlem made him an exception – for every one of me, he wrote, there were thousands of young Black boys dead, in prison, or "on the needle."[61] In Paris he found some form of freedom and could reinvent himself there. "I didn't have to walk around with one half of my brain trying to please Mr. Charlie and the other half trying to kill him," he recalled.[62] American society had consigned Black people to the bottom rung of society and the challenge was to avoid to succumbing to the three [false] senses of self, society, and history that determined one's fate.[63] We know from history that whenever the oppressed and marginalized attempt to wrest their freedom from their oppressors, it often ends in their death.[64] But Baldwin survived. He survived because he learned very early on that to be truly free is to confront pain and trauma without hating the one who inflicted them. He wondered whether "one of the reasons people cling to their hates so stubbornly is because they sense, once hate is gone, that they will be forced to deal with pain."[65]

One of Baldwin's renowned essays is his quasi-autobiographical *Go Tell It on the Mountain* in which the young protagonist John Grimes is depicted as standing on a hill in Central Park, New York, in the same way a biblical prophet would stand on a hill to deliver a saving message to a forlorn people in need of redemption.[66] Baldwin himself may well be the John Grimes of his own fictional work. "John Grimes is James Baldwin, and James Baldwin became that prophet. A Black American, born into the bleakness of poverty and the lie of the American Dream, who would rise up, with a voice dedicated like those of Ezekiel and Jeremiah, to tell his people, the American people, where they had gone wrong."[67] The prophetic voice of Baldwin shines supreme in truth-telling. In a 1963 speech to students of Howard University, Washington DC, Baldwin declared that the Black writer has a moral responsibility to excavate the real history of America to tell their fellow Blacks what really happened to get us where we are now. "We must tell the truth till we can no longer bear it,"[68] he declared. Former president Barack Obama has more recently acknowledged the vital role Baldwin occupies in the annals of Black history as a foremost truth-teller. Contrasting his own role as a politician with that of Baldwin the truth-teller, Obama frankly admitted, "If I spoke the language of James Baldwin as he speaks it on the campaign stump, I'm probably not gonna get a lot of votes in Iowa."[69]

It is not difficult to see the many similarities between contemporary racial tensions and the race-problem in Baldwin's time. From the contemporary race problem has emerged the Black Lives Matter (BLM) movement, in the same way that the race problem in Baldwin's time led to the growth of Black activism. The latter activists were fed up with the traditional models of Black leadership, particularly as represented by the Rev. Dr. Martin Luther King's nonviolent movement. Baldwin at the time lauded the courage of the Black activists and welcomed the challenge they posed to traditional forms of Black leadership. Baldwin, unlike many of the other civil rights leaders, was not romantically obsessed about hope. He understood the human capacity for evil and was pragmatic about what it means to be vulnerable and be living while Black. "If you're a Negro, you're in the center of that peculiar affliction," he wrote, "because anybody can touch you – when the sun goes down. You know, you're a target of everybody's fantasies."[70] What Baldwin was alluding to is the everyday biases the Black person is subjected to that are 'difficult to identity, quantify, and rectify because of their subtle, nebulous, and unnamed nature."[71]

In all, there are several noteworthy things we can learn from Baldwin's own life experiences. Chief among them is that Baldwin had a sacramental vision of human flesh because, for him, the human body is a site of grace.[72] He understood his sexuality and rejected very early on the life society had constructed for him. His theological imagination emphasizes the human capacity for love, "in the form of graced encounters, to dismantle harmful barriers and hierarchies that prevent freedom and full human authenticity."[73] His theological imagination points in the direction Black Theology needs to go because it "describes a vision of God that compels one to love unconditionally in a way that breaks down arbitrary boundaries. God permeates the messiness of life and is encountered within both the quotidian and the erotic."[74]

Naming the Seven Horse Riders of Racial Apocalypse

The American race problem is at its core a moral and a theological problem. Morally, it is "a disease and a crime."[75] The disease infects and lives within the nation and the illness "arises out of the injury and trauma of the Middle Passage, the slave plantation, the Black Codes, lynching, and segregation."[76] Theologically, the race problem stems from the surd of sin. What results from sin is, as Lonergan says, "a bias in favour of certain groups and against other groups, class opposition, the emotional charging of that opposition, and the organization of those emotions and that opposition in mutual recriminations and criticisms."[77] In the American cultural context, no one understands how this surd of sin plays out in favour of the dominant class better than Baldwin who lived through it and sought to establish a new form of humanism that will not be constrained by race, sex, gender, and class. Admittedly, racism today is no longer the old-school hard knocks kind that existed in Baldwin's time. But at its core racism still remains potent and ideologically driven. "Even if troglodyte racism no longer plies the surface of American life, it still hides out in subterranean fastness, to emerge now and again in episodes ranging from the trivial to the serious to the deadly."[78] Like many of his civil rights era colleagues, Baldwin understood that moments of genuine change around racial matters can suddenly hit a wall of resistance and even that some good laws can be distorted by the persistence of value gap.[79] The value gap is fuelled by the seven horse riders of racial apocalypse that are elaborated upon here using some theoretical concepts derived from Lonergan. My approach is to give them meanings somewhat different from their original usage in the Canadian theologian. My elucidation of the concepts will be complemented by some practical ideas garnered from the poetic imaginations of Baldwin who himself lived through the nightmare. The hope is that they can be of practical significance for a self-understanding of the monster of racism as Black Theology collaborates with the rest of society to work towards dismantling it.

1. The Racial Apocalyptic Problem of Tokenism

The first horse rider of racial apocalypse is tokenism. Black Theology must begin to respond to and renounce the pervasive problem of tokenism or symbolism around matters of racial justice. Tokenism or symbolism is a great hang-up in racial discourse. It is nothing but an emotional outlet that allows the privileged to feel like they are doing something about racism while they remain entrenched in the structure that produces the unequal power relations. They do not draw the ire of anyone because there is a make-believe that they are doing something about the unequal power relations. Symbolic efforts have far too often been passed off as a solution, even when it does not move the needle. It does not take a rocket scientist to know the system of tokenism is intentionally (in effect, *de jure*) and negligently (essentially, *de facto*) perpetuated,[80] especially in the academy, for a particular reason. Willie Jennings has spoken of "something sinister" in the academy. "Something that draws our energy and corrupts our desire in ways so subtle yet comprehensive that it is like toxic fumes covering the surface of our bodies, moving through our fingers and across our faces. This thing makes us sick."[81] Tokenism is that "something" that "needs to die."[82] Academicians love theories. They also revel in abstract concepts. For many in this white-dominated institution, racism is an abstract concept.[83] Racism is not something many of them can relate to. It does not touch their existential reality the way it touches the existential core of Black subjects. So it is understandable that many academicians approach racism as an academic exercise to be learned and debated, the way the scholastics of the Middle Ages debated abstract concepts. The Rev. Martin Luther King Jr. discovered later to his dismay that some of his loyal supporters in the desegregation efforts of the South, including some on the Board of his Southern Christian Leadership Conference (SCLC), were less enthusiastic when it came to supporting his agenda for equitable job distribution and ending poverty.[84] Regrettably, the abstract nature of the subject for academicians contributes to the failure to confront the invisibility of white privilege (the other side of racism). Even if for the sake of the argument we accept that troglodyte racism may break the surface only now and again,[85] office Karen far too often remains a workday reality for Black subjects. As will be demonstrated in chapter 3 and beyond, the root cause of these matters is dramatic bias. The same white faculty colleague who posts a big sign of Black Lives Matter on her door will be the very same faculty colleague to argue vehemently (and for frivolous reasons too) against advancing a Black faculty in the same department for tenure or promotion. The same white faculty colleague who organizes regular food donations in homeless shelters in Black neighbourhoods will be the same faculty colleague to be opposed to hiring an additional Black faculty in the department. Presumptions for hiring or advancement are always in favour of white faculty. Sometimes no harm is "intended" and the people who uphold these traditions of keeping things white are the first to tell you, "I am not a racist. You can check my record!" Ironically, it is no longer the Ku Klux Klan or Skinheads that pose the greatest threat to Black people in the workplace. Rather, it is now those "well-intentioned people, who are strongly motivated by egalitarian values, who believe in their own morality, and experience themselves as fair-minded and decent people who would never consciously discriminate."[86] Ta-Nehisi Coates thinks this obsession with politics of personal exoneration is part of what it means to be white.[87] On the one hand, they seem to endorse egalitarian values, on the other hand, they subconsciously harbour antiminority feelings.[88] This ingrained habit of maintaining unequal power relations stems from dramatic bias. Afterall, "unequal power relations and racialized location within the social hierarchy are preserved through the maintenance of the status quo."[89] Karen Fields and Barbara Fields could not have made this point any clearer when they surmised that those who create and re-create racial imbalance are not just the mob that kill African Americans on the streets or the Ku Klux Klan. "They are also those academic writers whose invocation of self-propelling 'attitudes' and tragic flaws assigns Africans and their descendants to a special category, placing them in a world exclusively theirs and outside history – a form of intellectual Apartheid no less ugly or oppressive, despite its righteous (not to say self-righteous) trappings, than that practiced by the bio-and theo-racists; and for which the victims, like slaves of old, are expected to be grateful."[90] Thus, the dissonance between the effort to achieve justice and the perpetuation of the self-interest of those leading the effort demands more serious attention than has previously been given.

2. *The Racial Apocalyptic Problem of White Privilege*

The second horse rider of racial apocalypse is the perduring problem of white privilege. Closet racism begins with white privilege. It is related to the racial horse rider of tokenism and more pervasive in the academy. Ta-Nehisi Coates says his own moment of epiphany came when he realized that the streets and the schools are arms of the same beast. "One enjoyed the official power of the state while the other enjoyed its implicit sanction."[91] In the academy, when "white privilege" is a topic for discussion, it is most often at the theoretical and broader social levels, not at the personal level and does not address individual concrete situations. The personal level is always bypassed and conveniently left unexamined because it is not only more difficult and challenging to examine, it can also threaten that which is held to be sacred, confidential, and private.[92] Far too many are less interested in taking the radical measures needed to attain equity. This makes the rhetoric seem dysfunctional.[93] Granted that the discourse is trying to describe "a force that inhibits justice in the ongoing social relations between races,"[94] the rhetoric, however, does not do much to advance change. First, the rhetoric is ambiguous and the term "white privilege" is non-differentiated.[95] Second, its appeal to action lacks the requisite nuance to dismantle the ubiquitous white privilege.[96]

Let me be clear, I am not saying nothing literarily is being done to address the phenomenon of white privilege. Far more than before, many schools and organizations have become more aware of the need for sensitivity on the issue of diversity. Many, including government agencies and non-profit organizations, have hired diversity and inclusion officers, instituted diversity and inclusion training programs, established special holidays to celebrate the contributions of certain ethnic minorities who previously were not honoured, and periodically organize departmental and school-wide conferences on equity, diversity, and inclusion to help foster tolerance.[97] They have also put in place laws that can limit people's biased behaviour and hold them accountable for flagrant discriminatory practices. On the theological front, some white theologians involved in the white privilege discourse are beginning to speak of how "embarrassed and uncomfortable"[98] they feel now that they are suddenly realizing that they have failed to address racism and white privilege in their writing.[99] So, there is no question that on the conscious level behaviours are changing.[100] However, even the people involved in the rhetoric of white privilege admit that their discourse "does not add anything to an objective analysis of racism."[101] Even where there is some semblance of change, the change remains fragile.[102] The fragility at times makes changes seem merely symbolic. No doubt, acknowledging one's failure to address and deal with the problem of racism is a good first step.[103] But it will take more than a polite acknowledgement to dismantle this invisible structure that is systemic and omnipresent in the everyday life of the privileged.[104] In the academy, beyond symbolic gestures at both the departmental and institutional levels of most schools, as it is for the most part in church and society at large, hardly anything meaningful is done to address racism and racial attitudes.[105] In the end what is achieved remains the same – just do enough to keep the Black subject content in their second-class status. This was the self-congratulatory exercise Baldwin warned against. Even the ever-optimistic Martin Luther King Jr. was forced to admit later in life: "I must honestly confess that I go through moments of disappointment when I have to recognize that there aren't enough white persons in our country who are willing to cherish democratic principles over privilege."[106] Baldwin was always clear that white privilege has to be confronted before there can be social transformation. He believed that the academician has a moral responsibility in society. The academician, for him, must put aside America's myths and legends and become "a disturber of the peace in doing so."[107] To put it simply, white privilege cannot be transformed unless attention is paid to dramatic bias.

3. The Racial Apocalyptic Problem of the "Already-Out-There-Now Real"

The third horse rider of racial apocalypse that Black Theology must take seriously is the problem Lonergan calls *the already-out-there-now real*. Its colloquial rendition is "the more you look, the less you see." It is what is expressed in the adage, "missing the forest for the trees."

Some people mistake knowing for taking a good look. Lonergan calls this wrong conception a myth about knowing. There are many facets of the American life that have the weight and force of *the already-out-there-now real* (taking a glance and losing perspective). It is a problem Lonergan first associated with the astronomer and physicist, Galileo Galilei (1564–1642). In order to show the seriousness of this problem and the context of its emergence, a lengthy quotation of Lonergan's indictment of Galileo will be helpful:

> Galileo discovered the law of falling bodies, but he failed to recognize its abstractness. Correctly, he grasped that explanation lies beyond description, that the relations of things to our senses must be transcended, that the relations of things to one another must be grasped, and that a geometrization of nature is the key tool in performing this task. Still, Galileo did not cast his methodological discoveries in the foregoing terms. Instead of speaking of the relations of things to our senses, he spoke of the merely apparent secondary qualities of things. Instead of speaking of the relations of things to one another, he spoke of their real and objective primary qualities, and these he conceived as the mathematical dimensions of matter in motion.[108]

Lonergan's point is simply that in spite of his laudable scientific achievements, such as the classical laws he helped to discover, Galileo's problem was that he made some indefensible assumptions about reality and objectivity. He thought of his classical laws not as abstractions that can be statistically united to the concrete but as concrete themselves.[109] Not only was his methodology erroneous, he also failed to grasp its ambiguities. His "fallacy of misplaced concreteness" misled him into believing that his own scientific discoveries were of the "really real concrete world."[110] Unknowingly, these ambiguities were passed on to Descartes and from Descartes to Hobbes, Locke, Berkeley and Hume, and from Hume to Immanuel Kant in whose work "the real and objective bodies of Galilean thought prove to constitute no more than a phenomenal world."[111] From Kant, *the already-out-there-now real* was transmitted to the rest of the Western world. It has since found expression in some misguided social realities. Its expression in the United States has come in the form of what Karen Fields and Barbara Fields call racecraft – a morbid problem that makes equal justice hard to imagine for all Americans.[112]

In simple terms, what Lonergan technically calls *the already-out-there-now real* is a warning against the mirages of life that make us confuse the abstract for the concrete, the token for the real. Let me cite a quick example of this mirage in Christian theology that mistakes the token for the real. Many Christian theologians, ethicists especially, are quick to speak of God's preferential option for the poor and they are correct because the scriptures bear them out (Psalm 140:12; Luke 10: 30–37; James 2:5). The problem, however, is that they hardly ever connect it to racism and hardly ever examine their own complicity in the systemic problem. When they do, it is always by way of "an occasional word or phrase."[113] This lack of desire on the part of Catholic theologians to address racism in any substantial manner left James Cone perplexed. He wondered why white Catholic theologians always remain "silent in regard to racism, even though they have been very outspoken about anti-Semitism and class and gender contradictions in response to radical protest."[114] Baldwin alluded to the same problem of mistaking the symbolism for the really real in society at large when he pointed out that, contrary to the dominant narratives, the race problem in America is not due to the pathologies of Black culture or the failures of Black subjects, but that the race problem is due to society's invention of the "nigger." Baldwin writes, "I didn't invent him; white people invented him. I've always known, I had to know by the time I was 17 years old, that what you were describing was not me and what you were afraid of was not me."[115] In indicating that the times demanded a new approach, Baldwin noted how there were no clear images and that everything seemed superimposed on something else.[116]

> There are no clear vistas: the road that seems to pull one forward into the future is also pulling one backward into the past. I felt, anyway, kaleidoscopic, fragmented, walking through the streets of San Francisco, trying to decipher whatever it was that my consciousness made of all the elements in which I was entangled, and which were all tangled up in me.[117]

What we see in the passage above is Baldwin's frustration about how the country keeps turning its back when it has opportunities to make appreciable progress. The country keeps turning its back when it is on the precipice of change. Rather than opt for the truly good, the country chooses to double down on its historic ugliness.[118] It is this doubling down that feeds *the already-out-there-now real* myth – the myth that we are already living in a post-racial society, as evidenced by the election of President Obama in 2008. Obama's election was "framed as an ending: a triumphant climax to the civil rights movement begun decades earlier."[119] The myth was meant to suggest that if a Black man could be elected the president of the leader of the free world, it meant that all constraints had been removed and America had finally overcome its racist past.[120] Obama's situation and the narrative around it is similar to that of the African American political scientist and diplomat to the United Nations, Ralph Bunche (1904–71). Bunche was a formative member and a United States delegate to the United Nations in 1946. He received a Nobel Peace prize in 1950 for his role in peace mediation in Israel. President John F. Kennedy awarded him the Presidential Medal of Freedom in 1963. Some race sceptics at the time used the success of Bunche to frame a narrative with which they judged all other African Americans: "If Ralph Bunche can be ambassador to the United Nations, what more do negroes want?"[121] There are two issues here. First, the idea of designating a person of colour as a proxy for the countless number of the group reveals a moral impotence. The moral impotence of the essentially free subject is neither grasped with perfect clarity nor totally unconscious.[122] Second, advancing one person's accomplishment as an argument against the demand of the rest of the group is no more than substituting the token for the proxy.[123] In the case of Obama, even as those who claim his election signalled the post-racial era continue to hone their deceptive narrative, "their very harping on Obama as a 'black president' reprised an age-old feature of racecraft: the turning of one person of African descent into a synecdoche for all."[124] To think we now live in a post-racial America is the political equivalent of the mistaken notion that knowing consists in looking, "missing the forest for the trees." It is this mirage that Lonergan finds disconcerting. The error consists either in seeing what is not there or in not seeing what is there.[125]

4. *The Racial Apocalyptic Problem of White Rage*

The fourth horse rider of the racial apocalypse is white rage. Black Theology must no longer neglect the reality of white rage and its triggers. "Whites don't understand themselves in abstraction from the cultural institutions and the critical mythologies that accrete around whiteness,"[126] Ronald Chennault writes. White rage is a problem that can no longer be taken for granted in Black circles. White rage is no longer the kind of visible and outlandish violence of groups like the KKK. White rage is no longer fringe, if ever it was fringe. Rather, white rage is organized and mainstream. It works its way through established structures and a range of bureaucracies. "It wreaks havoc subtly, almost imperceptibly."[127] Long before Carol Anderson articulated the phenomenon of white rage, Baldwin had written about its consequences on the life of Black subjects: "When a black man, whose destiny and identity have always been controlled by others, decides and states that he will control his own destiny and rejects the identity given to him by others, he is talking revolution."[128] Some modicum of white rage and anger came to the surface with the election of President Obama in 2008. During the State of the Union address in 2009, a congressman from South Carolina shouted "you lie" at President Obama. Although the congressman later apologized for what he termed his "lack of civility" and for letting "my emotions get the best of me,"[129] the genie was already out of the bottle. The congressman's public scream was seen by many as evidence of rage. Baldwin had written in a 1951 essay, in what seems now like a clairvoyance on his part, "Whenever the Negro face appears a tension is created, the tension is a silence filled with things unalterable."[130] In 1979, Baldwin came up with a book idea that began with him travelling to many of the cities in the south that were central to the civil rights movement, such as Selma and Birmingham, Alabama, and Atlanta, GA. In the end, the book was not published. What came out of it instead was a documentary that tells the story of how the gains of the civil rights movement were upended. It was released in 1982 under the title, "I Heard It Through the Grapevine." "The trigger for white rage, inevitably," writes Anderson, "is black advancement. It is not the mere presence of black people that is the problem; rather, it is blackness with ambition, with drive, with purpose, with aspirations, and with demands for full and equal [rights]. It is blackness that refuses to accept subjugation, to give up."[131] Baldwin understood very well what is at the heart of this moral psychology that inhibits Black advancement. Recalling his own experience, he calls it "a concentrated, malevolent poverty of spirit."[132] The academy is very good at making the Black person feel othered. It is either through microassaults (which are conscious) or microinsults (which are unconscious) or microinvalidations (which can be conscious or unconscious).[133] Minus physical harm and open picketing, Black faculty in many schools face a situation similar to what Black students and their parents faced during the busing controversy of the 1970s and 1980s. Following the landmark Board v. Board of Education (1954)[134] and the subsequent court-ordered school desegregation in the 1970s, some white parents, eager to maintain a racially homogeneous environment for their children, opposed busing under many pretexts.[135] The phenomenon still exists today but under modified forms of microaggressions.

5. The Racial Apocalyptic Problem of Mythic Consciousness

The fifth horse rider of racial apocalypse is a problem Lonergan calls mythic consciousness. He uses it to designate a nostalgic longing for a past, i.e., a past that reifies the search for essences of things. It is through mythic consciousness that the Greeks located the essence of culture and the proto human in the Greek (and by extension the Western) notions of these. He brands people with this kind of mindset as people having a classicist mentality. The classicist is no pluralist.[136] All they are about is reifying their own group as the gold standard or their own culture as the "high culture." Their main preoccupation is to set their own group or cultural traditions as the norm for human living. More importantly, Lonergan rejects any suggestion that mythic consciousness belongs to a past period of human history. "You can get right back to it very easily,"[137] he warns. Here I appropriate and extend mythic consciousness to designate a way of living and acting that makes certain privileged people feel entitled. They want to maintain their privileged status at all costs because they think of their group (consciously and unconsciously) as the gold standard. Black Theology must take seriously the racial apocalyptic problem of mythic consciousness because it is an instance of collective myth and delusion that hampers racial justice. It is an entitlement syndrome that is built on myths and false narratives. The narrative is that the rich are privileged because they work hard and the poor are destitute because they are lazy. This is how you maintain a "high culture." The Karen phenomena exposes the entitlement or "high culture" problem. The office Karen is no different from the department Karen. The department Karen is no different from the street Karen. To harken back to Ta-Nehisi Coates observation, the streets and the schools are arms of the same beast. The only difference is that one enjoys the official power of the state while the other only enjoys its implicit sanction.[138] There is a Karen in any system where there is an imbalance. What Lonergan calls mythic consciousness is ever present anywhere there is an ideology of inequality. Mythic consciousness is slick. It develops under a bias in favour of the rich and powerful and changes the creative minority into a dominant minority.[139] Mythic consciousness dreads equality, particularity of people it had once marginalized. What it can confer, at best, is "the bare privilege of not being chained."[140] Mythic consciousness makes real change seem cosmetic because it wants to maintain the privilege of the dominant class, i.e., white privilege. It also seeks to ensure that the old Jim Crow laws, which many assume to have been long dead, to metamorphosize and continue to rule from the grave.[141]

Race is not a biological or scientific fact. But unfortunately "Americans believe in the reality of 'race' as a defined, indubitable feature of the natural world."[142] In the United States also, "racial categories are so significant that knowing a person is black or white, for example, can shape how we see that person's facial features."[143] The social judgment that flows from such categorization "is so strong it affects not only how we see others but how we perceive ourselves."[144] The social categories "are filled with beliefs and feelings that may direct our actions."[145] Race is nothing but a social construct that is used to underpin inequality. Its father is racism. This was why Ta-Nehisi Coates speaks of this obsession for race construct as "the need to ascribe bone-deep features to people and then humiliate, reduce, and destroy them."[146] Some modern race theorists have taken to naming this ideology "racecraft." What they call racecraft "is a fingerprint evidence that racism has been on the scene."[147] Since what is called race is not based on nature or science (knowledge of facts), but human actions and imaginations,[148] the justification for racecraft, therefore, does not lie in science (knowledge of facts), but in a fabricated belief system that "presents itself to the mind and imagination as a vivid truth."[149] It is what Baldwin describes as the pervasiveness of "lies" in the narrative of American triumphalism. The Rev. Dr. Martin Luther King, Jr. also excoriated America for a moral vision that is clouded in "a fog of lies."[150] Following W.E.B. Dubois who attempted to expose the lies in both the narrative history of the United States and the reconstruction after the civil war, Baldwin concludes that what we see in American narrative history as a whole is one set of lies begetting another.[151] For Baldwin, as it was with both Dubois and King,[152] "lie" denotes a story that is used to warp reality.[153] It creates a "value gap" in our social imaginary.[154] Baldwin knew it was time to shatter the lies that secured America's innocence, as well as the myths of a "high culture" – that a particular group of people is superior by virtue of their race and another group of people is inferior by virtue of their race. So long as this narrative was believed, the brutality of conduct towards the Black subject becomes easy for the conscience to bear.[155]

In a fashion similar to the way Lonergan draws attention to interiority as a way of understanding the cognitional processes of the world of common sense and the world of science, Baldwin asked that everyone examines his or her interior ways of thinking. That way people may uncover what traps them in the lie.[156] White people, he said quite often, are trapped in their myths (or mythic consciousness in Lonergan's term). Non-whites catch hell because of that fact. Baldwin writes, "The American negro has the great advantage of having never believed that collection of myths to which white Americans cling: that their ancestors were all freedom-loving heroes, that they were born in the greatest country the world has ever seen, or that Americans are invincible in battle and wise in peace, that Americans have always dealt honourably with Mexicans and Indians and all other neighbours or inferiors."[157] Resisting lie or mythic consciousness means replacing it with a new consciousness that involves telling a true version of the story.[158] The Rev. Martin Luther King, Jr. had a dream that one day his children will "live in a nation where they will not be judged by the color of their skin but by the content of their character."[159] King has always been lauded for his optimism. His optimism echoes the famous lines of the eighteenth-century English poet, Alexander Pope (1688–1744), "Hope springs eternal in the human breast; Man never is, but always to be blest." While King's "I Have a Dream" speech has been celebrated because of his belief in the redemptive possibilities of human beings, it is rarely critiqued and often misunderstood.[160] King's celebrated speech does not account for the problem of undifferentiated consciousness and the ever-recurring problem of mythic consciousness. Undifferentiated consciousness does not know how to separate the mystery of human living from the myth that furthers human ideological divides. King's dream was inspired by a series of optimistic events, including the constitutional amendments, which abolished slavery and redefined U.S. citizenship to include African Americans. There was also some civil rights legislation that guaranteed and protected the African American right to vote that made King hopeful. But Lonergan's differentiated consciousness, which Black Theology aspires to, belongs to the realm of interiority. Interiority is a journey of self-discovery. It is this journey of self-discovery that Baldwin understood more than King. It was Baldwin who urged that African Americans see the connection between the disaster of their interior lives and "the mess of a country that believed, for some odd reason, that if you were white you mattered more than others."[161] As the Baldwin interpreter, Eddie Glaude writes, "even good laws are distorted by the persistence of the value gap, meaning that changes in laws, no matter how necessary, will never be sufficient."[162] Perhaps this is why Lonergan suggests that, "if myth is to be broken, more is needed. Man must discover mind."[163]

6. The Racial Apocalyptic Problem of Institutionally Embedded Racism

The sixth horse rider of racial apocalypse is institutionally embedded racism. Black Theology has a responsibility to do more to address systemic racism. Even in the academy, racism is hardly marginal. Only a somnambulist denies that racism is institutionally embedded. Racism camouflages inequality, making it harder to see, harder to discuss, and harder to tackle.[164] Inequality is a form of racism. Both "work together and share a central nervous system."[165] In the United States, at least, racism and class inequality have always been part of the same phenomenon.[166] Racism today may not be as overt as the old-school type, but "institutionalized racism and acts of white privilege continue to add subtle complexities" to the phenomenon itself.[167] Ta-Nehisi Coates wondered how it came to be that to be Black is to be naked before the elements of the world: "a society that protects some people through a safety net of schools, government-backed home loans, and ancestral wealth but can only protect you with the club of criminal justice has either failed at enforcing its good intentions or has succeeded at something much darker."[168]

Black people are not interlopers. They are not objects of charity that should be grateful for permission to exist. When institutions confront racism, they should not expect an accolade when they are not doing Black people any favours. They are only attempting to undo what should not have been permitted in the first place. Confronting racism should be seen for what it truly is – the institution's attempt to be a better version of itself. The same inner logic applies to those who think reading Black authors or adding a Black faculty to a curriculum or program is doing the Black subject a favour. It is absolutely not. Let me illustrate this with an idea Lonergan derives from Cardinal Newman's *Idea of a University*.[169] This idea that Lonergan chooses to call Newman's theorem is the idea that human knowing is to be conceived as a whole with individual parts organically related. Newman posed the question: What would happen if a significant part of knowledge were to be omitted, overlooked, and ignored by some individual or human cultural community? Newman contended that in such a situation there would be serious consequences. "First, people in general would be ignorant of that area. Second, the rounded whole of human knowing would be mutilated. Third, the remaining parts would endeavor to round off the whole once more despite the omission of a part, and as a result they would suffer distortion from their effort to perform a function for which they were not designed."[170] The same inner logic is at work when the experiences of Black faculty or Black writers are omitted, overlooked, and ignored in a human cultural community. Imagine the lacuna that will exist in an educational system if literary works of say, Toni Morrison, Langston Hughes, Alice Walker, and Maya Angelou were to be omitted. Perhaps this is why Lonergan wondered if common sense is at times not primitive ignorance.[171] It gives relevance to one of Baldwin's oft-quoted statements that ignorance, allied with power, is the most ferocious enemy justice can have.

7. The Racial Apocalyptic Problem of Misuse of Dialogue

The seventh horse rider of racial apocalypse is the misuse of dialogue for political gains. Black Theology must address the misuse of dialogue to score a political point. Dialogue is sometimes used to give the appearance of commitment to change, when in fact very little is being done to effect change. Dialogue is often used as a stop gap measure in a racially combustible environment. There is nothing wrong with that, if it is matched with a commitment to effect a lasting change. But unfortunately, quite often there is "little forward movement following the conversation."[172] This is unfortunate because quite often the stop gap does not even move the needle. Dialogue becomes useful PR, but the message is lost. No sector of society is guiltier of the misuse of dialogue than our schools and colleges. They are very good at putting on good fronts. It is akin to what the Uruguayan art critic, Ana Tiscornia said about the lack of will to tackle sexism:

> Our society is machista [sexist]: very machista and hypocritical, but very good at putting on a "good front," especially in the artistic, politically progressive and intellectual circles in which I move. With the way the left embraces certain lines of thought, the privileged intellectuals develop abstract concepts ... one would think that they would reject machista tendencies. Lamentably in this case, theory is not compatible with practice, and more than awareness is needed to transform daily habits.[173]

Ideally, dialogue ought to be used to reverse counterpositions, i.e., correct past wrongs and policy mistakes. In cases of racial tension, dialogue ought to be used as a means of reversing the lower viewpoints of ideologies of discrimination with a view to developing positions that are compatible with intellectual, moral, and religious conversion. But unfortunately, what passes for racial dialogue today has far too often been reduced to merely seeming to do something. In many cases the symbolic gesture or tokenism is confused for substance.[174] When counterpositions are reversed and positions are developed, what emerges is not tokenism, but something substantially better than what existed prior. Racial dialogue should, at least, be geared towards understanding each other's common sense because, let's be honest, the common sense of the privileged differs significantly from the common sense of the deprivileged and oppressed. Understanding each other's common sense is not a matter of making the other's common sense one's own, but a matter of fusing horizons.[175] It is only by so doing that one can acknowledge one's mistakes and the mistakes of those with whom one is allied. "Just as it is one's own self-transcendence that enables one to know others accurately and to judge them fairly, so inversely it is through knowledge and appreciation of others that we come to know ourselves and to fill out and refine our apprehension of values."[176] This is what Baldwin was alluding to when he insisted that it is not the task of Black people to save white people. He is emphatic that Black people can no longer afford to do what Henry Thoreau (1817–62) called us to do, which is to "awaken the sleeper."[177] Baldwin thinks the time has come for Black people to drop their "ready-made absolution," i.e., that White people will be forgiven for their sins because Black people will forgive them. Baldwin thinks ready-made absolution is folly.[178] This tendency to preach forgiveness without repentance or a change of heart was equally denounced by Dietrich Bonhoeffer and the Reformed Church as cheap grace (see chapter 6) That is not to say we need not be mindful of Jesus' own admonition, "be merciful, as your heavenly Father is merciful" (Luke 6:36).

Conclusion

Interiorly differentiated consciousness is a requisite demand for Black Theology. The biases of our interior mind that Lonergan suggests need to be examined have been illuminated in the last several decades by emerging new studies in the science of brain research. Although the brain still remains a great mystery, "breakthroughs in the neurological and cognitive sciences are teaching us more than we have known in all of our history of medicine. Great developments in the social sciences are teaching us more than we have ever known about human behaviour, both on individual and collective bases."[179] There was a time when Black Theology was quick to denounce racism, but slow to address sexism and homophobia within its ranks. Baldwin was a victim of the latter, as were many women of sexism. As a consequence of studies in brain research and human behaviour, we are gaining insight into how to critique prejudicial behaviours that lead to racism as well as prejudices we harbour ourselves, such as sexism and homophobia; these are what Lonergan technically calls "bias." Interiorly differentiated consciousness is a demand Black Theology must also make of society, starting with its own members. It is a demand for consistency in knowing and doing in matters pertaining to the common concerns of the dialectic of community.[180] The demand needs to be part of a grand plan of a larger conversation that will unfold in two contexts: ecclesial and societal. The first context, ecclesial, is necessitated by the fact that the church is a community of believers that understands how the power of love can transform human frailty, especially when good intentions are matched by good performance.[181] If Lonergan's observation is correct (and I know it is spot on) that the Church, like a sluggish sleeper, is "always arriving on the scene a little breathlessly and a little late,"[182] Black Theology's demand for interiorly differentiated consciousness and racial justice cannot be left in the hands of the ecclesiastical hierarchy alone. Black theologians must be in the forefront and need to be the drivers of the conversation. It is because the Church is a sluggish sleeper that it took almost forty years for the United States' Catholic Bishops to issue a major text on racism.[183] It is because the Church always arrives at the scene a little breathlessly and a little late, particularly in matters concerning Black advancement, that it took the American bishops decades to acknowledge what the rest of society had long moved on from – that the social structures of injustice and violence make all of us "accomplices in racism."[184] This late acknowledgement came on the heels of their paltry, "Brothers and Sisters to Us: U.S. Catholic Bishops Pastoral Letter on Racism" (1979).[185] The matter of ecclesial repentance will be raised in chapter 3 (in the context of the structures of sin) and in chapter 6 (on conversion). The second context of Black Theology's larger conversation, the societal environment, is necessitated by the fact that the society is the arena in which Black subjects suffer the evils of racism the most. Baldwin repeatedly pointed out the contradictions in our self-understanding as a society, i.e., "that in this so-called democracy, people believed that the color of one's skin determined the relative value of an individual's life and justified the way American society was organized. That belief and justification had dehumanized an entire group of people."[186] Baldwin continues,

> We know that we, the blacks, and not only we, the blacks, have been, and are, the victims of a system whose only fuel is greed, whose only god is profit. We know that the fruits of this system have been ignorance, despair, and death, and we know that the system is doomed because the world can no longer afford it – if, indeed, it ever could have. And we know that, for the perpetuation of this system, we have all been mercilessly brutalized, and have been told nothing but lies, lies about ourselves and our kinsmen and our past, and about love, life, and death, so that both soul and body have been bound in hell.[187]

Black Theology can bring a theological component to society's social analysis of racism. It can help direct the attention of society to the otherworldly through religious, intellectual, moral, affective, and psychic conversions. It can help society appreciate what it means to say, "God was in Christ reconciling the world to himself, not counting their trespasses against them, and entrusting to us the message of reconciliation" (2 Cor. 5:17–19). Reconciliation and the different conversion processes will be discussed in chapter 6.

In a speech he gave (12 October 2016) at a reception in honour of his 2016 Peace Prize for the Universal Peace Project, George Weigel reflected on the meaning of peace. Drawing from St. Augustine's City of God (XIX, 13), Weigel characterized peace as *tranquilitas ordinis* (the tranquillity of order). He surmised that when Augustine speaks of tranquillity of order, he is not referring to any ordinary order, but an order rooted in justice. Such an order is one that promotes the common good and makes virtue possible in public life.[188] Weigel went on to suggest that we can think of *tranquilitas ordinis* today as "dynamic, rightly ordered political community" – an order in which human rights are respected and individuals have the opportunity to participate in public life.[189] This brings us to the question "colour-blind" people ask to the point of annoyance: what do Black people want? Baldwin answered with candour – that white people know what they want and what they do not want (not to be like the Black people) and yet they ask, what do Black people want? To situate it in the context of Weigel's appropriation of Augustine, Black people want the same *tranquilitas ordinis* of dynamic, rightly ordered political community that white people want. In this *tranquilitas ordinis* must be a genuine pluralism. Genuine pluralism, is not mere difference, but "an orderly public conversation about those differences, conducted against that horizon of moral truths."[190] Tolerance does "not mean avoiding differences or denying differences, but engaging and exploring differences within a bond of civility and respect."[191] That bond, Weigel reminds us, "can only be built on the foundation of convictions about the dignity of every human being."[192] The critical question, as we search for racial justice, is whether the Church and the society have a sufficient moral capacity for *tranquilitas ordinis*. Thankfully, the Catholic tradition, stemming from St. Augustine through Thomas Aquinas to the Second Vatican Council, sees peace as inseparable from security and freedom in a well-ordered political community.[193] When people ask, what do Black people want? The answer is simple – *tranquilitas ordinis* of dynamic, rightly ordered political community.

Chapter Two

The Perplexing Matter of Black Theology

On 25 May 2020, George Floyd, a forty-six-year-old Black man, was killed in Minneapolis, Minnesota, in the United States, during an arrest by police for allegedly using a fake U.S. dollar bill at a neighbourhood store in Minneapolis. The death of George Floyd was met with horror by many who saw the video on social media. It sparked nationwide outrage and protests all over America and in other parts of the globe, particularly Europe and Australia. For many white subjects who took part in the protests, the chilling death of Mr. Floyd was unimaginable. But for many Black subjects, the death of Mr. Floyd reveals the existential reality of what it means to be Black in America. Thus, for many Black Americans who took part in the protests, it was part of an ongoing protest against the civic and economic oppression that is rooted in American history. It is about the systemic racism that plays out in different shapes and forms in American socio-political life, namely mass incarceration, unemployment, unfair housing policies, lack of educational opportunities, inadequate health care, and a ground zero in the face of a system that is stacked against them. Most intriguing, however, is that more than ever in the history of civil rights protest in the United States, more white people took part in the protests, particularly young white millennials. Some of the protests were even organized by these millennials and in places where there are few or no Black residents. It became a trend to see a mass of white people holding "Black Lives Matter" signs. A survey by Pew Research in the months following the death of Floyd reveals that two-thirds of Americans are now supportive of the Black Lives Matter movement. Among Americans, 67% of those polled say they strongly (38%) or somewhat (29%) support the Black Lives Matter movement. Only a smaller share (31%) oppose the movement. The majority support for the movement among adults, according to the Pew Research, cuts across racial lines: 86% of Blacks, 77% of

Hispanics, 75% of Asians, and 60% of whites. About one in ten Black, Hispanic, and Asian respondents also reported that they have attended rallies for racial justice in the same period. Among those active on social networking sites, 51% of Blacks surveyed reported they have posted or shared content related to race or racial equality in the same period, 38% of Hispanics and 34% of whites also posted or shared content related to race or racial equality in the same period.[1] The scale and depth of the protests, including support for the Black Lives Matter movement show that a new race awareness is taking place in America. The American novelist, essayist, and civil rights leader, James Baldwin (1924–87), like many other civil rights activists of his time, once cast doubt on the moral conscience of white America and the Christian West on the race question. In an archival interview, he asked if it was ever possible to reach the conscience of a people who on the fundamental level have no conscience. We can at least say that the death of Floyd, if nothing else, has reached the conscience of white America. The furor over his death reveals that something is happening, more than ever before, in the consciousness of white America. But what that "something" is, is a different question altogether. One thing is clear, though. "Children who enter a society different from the one their parents entered will eventually have their own opportunities to distinguish between social *is* and moral *ought*."[2] That critical attitude has been unleashed.

America, from its inception, has been defined by volatile race relations – racism. Black Theology has always had something to say about racism. In fact, racism has been the linchpin of Black Theology. Take racism away, Black Theology falls apart. To apply one of Bernard Lonergan's transcendental precepts to American race relations, "Acknowledge your historicity,"[3] means we have to face the truth of our racial past to be able to confront the truth of our racial present.[4] In the American context, it is the history that shapes "the material and structural racism of separate and unequal schools, of segregated ghettos, of employment discrimination, of mass incarceration, police killings, border walls, and brown children held in cages."[5] Baldwin explains acknowledging one's history this way: "To accept one's past – one's history – is not the same thing as drowning in it; it is learning how to use it. An invented past can never be used; it cracks and crumbles under the pressures of life like clay in a season of drought."[6] Unfortunately, outside of Black circles, Black Theology is often poorly understood and at times badly framed because of the failure to acknowledge historicity. This poor understanding also stems from an inadequate framework for understanding the reductionist philosophies that engender institutional racism, as well as the effect of racism on mainstream Christian theology. Black Theology is a protest against institutional racism in all its forms – political, social, economic, and religious. Lonergan has a framework that can help refine the categories of meaning and understanding of Black Theology. Throughout this work, I shall exposit how Lonergan's critical realist theology helps Black Theology (and by extension, critical race theory) countenance the counterpositions of race classifications in the United States. As a category, race is usually applied to the so-called people of colour, i.e., nonwhite subjects. The subliminal message is that "others" are raced and white subjects are "centered as the human norm."[7] The way Lonergan clarifies the reflexive and objectifying superstructure in modern culture can enhance societal understanding of the effect of racism in all its forms on individuals and society. His framework captures why and in what ways reductionist philosophies omit the meanings and values that inform human living and acting. In this chapter, I flesh out this category of meaning to set the stage for discussion in the chapter that follows of his analysis of what he technically calls bias, which I interpret as including race-based discriminations. Bias is Lonergan's technical word for all forms of ideologies that demean and depersonalize the other. Foremost among these ideologies are those human policies and actions that alienate. His analysis of bias is psychologically and philosophically grounded. He also provides theological resources for overcoming these odds. The resources, most of which are premised on God's ability to bring good out of evil (Romans 8:28), will be discussed in chapter 6.

Contexts of Black Theology and the Category of Meaning

In Africa, it is hard to separate the Black Theology movement from the post-colonial theory of the mid-twentieth century, even though postcolonial theory was the backbone on which Black Theology, which came much later, was built. Postcolonial theory was pioneered by the likes of the Martiniquan French political philosopher, Frantz Fanon (1925–61),[8] his fellow Martiniquan poet, Aimé Césaire (1913–2008), and the Sephardic Jewish French-Tunisian, Albert Memmi (1920–2020).[9] Their works influenced many African nationalists to develop their own postcolonial responses to colonization. Notable among these were Kwame Nkrumah (1909–72) of Ghana who developed a theory of African personality, Leopold Senghor (1906–2001) of Senegal who developed the philosophy of *Negritude*, Julius Nyerere (1922–99) of Tanzania who developed an *Ujamaa* political philosophy, and Kenneth Kaunda (1924–2021) of Zambia who developed a philosophy of African humanism. From these postcolonial theories and responses also came different forms of religious movements, including African Independent Churches. Many of these movements complemented the existing protests against colonialism. Although they were at the beginning separate from Black Theology, they were still part and parcel of the emerging Black Consciousness Movement of the time. It was much later, as the South African example demonstrates, that the Black Consciousness Movement was linked to Black Theology and to other social, political, and theoretical forms of protests for the liberation of the oppressed Black people of South Africa. The Black Consciousness Movement, especially under Steve Biko (1946–77), helped to dismantle Apartheid. Biko thought any revolution must begin with the consciousness of the Black majority, i.e., their self-affirmation and re-evaluation of their relations with the white minority.[10] The political, economic, and theoretical sources of this movement, which gathered momentum in 1970, were derived within Africa itself, particularly within Black experience. At the political level, it was influenced by decolonization or the "wind of change" in the rest of the continent where movements for independence were already taking root. At the theoretical level, the movement was influenced by the Negritude program in Francophone Africa. Thus, Black consciousness in South Africa emerged as a response to the system of Apartheid (separation of the races) that was introduced in South Africa in 1948 by the National Party under the leadership of D.F. Malan.[11] In South Africa at the time, "being non-white is not the same as being Black. Being Black is a mental attitude. Non-white refers to someone whose aspirations are to be white, but who is prevented from achieving this because of pigmentation."[12] Biko thought that traditional Christianity moulded the consciousness of the African towards compliance with the law, not towards justice. The Bible, he insisted, must speak to the oppression of the Black people.[13] He "frequently quotes Aimé Césaire, and to a lesser extent Franz Fanon."[14]

Post-colonial theory was Africa's own intellectual response to colonization and imperialism following the new awakening that came with the independence movements of the 1950s and 1960s. It was an attempt, on the part of Africans, to articulate their shared experiences and identify and name colonial methods that were used to subjugate them in the process. In this intellectual response, Africans would no longer be dependent on the benevolent western "outsider" for their liberation, but would now begin to look inward for sustainable and self-directed resources of their empowerment and emancipation.[15] In the field of theology, some of these resources were varieties of African theology, like the kind of Black Theology employed in South Africa in the fight against the institutionalized system of racial segregation – Apartheid (1948–94).

In Catholic circles, people began to speak more of Black Theology and Black Theology soon became a catchword for freedom.

Two factors contributed to the rise of Black Theology in Africa in the 1960s. Many African countries were gaining independence in this period and with independence came theological voices that sought to address the identity crisis brought about by colonialism. It also sought to restore the African sense of pride, as well as their self-understanding of their Blackness. In the heyday of colonial practice, the Dutch used a system of racial-segregation (separating the races according to colour), the British used the system of indirect rule (a policy of using pre-existent indigenous structures to control the colonies) and the Portuguese and the French both employed a policy of assimilation – a system that imposed Portuguese and French cultures (including language, religion, modes of dressing, and systems of law and governance) on the African. In the case of the French, when assimilation had to be abandoned after stiff resistance from the Africans, Charles de Gaulle (1890–1970) replaced it with his policy of association. The policy of association, in theory at least, was intended to resolve the problems connected with the dehumanizing tendencies of assimilation. In theory, the idea was that it would no longer make Africans feel like Black Frenchmen, but would instead help them acknowledge their African roots. While the policy was intended to respect African political and social institutions, its implementation and practice were anything but. The practice and implementation of association were no different from assimilation. In fact, it continued the same French policy of "civilizing" its colonies and absorbing them administratively and culturally for French gain. In sum, whatever system was adopted by the colonial powers, they were all basically the same systems of oppression and exploitation of the natives.[16] In the end, the colonial policy that was adopted in Africa became no different from the colonial policy that was adopted in the New World in which every Black person was classified as a "Negro" and no amount of white ancestry, except one hundred percent, permitted entrance to the white race.[17] Colonial racism, as Albert Memmi brilliantly captured it, was built on three major ideological components: the gulf between the culture of colonialist and the colonized; the exploitation of these differences for the benefit of the colonialist; and the use of these supposed differences as standards of absolute fact.[18] In the Americas, the 1960s were also a period of unrest for Black people there, particularly in the United States. The same Negro racial classification was used to identify anyone with African origins, albeit employed somewhat differently when compared to that used on the African continent. Black Theology in the United States emerged out of the civil rights movement and the Black quest for liberation. It became an indispensable part of Black revolution.[19] Thus, in all its manifestations in Africa and the Americas, Black Theology became a theology of liberation – economic, political, social, and cultural. In most of sub-Saharan Africa, except for the then-Apartheid South Africa where it retained its original name, Black Theology of liberation took the label Theology of Inculturation. The term "inculturation" is a twentieth-century term that derives from the Jesuits in their missionary practice in the new world. Some people misunderstand the term to mean only liturgical adaptation or reforms. This restrictive meaning is rather unfortunate. Inculturation involves liberation and self-determination of the oppressed in all its forms – economic, political, social, religious, and cultural.[20] In South Africa and the United States, where the theology of liberation retained the label "Black," the choice emphasized that it is a protest against white people's way of doing theology. Its basic assumption is that the starting point of Christian theology must be the experience of Black people and that no one can claim to be doing Christian theology in the postcolonial context without making the liberation of Africans and the so-called people of colour from the hands of white people of the First and Second worlds a central aspect of this theology.[21] "Black Theology is a theology of black liberation," declared the National Committee of Black Churchmen, at their 1969 Congress in Atlanta, Georgia. "It seeks to plumb the black condition in the light of God's revelation in Jesus Christ, so that the black community can see that the Gospel is commensurate with the achievement of black community."[22] Black Theology, in other words, is a theology that promotes political action in the light of the lived experiences (slavery and colonialism) of Black people.

But there are those who find Black Theology odious and even contemptible. How can theology be "Black" or "white," they ask, without losing its Christian character? Is the very fact of theology of Blackness not an assault on the Gospel of Jesus Christ and the nature of theology as a whole? In the light of liberation theology, which begins theological reflection from the experience of the poor and oppressed, the question whether theology can be done from the standpoint of the poor and marginalized is taken for granted. Since Lonergan is central to the Black Theology advocated here, justification for Black Theology is implicit in Lonergan's own way of doing theology in a world culture. For "a theology mediates between a cultural matrix and the significance and role of a religion in that matrix."[23] This means that in a world culture one cannot simply follow blindly old-style theology. In a world culture, one cannot simply be content to speak with categories derived from Greek or Teutonic metaphysics. These may or may not speak to the people who are non-Greeks or non-Teutons. To insist on doing theology without attention to the local context and the human experience arising from it would be to emasculate theology and empty it of its serious content.[24] Black Theology attempts to address the issues surrounding the lived life-experiences of people who are racialized as Black or coloured. It takes for granted that the classical mediation of meaning, i.e., the ancient way of controlling people's thought, has broken down. It also seeks to replace them with modern mediations of meaning, i.e., new ways of thinking. A modern mediation of meaning interprets and thematizes a people's cultural artefacts, history, and experiences.[25] Theology mediates between a religion and culture because theology is not done in a vacuum or in a laboratory. Just like the Jews articulated their experiences of God in the light of the oppression they faced in their Ancient Near Eastern context, Black Theology articulates its experiences of God in the light of its history of slavery and colonialism. Black Theology, therefore, cannot be understood without a keen knowledge of these issues. Not to be attentive to these is, as Lonergan says, to fall victim "to the up-to-date myth of ideology and the hypnotic, highly effective magic of control of thought."[26]

Why the American Situation Finds the Term "Black" Appropriate

Why is this theology called Black Theology in the Americas, especially when most of sub-Saharan Africa has opted for a theology of inculturation? Is it "Black Theology" because mainstream theology is considered a "white theology?" Absolutely. There are many who think so. This question will be answered fully in the next section when we consider James Cone's contribution to Black Theology. It is enough to say that the name "Black Theology" is related to the Black Power movement that emerged in the 1960s. In the quest to affirm their Black identity, the philosophy of *negritude* that was developed in French-speaking parts of West Africa began to spread even to the English-speaking parts of the continent.[27] This consciousness helped those in the Americas to develop the Black Power movement. The appearance of the Black Power movement and Black Theology that developed from it on the American scene was "due primarily to the failure of white religionists to relate the gospel of Jesus to the pain of being black in a white racist society. It arises from the need of blacks to liberate themselves from white oppressors."[28] The African American sociologist, civil rights activist, and Pan-Africanist, William Edward Burghardt Dubois (1868–1963), wrote in 1903 and repeated many times thereafter, "The problem of the twentieth century is the problem of the color line." By colour line, he was referring to the problem of race classification and racism that this classification birthed – domination and exploitation of people of colour. In an address he gave at the first Pan-African Congress, Dubois again repeated this line for which he is famous: "The problem of the twentieth century is the problem of the color line, the question of how far differences of race – which show themselves chiefly in the color of skin and the texture of the hair – will hereafter be made the basis of denying to over half the world the right of sharing to their utmost ability the opportunities and privileges of modern civilization."[29] Theology is one phase in the many phases of addressing the problem of the colour line. Black Theology is an attempt to confront this problem squarely and turn what was considered abject and detestable (Blackness) into something of hope. This is why Black Theology is a theology of hope for oppressed Blacks.

Contemporary Mediating Writers and Theologians

Black Theology has a long and varied history. Its development can also be traced to the distant past – to the spirit of liberation that motivated many of the slaves in the New World to seek their liberation, to the spirit of liberation that led Nat Turner (1800–31) to use Christianity as a tool of insurrection against the slave system in Virginia in 1831, to the spirit of liberation that led Harriet Tubman (d. 1913) to leave the slave plantation in Maryland in search of freedom in the north, and to the spirit of liberation that led Henry McNeil Turner (1834–1915) to proclaim that God was a negro, and for Marcus Garvey (1887–1940) to build in 1923 "a six-million-member organization in his universal Negro Improvement Association and preached that God and the Madonna were both Black."[30] In the twentieth century, as the United States struggled with its racist heritage, prominent African American leaders, such as Martin Luther King Jr. (1929–68), Malcolm X (1925–65), and James Baldwin (1924–87), wanted to make a contribution and be heard. Some became civil rights leaders and preachers and others took the stage as artists, public intellectuals, and civic leaders.[31] Here I classify these civil rights icons and early pioneers of Black Theology as mediating theologians because of the way they articulated the Black experience from which emerged the substance of what we now call Black Theology. These mediating theologians reject purely speculative theology and all forms of rationalism. They also see religious consciousness as belonging to the essence of humanity. In the end, some (Martin Luther King Jr., Malcolm X, and Medgar Evers especially) sacrificed their lives and others faced the crucible (Baldwin in particular), in the effort to help Black people find hope and guidance in the tangled web of racism, trauma, and memory in the difficult truth of race in America. Let me be clear that the discussion here of the mediating theologians is not intended to be a detailed or comprehensive history of Black Theology. In fact, the history of Black Theology, in terms of its variety and its forms of expression, is very complex and cannot be done in one book chapter. What I present here is a snapshot and is by no means exhaustive.

(a) James Baldwin (1924–87)

James Baldwin was incisive and honest in his criticism of America and its race problem.[32] He was catapulted to literary fame with his views on the moral role of the writer and his faith in the redemptive possibilities of the human subject. He expressed these in works such as *Go Tell It on the Mountain* (1953), *Amen Corner* (1954), and *Notes of a Native Son* (1955).[33] Baldwin was born in 1924 in Harlem, New York. His mother, Emma Berdis Jones, was unmarried when he was born. Three years after his birth, his mother married a factory worker and a preacher named David Baldwin. But James' mother never told him David was not his biological father. This was during the Great Depression. Later in life, Baldwin would recall how not knowing his biological father was symbolic of the problems of African American identity in which a people descended from slavery find themselves trapped in a system that hides or masks their family ancestry and distances children from both their parents and their ancestral homeland.[34] Emma and David had eight other children whom they raised together with James in Harlem, New York. Harlem at this time was a difficult place to live for African Americans. Not only was it a poor ghetto, it was also plagued by drugs and alcohol. The young James was shielded from the dangers of street life in Harlem because he was raised in the church, in the Pentecostal Holiness tradition. At the age of fourteen, he became a junior minister in one the churches in Harlem. "The combination of multiple children, Depression-era conditions in Harlem – where unemployment in the 1930s reached 50 percent – his father's low-wage job, and the oppressive ceiling of racism in America enabled Baldwin to see his family life and upbringing as allegories for the systemic, historic oppression and struggles of African Americans."[35] Later in life, Baldwin recalled that the worst thing to have happened to his father was that he was a proud man who had no power and could not feed his children. He said his father "was always at the mercy of some other man, some other man who was always white."[36] This always filled James' father with rage, leading him to develop an authoritarian personality. Baldwin saw his father's entrapment and rage as microcosms of the life of Black people and Black families in America.[37]

In 1938, Baldwin attended DeWitt Clinton High School in the Bronx. Reading novels by the likes of Charles Dickens and Fyodor Dostoevsky began to change his perspective about life, even challenging some of his religious beliefs. Like every African American living in the United States at the time, Baldwin experienced the horrors of racial prejudice in Harlem. At 16, he became convinced that he was not cut out to be a preacher anymore. "Baldwin knew intuitively, and came to know it experientially from the example of his family, that racism and capitalism combined to try and crush the life from what W.E.B. Du Bois called defiantly the 'souls of Black folk.'"[38] Baldwin graduated from high school in 1942 and moved to New Jersey to work on a railroad track. After a year, he lost his job and returned to Harlem. His stepfather died soon after. James felt compelled to remain in Harlem to help his mother raise his siblings. He took on odd jobs to make money. But he was convinced he wanted to be a writer. He was attracted to the African American novelist, Richard Wright (1908–60) whose work he greatly admired. Wright helped Baldwin secure a grant for young writers from the Eugen F. Saxon Trust, which enabled him to complete a novel he was writing. By a stroke of chance, in 1947, he also came under the influence of Randall Jarrell (1914–65), a poet and editor of *The Nation Magazine* who helped Baldwin to get some work published. One of Baldwin's first essays published in 1948 was "The Harlem Ghetto," an essay that deals with the relationship between the African Americans and the Jews in New York. Several other magazines also published some of his essays. Wright left the United States in 1947 to escape America's racial problems. Baldwin soon followed suit in 1948. Baldwin lived in Paris from 1948–57 to escape what Eddie Glaude calls America's "value gap," i.e., the idea that in America white lives mattered more than the lives of the others, and the "powerful architecture of false assumptions by which the value gap is maintained."[39] Even when he returned to the United States a decade later, he did not give up the idea of living abroad, an idea he would later call his "transatlantic commutes."[40] Living abroad actually helped him become an American writer. He said, in fact, that the best thing he ever did in his life was leave America and go to Paris. "The distance from his birthplace allowed him space to start deconstructing our myths, come to the terms with the fact that he was American."[41]

Under the influence of Wright, Baldwin continued to write novels in Paris. His first novel was *Go Tell It on the Mountain* (1953). Some of the verses of this novel, "When I was a sinner / I prayed both night and day. / I asked the Lord to help me / and He showed me the way," evoke the themes of salvation and renewal.[42] They also capture the biblical narrative of conversion of the novel. This conversion narrative will also become central in Baldwin's other works. This first novel "is largely a work of autobiographical fiction, focusing on the story of young John Grimes, who functions as a fictionalized version of Baldwin's younger self."[43] While the first novel was on a Black theme, the second, *Giovanni's Room* (1956) departs from it. In fact, all the characters of this second novel are white. The novel was somewhat controversial because it deals with the story of a homosexual bartender in Paris. The publishers at first refused to publish it. With this novel, Baldwin attracted a new homosexual audience. "Giovanni's Room was a bold step. Not only was homosexuality still considered a crime at the time – in the United States where he was from, in France where he wrote it, and in the United Kingdom where it was first published – but Baldwin wilfully wrote outside of the box his publishers were trying to put him in: that of 'the next big Negro writer.'"[44]

Although Wright was his mentor, Baldwin had his disagreements with his mentor and would later separate from him. Wright told Baldwin, all literature is protest. Baldwin replied, all literature may be protest, but not all protest is literature. Baldwin left Paris in July 1957 and returned to the United States. He said he left Paris to return home because he was tired of being referred to by the Parisians as an Algerian (the "nigars" of France). At this time, the push for desegregation was taking place in the United States. Baldwin travelled to the racially segregated South where he had never been before: North Carolina, Georgia, Alabama, Mississippi, and Arkansas. He was horrified by what he found there. He met with Dr. Martin Luther King Jr. The trip to the South was a continuation of his learning about racial issues in America. In Mississippi, he was moved by the lynching of the fourteen-year-old African American boy, Emmett Louis Till (1941–55) in 1955 who was accused of making a pass at a white woman. The tragedy inspired Baldwin to write the play *Blues for Mr. Charlie* (which premiered on Broadway in 1964). He returned to Paris in 1959 and continued his writing and from there travelled from time to time to the United States where he took part in the civil rights movement. The assassination of Martin Luther King Jr. made him cynical of racial reconciliation in the United States. He continued to write and teach, nonetheless. He served as a visiting professor at Bowling Green State University, Ohio, and the Five Colleges in Amherst, Massachusetts between 1978 and 1986. He died on 1 December 1987. Throughout his career, "Baldwin routinely questioned the doctrine of the fundamentalist Christian tradition in which he was raised, and often directly challenged those beliefs that he considered to be most damaging. In so doing, his approach to supposedly sacrosanct beliefs was to hold the 'truths' of Christianity up to a critical light."[45] The Black church and religion represent, for Baldwin, "the sigh of the oppressed" in a hopeless world.[46]

Baldwin wrote on a variety of topics, including religion, politics, and history, and never confined himself to one single genre. "As an activist, he inhabited a peripheral role in several political movements throughout his life, never confidently identifying with one specific organization over another."[47] His work as a whole was intended to be a critique of a US Civil Rights society that thought it had cleansed itself of "its hateful ideology and oppressive practices"[48] because of its devotion to the practice of democracy. Baldwin called on the nation to confront its history and challenged its superficial notion of conversion on both the individual and collective levels. He advocated "instead for wholesale change – a more honest 'conversion' of ideologies and practices – through which true transformation might be realized."[49] Although not often credited for opening up space for Black women in Black Theology, it was Baldwin who, in his conversations with Black women in the 1970s, opened space for critique of a dominant ideology that represses Black men and Black women, "recognizing in black feminism a parallel struggle to his own to disrupt and dispel white, middle-class hegemony in both the women's movement and the gay and lesbian movement (this was before transgender rights were attached to those two, and before the common self-designation 'queer')."[50]

(b) James H. Cone (1938–2018)

James Cone is one of the founding fathers of Black Theology in the United States. He laid the foundation for a liberation theology that would speak directly to the injustices and pain of being Black in America. Born in Arkansas in 1938 and raised in the segregated town of Bearden, Arkansas, Cone later recalled that he grew up in a town where white people sought to make them believe "that God created Black people to be white people's servants."[51] Growing up, Cone endured racism and saw first-hand what the destruction of Black lives meant. He had to come to terms with his Blackness amid the racism and Jim Crow laws in the United States of that era. As a theologian, he would claim that he was only interested in a theology that would empower people to be more creative and constructive.[52] In his theology, he chronicled his experiences coming of age in the face of white supremacy in Bearden, Arkansas, how Black Theology found him and gave him a voice, and how the church he grew up in, Macedonia AME Church in Bearden,

Arkansas, "could not speak to Black Power" because it was "too outrageous," even though Black Power was what attracted him to the church in the first place.[53]

In 1966, the National Committee of Negro Churchmen issued a position statement in support of Black power.[54] Three years later, on 4 May 1969, the National Black Economic Development Conference took place in Detroit, Michigan. The Conference released a manifesto that was delivered by the African American civil rights leader and a member of the Black Panther Party, James Forman (1928–2005). The opening lines of the manifesto read: "We the black people assembled in Detroit, Michigan, for the National Black Economic Development Conference are well aware that we have been forced to come together because racist white America has exploited our resources, our minds, our bodies, our labor." They demanded that white churches and synagogues pay reparations for slavery and for the continuing discrimination and racism in America.[55] These two events became a catalyst for Cone to begin analyzing Black power from a theological perspective.[56] Cone himself insisted that his work "cannot be understood without a keen knowledge of the civil rights and black power movements of the 1960s and a general comprehension of nearly four hundred years of slavery and segregation in North America, both of which were enacted into law by government and openly defended as ordained by God by most white churches and their theologians."[57]

In the preface to his 1991 book where he related the "dream" of Martin Luther King Jr. to the "nightmare" of Malcolm X to show how the dialectical tension of integrationism and nationalism plays out in African American life, Cone acknowledged two particular influences in his life: "I am an African American theologian whose perspective on the Christian religion was shaped by Martin Luther King and whose Black consciousness was defined by Malcolm X,"[58] he wrote. These two, for Cone, show that, as far as African Americans are concerned, justice and Blackness are two essential ingredients in the identity of the Christian faith.[59] Malcolm X in particular taught him that genuine religion must lead to liberation. He writes, "I do not think that anyone can be a real Christian in America today, or perhaps anywhere else, without incorporating Malcolm's race critique into his or her practice of and thinking about the religion of Jesus."[60] Following Malcolm, what Cone calls Black power is "complete emancipation of black people from white oppression by whatever means black people deem necessary."[61] He believed strongly that the time had come to expose white theology for what it is: racist.[62] Since Christianity, for Cone, is essentially a religion of liberation, "any message that is not related to the liberation of the poor in a society is not Christ's message. Any theology that is indifferent to the theme of liberation is not Christian theology."[63] Writing from his American context, Cone observed that in a society where Black people are oppressed because they are Black, "Christian theology must become a black theology, a theology that is unreservedly identified with the goals of the oppressed."[64]

To return to a question we posed in the previous section regarding whether the name Black Theology is appropriate, Cone addresses the question squarely. He states unequivocally that the name Black Theology is appropriate for many reasons. First, "Black" has the "symbolic power to convey both what whites mean by oppression and what blacks mean by liberation."[65] Black Theology is, as it were, a protest against white theology. Second, white theology may simulate neutrality, but it is "preoccupied with the conciliation of things that cannot be conciliated."[66] While white theology denies the differences among social classes and their struggles, its efforts for social good do "not go beyond the kind of modernizing reformisms that only shore up the status quo."[67] Third, in a revolutionary situation, "there can never be nonpartisan theology. Theology is always identified with a particular community. It is either identified with those who inflict oppression or with those who are its victims."[68] Fourth, in a racist society God is never colour-blind. "To say God is color-blind is analogous to saying that God is blind to justice and injustice, to right and wrong, to good and evil."[69] The God of the biblical tradition is always involved in human history and is never neutral, always taking sides with the oppressed. "If God is not involved in human history, then all theology is useless, and Christianity itself is a mockery, a hollow, meaningless diversion."[70] Fifth, Black Theology takes seriously the symbolic nature of speech. The focus on Black people in Black Theology "does not mean that only blacks suffer as victims in a racist society, but that blackness is an ontological symbol and a visible reality which best describes what oppression means in America."[71] The persecution of Jews, the extermination of Native Americans, the oppression of Mexican-Americans and the inhumanity done in the name of religion, are all, for Cone, a testimony to the White American inability to recognize the humanity of people of colour. Blackness, then for Cone, "stands for all victims of oppression who realize that the survival of their humanity is bound up with liberation from whiteness."[72] Let me add that what Cone is doing here with the two categories of Blackness and whiteness, which he brings in apposition and places in dialectical tension, is in line with critical race theory, a matter we shall engage in the next chapter. Without mentioning Cone by name, but certainly not unaware of Cone's critique, some white subjects sympathetic to the line of reasoning of critical race theory are also beginning to question the construction of racialized identity in which "whites are taught to see their perspectives as objective and representative of reality."[73]

Cone castigates mainstream Christian theology for the racism that undergirds its theological reflections. Although Cone was not trained in the theology of Lonergan, his idea that theology cannot be done in a vacuum or from an abstract position is very much in the tradition of the theology Lonergan suggests for a world cultural matrix. Cone adroitly argues that theological reflection ought to start from the lived life experiences of the suffering poor. He castigates white Christian theology for being overly concerned with the plight of the ruling class, and for saying nothing about the oppressed condition of Black people. What Cone will call Black Theology is going to be a multilayered story of Black people's search for freedom. This means, for him, that in this struggle for freedom, Black Theology cannot divorce thought from practice or worship from theological reflection, the way white theology does. He berates contemporary theology, not only for not confronting racism, but also for its silence on "the enslaved condition of black people." Mainstream white theology, he insists, has distorted the Gospel of Jesus Christ. In his first book, *Black Theology and Black Power* (1969), which he wrote immediately following the assassination of Rev. Dr. Martin Luther King Jr. in 1968, Cone argues for a desperate need for a Black Theology, "a theology whose sole purpose is to apply the freeing power of the gospel to black people under white oppression."[74] He continued the same theme in his second book published a year later, *A Black Theology of Liberation* (1970), insisting, "Any message that is not related to the liberation of the poor in a society is not Christ's message. Any theology that is indifferent to the theme of liberation is not Christian theology."[75]

In general, the themes that recur in Cone's work are the following: God is Black; theology must be done from the perspective of the poor Black; and the task of doing theology is liberation. The societal and theological problems he generally denounces are racism, sexism, classism, exploitation of the Third World, and theology's inordinate dependence on European theologians. Cone thinks he can help African Americans overcome these odds through two things he learned from Martin Luther King Jr. and Malcolm X: to fight for justice the way Martin Luther King Jr. did and to love one's Black self the way Malcolm said and did. Cone's last book, *The Cross and the Lynching Tree* (2011), can be summed up as a fitting conclusion to his work on Black Theology. The lynching tree is, for him, a symbol of white power and Black suffering; the Cross symbolizes God's power aiding and prodding the endangered

Black people from the trauma of suffering and death. Cone writes: "The Cross and the lynching tree are separated by nearly 2000 years. One is the universal symbol of Christian faith; the other is the quintessential symbol of Black oppression in America. Though both are symbols of death, one represents a message of hope and salvation, while the other signifies the negation of that message by white supremacy."[76] *The Cross and the Lynching Tree* is a rejection of white supremacy and the sufferings they inflict on Black people. He puts the premium on Black resistance, arguing that it is resistance that redeems the lynching tree. Black people must continue to resist the pain of white supremacy and racism. Cone is shocked that in spite of "the obvious similarities between Jesus' death on a cross and the death of thousands of Black men and women strung up to die on a lamppost or tree, relatively few people, apart from Black poets, novelists, and other reality-seeing artists, have explored the symbolic connections."[77]

(c) J. Deotis Roberts (1927–2022)

If Cone is considered the father of Black Theology in the United States, then James Deotis Roberts is its grand seigneur.[78] Roberts held various academic positions and taught Black Theology for many years at prestigious schools in the United States, including the University of Virginia, Howard University, and Duke University. He was very active in the Black Baptist Church. He was also active in various organizations, such as the National Council of Black Churches, the Albert Schweitzer Fellowship, the Ecumenical and Cultural Institute, and the Foundation for Religious Exchange, the latter of which he founded. His involvement in these organizations centred around locating a model for the interaction of contextual theology and ethics. Roberts honours Cone for his pioneering work in Black Theology, but insists that no one person has the last word on Black Theology. Black Theology, he argues, is a theology in the making. Very much like Cone, Roberts defines Black Theology as a theology of liberation. Like all theologies of liberation, Black Theology moves from practice to reflection, the particular to universal. "Without a particular, concrete experience, the universal is abstract. It is by involvement in the experience of oppression – it is by developing solidarity with the oppressed that we understand the meaning of liberation."[79]

Roberts finds it pertinent to make a distinction between the various forms of oppression: racism, sexism, and classism. "Oppressions based upon race and class involve the wholesale suffering of an entire people. Sexism, on the other hand, is a form of oppression which is internal or ingroup suffering, exploitation or privation."[80] He argues that racism in the United States "cannot be toned down by any comparison with any other form of oppression." Racism, as he sees it, "is the oppression of a whole people over hundreds of years. This includes men, women and children. Therefore, Blacks must be concerned with building stronger families. This does not mean that Black women do not need to be liberated; for they suffer from both race and sex discrimination. Black male-female problems are Black family problems and not merely male-female problems."[81] Black people have been oppressed and they know it. "In a real sense, only those who are aware of their oppression and God's liberating word to them in the midst of their oppression can write a theology of liberation."[82] Black Theology, Roberts insists, must be one of liberation. Reconciliation is the handmaiden of liberation. Theological ethics must be an integral part of Black Theology and must have as its goal the reconciliation of Blacks and whites. This will help the church to be a liberating and reconciling church.[83] Black Theology, in other words, is essentially a theological ethic and is primarily concerned about Black protest, survival, liberation, and reconciliation. Roberts concentrates his efforts on political theology, rather than on creeds and dogma, because of his firm belief that theology must be involved in the human quest for freedom.[84] His starting point is the African American experience. He argues that in so far as white America has taken to destroying the humanity of Black people in America, the theological enterprise has to begin by declaring the dignity and sacredness of all of God's creation, particularly the humanity of Black people.[85]

Roberts thinks theology can be used to foster reconciliation. In ways different from Cone whose theology was influenced more by Malcolm X, Roberts draws most of his influences from the non-violent movement of Martin Luther King Jr. and the peace and reconciliation efforts of Archbishop Desmond Tutu of South Africa. Roberts thinks the volatile race relations in American society notwithstanding, reconciliation can still be achieved through non-violent means.[86] Another theologian he reveres is Dietrich Bonhoeffer. He compares the theology of Bonhoeffer to that of MLK Jr., two people he sees striking parallels in their biographies and theological commitments. He sees the theologies of these two activist theologians as deeply rooted in their social, religious, and political contexts. These two activist theologians who fought against racism in their respective social milieus and who both were martyred at the age of 39 because of their religious commitment, teach us that "religious faith can have a positive side."[87] Religious faith can be used to advance positive social change because "Bonhoeffer and King demonstrated for us that one could make a lasting contribution to humanity with a short life dedicated to a worthy cause."[88] In *Roots of a Black Future: Family and Church,* Roberts again takes up a discussion of African traditional influences on Blacks and the religio-cultural origins of some Black American practices, a theme he had begun earlier in *A Black Political Theology.* Here he examines afresh the complex interrelationships between the Black family and the church, two institutions he believes have helped the Black people of America survive slavery and racism in America. In spite of the systemic disruption of Black life, these two institutions have become for Black America the symbol of freedom. He suggests that to understand Black theology one must first seek to understand African theology because the Black religious experience has its roots in Africa. He maintains that we need to take seriously the African roots of Black family and church; that the two are connected. It is only when this is properly understood that the people will develop a sense of kinship in the family of God, which is the church.

(d) Katie Geneva Cannon (1950–2018)

Katie Geneva Cannon was a Black female theologian. Black women theologians differentiate their work from that of their male counterparts, preferring instead to call it Womanist theology. Cannon was a foundational voice in this theology that seeks to escape all forms of male-centred (white or Black) views of religion and ethics so that the experiences of Black women in those areas could be better appreciated. Cannon studied under James Cone at Union Theological Seminary, becoming the first African American woman to earn a Ph.D. from Union (1983). Earlier, in 1974, she had become the first African American woman to be ordained in the United Presbyterian Church. Her work highlights the triple oppression Black women face: race, gender, and class. Rephrasing W.E.B. DuBois' phrase that the problem of the twentieth century is the problem of the colour line, Cannon states, "The problem of the twenty-first century is the problem of the color line, the gender line and the class line."[89] She argues that Black women are the most vulnerable and the most exploited members of the American society. "The structure of the capitalist political economy in which Black people are commodities combined with patriarchal contempt for women has caused the Black woman to experience oppression that knows no ethical or physical bounds."[90] In fact, it was the pioneering work of Cannon that resulted in Womanist theology. It was Cannon who appropriated, in 1985, from Alice Walker's book, *In Search of Our Mother's Gardens,*[91] the term "womanism" and gave it its definition as she puzzled over the invisibility of Black women in both Black

Theology (a movement comprising mainly Black men) and white feminism (a movement almost exclusively comprised of white women).[92] Feminist theology represents mainly highly intellectual middle-class interests. "It is also mainly Western in orientation and is limited to the intellectual-linguistic tools of the very males being criticized. It is primarily Euro-American and its scope is the North Atlantic community."[93] Cannon does not reject Black Theology and feminism outright, she only intends her criticism to specify the limitation of these theologies,[94] as she embarks on her womanist project of "debunking, unmasking, and disentangling."[95] What she tries to unmask, debunk, and disentangle are ideologies, theologies, and systems of values that are operative in society, systems such as the monochrome of the generic woman (critique of feminism) and the monochrome of the generic Black experience (critique of Black Theology). She writes:

> I first began pondering the relationship between faith and ethics as a schoolgirl, while listening to my grandmother teach the central affirmations of Christianity within the context of a racially segregated society. My community of faith taught me the principles of God's universal parenthood, which engendered a social, intellectual, and cultural ethos that embraced the equal humanity of all people. Yet, my city, state, and nation declared it a punishable offense against the laws and mores for blacks and whites to "travel, eat, defecate, wait, be buried, make love, play, relax and even speak together, except in the stereotyped context of master and servant interaction."[96]

Cannon wondered, "How could Christians who were white, flatly and openly, refuse to treat as fellow human beings Christians who had African ancestry? Was not the essence of the Gospel mandate a call to eradicate affliction, despair, and systems of injustice?"[97] In *Katie's Canon: Womanism and the Soul of the Black Community*, she shows how any sin committed against humanity is a flagrant opposition to divine goodness.[98] Cannon's work has gained a wider appeal and her criticism of the triple oppression Black women face because of group egoism is recognized even in feminist circles. The white feminist theologian, Rosemary Radford Ruether, echoing Cannon's critique of structural racism in its triple manifestation, writes, "For intellectuals, categories such as race, class, and gender trip off the tongue as though they were so many abstractions, each separate from the other. The reality is that our racist, classist and sexist societies have one complex system of exploitation which sets different groups in different relations of oppression."[99]

Shifting towards a Second Stage of Meaning

Black Theology is at a critical juncture and needs to move into a second stage of meaning. Whether it will is a different matter altogether. Stages of meaning, in the Lonergan sense of the term, are ideal constructs. They are determined by differentiation of consciousness.[100] The stages are common sense, theory, and interiority, in that order. These are ideal types. They come into play when a culture moves to a new understanding of itself and of the world around it. Lonergan says to move from one stage of meaning to another requires an "intrusion of the systematic exigence."[101] What he calls the systematic exigence is what helps to provoke questions that common sense cannot answer and also what leads to answers that common sense cannot provide.[102] The Black Consciousness Movement in Africa in the early part of the last century and the Black Power movement of the 1960s in the United States, for example, can be conceived of as instances of Lonergan's systematic exigence because they raised critical questions regarding racism and oppression and matched those questions with steadfast demand for liberation of Black people. In contesting the evils of oppression, their key question was whether the necessary decolonization of Africa requires the dechristianization of Africa[103] in the South African case, or whether a liberation of Black people must do away completely with white-European theology in the American case. These questions became catalysts for the emergence of Black Theology. In the United States, the space for this stage of meaning was occupied by the likes of Baldwin, Cone, Roberts, and Katie Cannon. They focused on articulating what it means to be Black and female and Black, female, and Christian in an exploitative system that knows the scriptural basis of God's preferential option for the poor and vulnerable, but does not have the will or desire to see to the liberation of Black people who have been rendered poor and marginalized by an exploitative capitalist system. In this stage, Black theologians were motivated by both the civil rights movement of the 1950s–1970s and the spirit of resistance of the Black Power movement. These two movements helped them to articulate what that liberation may mean for both white and Black subjects, as well as what a true Christian reconciliation will look like. As Roberts puts it, the liberated person is also a reconciled person.[104]

The emergence of racial justice movements in the United States today, like Black Lives Matter (BLM), following the death of Floyd (May 2020) and other Black people who have died either in police custody in the years leading up to this momentous event of 2020 or who have been singled out and targeted because of their race, is resonating across

Europe, Australia, and all over the world. Bias against African Americans is nothing new. The killing of African Americans because of their race is also not new. There has been media coverage of these events for years and nothing happened. Why is the killing of Floyd different? Why is it arousing so much passion and evoking support all over the world? Could the pandemic (public health crisis of 2020) and the global lockdown that followed it have played a critical role in the support for the movement for racial justice? Could the questions arising from the different parts of the globe and by all kinds of people, irrespective of race, creed, or code, be the intrusion of systematic exigence needed to move Black Theology to a second stage of meaning? To see how this plays out will require time. But what we do know for now is that Black Theology is at a critical juncture. The question is, will it profit from this and get to the critical second stage? Does it have the wherewithal to make the much-needed reflexive turn? The spirit of resistance of the Black Power movement of the 1960s is in some ways different from the spirit of resistance of the present movements for racial justice led by the BLM movement. If the sample of what we saw in the protests that followed the death of Floyd is any indication, then it means that there may be as many whites as there are Blacks in the BLM movement, even if they are unaffiliated. If the method of the Black Power movement of the 1960s was captured in the slogan of Malcolm X, "by any means necessary," then that method may be in the present context a fad and may no longer be sustainable. This means that more than ever, Black Theology is now faced with the enormous challenge of reformulating its positions and backing them up with a well-developed theological method that can speak to all of its new constituents. In the first stage of meaning, Black Theology was content with telling stories and doing away with philosophical logic. It was content with reading scriptures and seeing itself in the images of the oppressed people of Israel and expressing the eschatological hope of its sufferings in liturgy and worship. Understandably, because it was meant mainly as a social critique of mainstream theology, Black Theology became more of a hermeneutic or what one scholar has called "a modernist genealogy of critique."[105] Edward Antonio who buttressed this idea and who taught "that Cone's theology was from the beginning to the end a critical theology,"[106] also admits "that Black Theology has largely, critically, and consciously not engaged with its own status as an intellectual activity, which *qua the category of theology*, always already borrows heavily (also, albeit, dialectically) from another *Sitz im leben*."[107] To be clear, I am not suggesting that Black Theology was wrong to have employed experience as a hermeneutic in the first stage. Far from it. Theology, after all, has to be "authentically autobiographical," if it is to enflame the heart with the love of God.[108] But experiential knowledge is not enough. To move from one stage of meaning to another, experience must be anchored in a thorough knowledge of history and a solid philosophical method that can dialogue with the sciences. It is in this way that what Lonergan calls the second stage of theory can be achieved. Understandably, Black Theology, like African theology, has always lived in suspicion of theory and there has been no critical exigence toward theory.[109] This is why I suggest that an adequate method that can meet the changing needs of the times is required if Black Theology is to move to a critical second stage. Moving to the second stage does not mean that the gains of the first stage are discarded. Lonergan himself was clear that when one moves from common sense to theory, one can still use common sense to correct theory. Ours is a time of social change and unprecedented social movements. A time of great social upheaval can be transformational and can become a time of great social change. This is why I believe the social upheaval and the apparent racial awakening following the killing of Floyd can help launch Black Theology into a new stage of meaning, i.e., theory. The recent racial awakening is causing people to ask questions about the United States of America's historical past and the continued oppression, denigration, and silencing of Black people and all people of colour.[110] What we are witnessing is a demand for an unrestricted intelligibility with respect to Black lives. The intelligibility may be the systematic exigence Black Theology needs to propel it to a new stage of meaning because more non-Blacks have joined ranks in questioning the reasons for the persistence of racial bias and bigotry, in spite of widespread public condemnation.[111] In the first stage, Cone may have experimented with Tillich and Barth in his search for method, but the fact that there is still a lack of an adequate method shows that that search has not been successful.

No doubt, some Black theologians work with a different schema or periodization than the one I am using. The Scottish theologian and well-known critic of Black Theology, Alistair Kee (1937–2011), himself speaks of three waves of Black Theology in South Africa. He thinks that the first wave was ushered in by the South African anti-Apartheid activist who was brutally murdered in 1977, Steve Biko (1946–1977). The second wave, according to Kee, is represented by work of the South African Dutch Reformed Mission Church cleric, Allan Boesak (1945–). The Dutch Reformed Mission Church was created in 1881 "when the Dutch Reformed Church created separate institutions for blacks and whites."[112] In 1982, Boesak became president of the World Alliance of Reformed Churches. He played a prominent role in the Dutch

Reformed Church's condemnation of Apartheid.[113] As Kee understands this wave, the emphasis was on including Indians and coloured people (people of mixed race) in the Black Consciousness Movement. In the race categorization in South Africa, one drop of Black blood makes a person Black.[114] The coloured, being a product of mixed races (white and Black), are more likely to be rejected and discriminated against by both groups. "It was the strength of black consciousness to insist that they be included."[115] Boesak also helped to "place South African Black Theology in a world, ecumenical context."[116] The seed of the third wave of Black Theology in South Africa, according to Kee, was planted in the 1980s and came to fruition in the post-Apartheid era. Its task is to address the issue of land and the "redemption of the peasantry."[117] In this wave, Black Theology becomes a part of the ongoing liberation movement and is tasked with turning "attention to any persisting or emerging forces which cause human alienation."[118] Disappointed that this third wave has dissipated because many of the activists are now either church leaders or holding various administrative positions, Kee notes, "Under Apartheid, creative black leaders were silenced by banning orders. Now they are silenced by administrative duties."[119] Kee's outline of the different waves of Black Theology in South Africa is legitimate. However, his outline of the wave of Black Theology in South Africa is not the same as what I mean by stages of meaning.

In the United States, Cone speaks of many changes in the evolution of Black Theology, observing that between 1966 and 1984 Black Theology "went through many changes, from hostile rejection by both white and black churches to tolerance by many whites and increasing acceptance by many blacks."[120] The reader may also want to refer to Dwight Hopkins' *Heart and Head: Black Theology – Past, Present, and Future* (2002), who suggests that Black Theology has entered a stage 4, beginning in the 1980s "when the first generation began to produce doctoral students."[121] Stage 1, according to him, began in 1966 with the formation of the ad hoc National Committee of Negro Churchmen (NCNC) and "included primarily radical black clergy who were connected to churches and community movements for justice."[122] Stage 2, for him, began in 1970 when Black Theology became an academic discipline with the creation of the Society for the Study of Black Religion; stage 3 began in the mid-1970s with the birth of a new organization created in 1975, the Black Theology Project, which made a strong connection between African Americans and the Third World.[123] This important work is not without some obvious problems. One key drawback is that the book is a collection of essays originally written as standalone pieces "at different times and in different contexts."[124] Because it is a collection of essays, it has no central or unifying theme. The book, however, provides a good overview of Black Theology in general, paying great attention to Black Theology's historical and ideological contexts, particularly slavery, racism, and the emergence of the civil rights movement. It is in the last part of the book that Hopkins attends to the challenges for the future. Here he speaks of his hope for and the challenges facing the "second generation" of Black Theologians (his stage 4), such as Cain Hope Felder, Josiah Young, Katie Cannon, Delores Williams, and Emilie Townes. Being a disciple of Cone himself, he groups himself among the "second generation" of Black theologians and even scolds his own "second generation" for concentrating too much on the issue of race, sex, and class. It would seem that by "second generation," Hopkins means "young scholars" because he excoriates these "younger scholars" as being part of the status quo, i.e., as scholars who operate as individuals.[125] Many of these young scholars in the second generation were themselves students of the first generation of Black theologians. Many of them now occupy positions in universities in the United States. Their main task is to return to the "sources." The danger Hopkins sees in their scholarship "is that their closeness to the mainstream can seduce them into exclusive reliance on the experiences and opinions of white elite thinkers."[126] The contrast between my periodization and that of Hopkins is stark. First, I am working with a schema that differs from that of Hopkins. Hopkins is alluding to generational shifts, which do not necessarily equal a new stage of meaning. Second, Hopkins' division of generational groups raises many questions: Are all African American academic thinkers Black theologians? Granted, there are many African American academics of a younger generation who are speaking out forcefully in their respective fields against racial injustice and bias, however I doubt if that makes them all Black theologians. Is it not possible to be an African American academic scholar without being a Black theologian? The seemingly unending diversity of research within Hopkins' "second generation" has led some to wonder whether his "second generation" of Black Theology is really Black Theology or whether a great deal of what they are doing is in actual fact cultural studies, ethnography or even therapy.[127] Third, since Hopkins speaks in terms of "generations" and since it is conceivable for two or more generations of Black Theologians to repeat and do the same thing, it is obvious that Hopkins and his teacher, Cone, though of different generations, are doing the same thing because of the influence of the master-teacher on the student. In my schema they both inhabit the same first stage of meaning. In the foreword to the Hopkins' book, Michael Eric Dyson notes that what Hopkins has helped to do is simply "expand the intellectual gestures and scholarly impulses of first-generation black theologians and religious thinkers," such as Cone, Vincent Harding, Jacqueline Grant, Gayraud Wilmore, Albert Cleage, William Jones, and Deotis Roberts."[128] I could not agree more. Fourth, I use the term "stages" in the sense of stages of meaning.[129] Lonergan locates the source of stages of meaning in human conscious intentional operations and explains how it develops and functions in human living.[130] What is called Womanist theology, which Hopkins correctly characterizes as "the most important and innovative creations in the method of black theology,"[131] however, does not correspond to a stage of meaning. There are some who think that the Womanist theology of the likes of Katie Cannon (1950–2018), Emilie Townes (1955–), and Delores Williams (1937–), etc., may have ushered in a different phase of Black Theology. If by phase they mean "development," I have no objection. But if by phase they mean a stage of meaning, that is not accurate. They all belong to the same first phase of Black Theology. Womanist theology is mainly a corrective to the Black Theology program of Cone and the early pioneers of the movement who neglected the experience of Black women. What Womanist theology adds to this first stage of meaning is an interpretive tool for overcoming patriarchy and sexism. Thus, Womanist theology is rather a development within Black Theology itself. In opposing racism of white women and sexism of African American men in both the academy and the church, these African American women gifted Black Theology a deeper understanding of texts and provided a new lens for interpreting them. Anthony Bradley could not have put it more bluntly – "There have been no new developments in black liberation theology, other than womanist theology, since James Cone completed his corpus. Current publications in this area are nothing more than regurgitations of Cone."[132] Let me use a Lonergan-derived idea to support this claim that there has been no new development in Black Theology since Cone. Lonergan makes it clear that when a new stage of meaning is reached, there is a priority given to what is needed moving forward. Using the examples of the Greeks, he writes:

> The Greeks needed an artistic, a rhetorical, an argumentative development of language before a Greek could set up a metaphorical account of mind. The Greek achievement was needed to expand the capacities of common-sense knowledge and language before Augustine, Descartes, Pascal, Newman could make their common-sense contributions to our self-knowledge. The history of mathematics, natural science, and philosophy and, as well, one's own personal reflective engagements in all three are needed for an entry into the world of interiority.[133]

Hopkins is correct that the challenges of the twenty-first century demand an ongoing Black Theology.[134] But it will take a well-developed theological method that can facilitate entry from one stage of meaning to another to meet these challenges. It is that method that will help propel Black Theology to the critical second stage of meaning. That method must be grounded in a critical realist philosophy that can speak to all the publics of Black Theology and outside of Black Theology, like the one that has been developed by Lonergan whose starting point of theology (human experience) gives validation to Black Theology's turn to experience. In this method, Lonergan shows how consciousness can be differentiated in various ways – scientific, theoretical, artistic, and religious. Knowing oneself as subject (which Black Theology knows too well), something Lonergan technically calls self-appropriation, yields a further differentiation of consciousness which Lonergan terms interiorly differentiated consciousness.[135] "The person of interiorly differentiated consciousness has developed a habitual understanding of the operations and states of his or her consciousness in their relations with one another."[136] Interiorly differentiated consciousness provides a context for Black Theology's self-understanding and self-constitution.

The new method Black Theology needs, therefore, can be appropriated from the theological method of Lonergan, for Black Theology is a search for meaning and a search for interiorly differentiated consciousness. To say that Black Theology needs to appropriate the theological method of Lonergan is counterintuitive. At first glance, this suggestion seems diametrically opposed to what Black Theology stood for, at least in its first stage of meaning, i.e., disengaging and dissociating with white theology. But the theological method of Lonergan is anything but white theology. In its essence, it is a method ready-made for Black Theology even before the coming to birth of Black Theology in that it is existential, transcultural, and experience-based. It is a method rooted in a common humanity that is open to anyone with intelligence who wants to understand oneself as a human subject. In other words, the very thing Black Theology wants to achieve (liberation) is a miniature of what Lonergan calls everyone to find out for oneself in the processes he articulates for self-discovery. Lonergan himself was averse to taking credit for this theological method that goes by his name because he understands that the method itself is transcultural in nature. It is a method that is open to everyone. "What I'm asking people is to discover themselves and be themselves," he writes. "They can arrive at conclusions different from mine on the basis of what they find in themselves."[137] Appropriating the theological method of Lonergan will help Black Theology fill a void. One of the problems with the first stage of meaning of Black Theology is that it does not know to distinguish adequately between the data of sense and the data of consciousness. Since the landmark works of Cone, Roberts, and Katie Cannon and others who came after them, much attention has been on the data of sense (the lived experience of race. class, and gender bias), to the neglect of the data of consciousness (the inward cognitive operations that produce these biases). This distinction was implicit in the poetic imaginations of Baldwin, but his work was not given the kind of attention it deserves in Black theological discourse, perhaps because he was classified as a poet (and not a theologian) and, sadly too, because of his sexuality. Conservative Black Theology at the time had no room for LGBTQ perspectives. In contemporary discourse, however, Shawn Copeland has been moving Black Theology in the direction of data of consciousness. She has been using the framework of Lonergan to construct a theological anthropology that pays attention to why human subjects are prone to acts of bias. She insists, correctly, that theology must play a "vital task of abstraction: grappling with concrete data to discern, understand, and evaluate their emerging patterns in order to interpret their meanings."[138] By helping Black Theology pay attention to the data of consciousness, Copeland has begun the difficult task of unmasking "the thought-systems that would allow for the stigmatizing, identifying, and eradicating of whole groups of persons – persons deemed different, inferior, dangerous."[139] As will be discussed in detail in the next chapter, racism, like sexism and classism, is fuelled by what Lonergan technically calls bias. If bias is to be identified, named, addressed, and hopefully overcome, the question Copeland raises in appropriating the work of Lonergan becomes ever more relevant: "How is a mind to become conscious of its own bias when that bias springs from a communal flight from understanding and is supported by the whole texture of a civilization?"[140] In *The Subversive Power of Love*, Copeland shows how the bias from understanding supported the worldview of chattel slavery in the United States. That worldview created "a laissez faire morality and casual religiosity that shaped the environment in which black bodies were objectified and used, abused and desecrated."[141] Following the line of argument Lonergan suggests for remedying bias, Copeland makes the case for a critical consciousness, not only for Black women to understand the ways their bodies are framed and read socially, but also how they are read and framed by both white and Black people.[142]

Conclusion

In its search for interiorly differentiated consciousness, Black Theology faces enormous challenges, the greatest of which is "to develop an enduring race critique that is so comprehensively woven into Christian understanding that no one will be able to forget the horrible crimes of white supremacy in the modern world."[143] In Catholic circles, some white Catholic theologians are slowly, but increasingly becoming somewhat conscious, and even "embarrassed" and "uncomfortable" about their failure "to recognize the problems of racism in the United States and in the Catholic Church."[144] One such theologian, Charles Curran, has courageously detailed his own epiphany: "In the last few years, I have become somewhat educated about racism and white privilege. I have to face the reality that I barely recognized the problem of racism in my own somewhat extensive writings and was blithely unaware of my own white privilege."[145] In this new awakening, Curran now admits that "despite having the tools that should have made me more aware of the problem of racism, I never really addressed racism in my writings."[146] To this end, he is now joining forces in calling for a "spirituality that prays to a God who is black and female" as a way of helping to open the eyes of mainstream white theologians to the problem of systemic racism.[147] Curran's courageous example is in line with the suggestion I made in the previous section – that the long-range plan of Black Theology has to be one that pays attention to the data of consciousness.

A recovery of data of consciousness is key to understanding cognitive mediation and social behaviour – how bias operates in the mind of the conscious subject. As Lonergan explains it, there are two dimensions of awareness to be identified in a person's cognitional operations – what the person is conscious of and what the person intends.[148] Gordon Allport long ago declared attitudes to be social psychology's "most distinctive and indispensable concept."[149] In the next chapter, following Allport's lead, we will show how social psychology began developing methods for measuring attitudes in the 1930s,[150] methods that will later be extended to investigate stereotypes and attitudinal constructs.[151] In investigating stereotypes, social psychology now distinguishes "automatic" (intuition) from "effortful" (reason) mental processes. The operations of the intuitive system, according to these social psychologists, are "fast, automatic, effortless, associative, implicit (not available to introspection), and often emotionally charged."[152] By comparison, the operations of the reasoning system are "slower, serial, effortful, more likely to be consciously monitored and deliberated and deliberately controlled."[153] While the operations of the intuitive system are governed by habit and, therefore, difficult to control or modify, the operations of the reasoning system are relatively flexible and rule-governed.[154] In chapter 5, I will flesh out what will be identified as implicit attitudes and their correlative implicit bias, i.e., that they belong to intuition and are more likely to exist outside of conscious awareness. They are also easier to activate and more difficult to control, unlike explicit attitudes and their correlative, explicit bias, which belong to reason and are easier to control or modify.[155]

Appropriating the theological method of Lonergan in this way will, in the end, help Black Theology in the task of self-appropriation. Let me try to explain, as clearly as I can, what I mean here. In my conversations with colleagues (white theologians in particular) about the state of Black Theology, I discover that many still have the perception that Black Theology is all about proof-texting of Scripture, lived-life experiences of Black people, and story-telling. There is still the perception that Black Theology lacks theory and solid philosophical foundation. They think the lack of theory makes it difficult to take Black Theology seriously as an avenue of rational theological discourse. Their criticism suggests that Black Theology is still caught in some sort of cul-de-sac. The criticism may be a little harsh, but there is something to be said about not properly distinguishing between the realms of common sense and theory (intellectual pattern of experience). There is nothing wrong with relying on and quoting scripture. In fact, systematic theology should do more to engage scriptural exegesis. But scripture, as Lonergan noted, corresponds to the undifferentiated consciousness. Magisterial and conciliar documents correspond to the differentiated consciousness. What the theologian needs to do is learn to make a transition from undifferentiated common sense to the intellectual pattern of experience.[156] This will involve engagement in self-appropriation that is far more nuanced than what Black Theology is presently doing.

My task in the chapters that follow will be to unearth, even if implicitly, how Black Theology is, as it were, a movement from attention to intelligence, to reasonableness, to responsibility, and to the religious experience of Black people. Self-appropriation, i.e., coming to know oneself and one's operations as a believer, a religious thinker, and a theologian,[157] will help to objectify and heighten this religious experience – and that objectivity is the fruit of authentic subjectivity.[158] Self-appropriation will help Black Theology develop a heuristic structure (theory) for conceptualizing its fundamental terms and relations within the horizon of its experience. In Lonergan's notion of self-appropriation, he "moves theory into a higher context where it becomes an aid to the concrete articulate self-possession of the human person in self-knowledge and self-constitution."[159]

Chapter Three

The Nature of Prejudice: A Psychological and Theological Understanding

The death of George Floyd (25 May 2020) in Minneapolis, Minnesota and the deaths of other African American males and females at the hands of police, brought to light by social media in 2020, have necessitated a re-examination of race in American social and political life. It is also forcing a long overdue conversation about America's racial history, its racial present, and racial future.[1] Long before this social media-inspired activism and discourse on race came to the fore, Black Theology had appeared on the American scene primarily because of "the failure of white religionists to relate the gospel of Jesus to the pain of being black in a white racist society."[2] This chapter re-invigorates this discourse. I show why the conversation on racism and theology must engage Bernard Lonergan's work on bias. Lonergan's definition of *bias* is philosophically sound, psychologically grounded, and theologically sophisticated. His notion of bias can also be a catalyst for engaging the new critical race theory that Black Theology must pay attention to because it exposes many of the counterpositions in common-sense-derived remedies to the American race problem. This engagement with Lonergan will also help to show more clearly that race or races do not correspond to any biological or genetic reality, but are rather "products of social thought and relations."[3] It exposes that what goes under the garb of race and races are categories that society invents, manipulates, and at whim retires, when convenient.[4]

As a concept, critical race theory has a long history that goes back to the Pan-African sociologist W.E.B. DuBois (1868–1963) and the African American womanist activist Fannie Lou Hamer (1917–77), among many others. Although it began within the system of law, critical race theory has now spread to other disciplines, and today has an activist dimension.[5] The activist dimension has in more recent times been controversial in the United States. The critical race theory of which I speak here pertains, not to the activist dimension, but to the insights it offers about discrimination and exclusion of peoples. If Black Theology is to be a genuine protest against racism, it must engage this new way of understanding and reading discrimination, because critical race theory seeks to understand and combat racism and inequality in the United States, using new strategies in social and scientific methods.[6] Granted, today critical race theory has splintered into sub-groups. There are now such sub-groups as the Latino-Critical group (LatCrit),[7] Asian-American jurisprudence group,[8] and Queer-critical interest group.[9] Although each of these groups has its own distinctive features and turf interests, for example, Latino-Critical group focuses on immigration theory, policy, and issues of discrimination, the Asian-American jurisprudence group focuses similarly on immigration and issues of discrimination, and the Queer-critical group focuses on human rights and discrimination, all still converge for a common goal – the defense of human rights and the fight against racism and discrimination.[10] They all share the unique insight that racism, to use the language Delgado and Stefancic employed so well in their work, is not aberrational, but a "normal science" in American social and political life. In other words, racism is "the usual way society does business, the common, everyday experience of most people of colour" in the United States.[11] Black Theology, like these sub-groups, understands that the American system of "white-over-color ascendancy serves important purposes, both psychic and material."[12] What Lonergan brings to the discourse further advances this critical race theory that began as a way of examining how laws and systems promote inequality in American society.[13] Lonergan's critical-realist approach to bias, if appropriated by Black Theology, will help Black Theology to properly engage what critical race theory has to say about prejudice. The conversations on racial prejudice by Black Theology and critical race theory seem to be happening independently of each other. They need to be brought together. Although the task of bringing them together is by no means easy, the tool Lonergan offers can be an aid in this effort. It can help Black Theology articulate not only how racism is an everyday experience of Black people, but also more importantly how and why society is not interested, at least in the long run, in doing away with it. It benefits certain groups, the elite class. Thus, bringing to bear what Lonergan articulates as the four types of common-sense bias can help steer Black Theology in the right direction. His insights into the data of human consciousness, which are consistent with new studies emerging from social psychology about human consciousness and behaviour, will offer the possibility of a new leap forward.[14]

Why Black Theology Has Not Paid Attention to the Data of Consciousness

Black Theology was validated by a psychological study of the nature of prejudice in Gordon Allport's *The Nature of Prejudice* (1954).[15] But the gift has yet to be fully harnessed. Focusing primarily on the contentious race relations in the United States, Allport (1897–1967), an American psychologist and a key figure in the emergence of personality psychology as a new field of investigation, drew from cognitive psychology to explain how stereotypes are acquired and sustained in the everyday life of community. He saw prejudice to be not only the cause but also the key problem in any majority-minority intergroup relations. He also noted that prejudice is the fundamental cause of socio-political and economic inequalities between groups and "the most formidable barrier to change in the status quo."[16] Before Allport's groundbreaking work, psychologists in the field of inter-group relations had spoken of six main approaches to the problem of racial prejudice: the historical, sociocultural, situational, personality, phenomenological, and stimulus-object level. As helpful as these approaches were, the problem was that different researchers focused almost exclusively on only one aspect of the six, depending on the subject and the time frame of their investigation. To Allport's credit, he not only acknowledged but also saw value in all six approaches to the problem of racial prejudice.[17] He admits, however, that it is not possible to reduce all six approaches to a single theory of human action. He therefore suggests that, since there is "no master key" to understanding prejudice, it is better to adopt an eclectic approach that will open the gate of understanding. That way, "the principal points of view will fall into a clear perspective."[18] The eclectic approach that Allport sought is his own way of ensuring that we advert to what we are doing when we are conceptualizing racial prejudice. This idea resonates with Lonergan who also takes seriously what he terms the data of consciousness.

What Allport presents in his landmark work is an empirically grounded analysis of prejudice. He sees prejudice as social attitudes that are acquired and maintained through the interaction of external influences, ordinary psychological functions, and personality structure.[19] Black Theology, unfortunately, has not fully embraced Allport's work and has done little to engage it, not that it dismissed it altogether. The reason Black Theology has not paid much attention to Allport's work is because Black Theology (in all phases of its manifestations in Africa, the United States, and the Caribbean) has seemed less interested in what Lonergan correctly distinguished as the data of consciousness and more interested in the data of sense. There are some who may think Black Theology has always paid attention to the data of consciousness. This reasoning at times stems from a dubious understanding of how the word "consciousness" is used in the South African and other African contexts. What was called Black Consciousness was an important movement in Southern Africa in the fight for freedom. In the early twentieth century, the Black Consciousness movement in South Africa led to the formation of many other allied movements, including the Congress of Youth League (formed in the 1940s) and the Pan Africanist Congress (1959), and South African Students' Organization (SASO) led by Steve Biko (1946–77). Although they all had their own specified agendas, all the movements saw oppression as largely psychological and thought consciousness raising was a *sine qua non* for liberation. One of their main contentions was that "the most potent weapon in the hands of the oppressors is the mind of the oppressed."[20] To counter this mind game, some of the cultural emphases of the Black Consciousness Movement were placed on Black pride, Black art, Black poetry, and Black solidarity. In this way, the Black Consciousness Movement in that region of Africa was part of a lengthy struggle for self-determination in southern Africa as a whole. Its goal was to intensify political and psychological pressure on the leaders of these southern African countries and the system of Apartheid wherever it was practiced. There was, for example, a students' revolt in South Africa in 1976, an uprising in which students refused to use Afrikaans as a medium of instruction.[21] They wanted instead a new Bantu education program. In emphasizing Black awareness, Biko adopted the slogan: "Black man, you are your own." Many in the United States and in the Caribbean were influenced by their consciousness-raising and Black activism, and particularly by their Black Theology, "which was self-confident, proud, and pictured Christ as a radical activist on behalf of the downtrodden."[22] The Black Consciousness Movement of the early 1970s in South Africa helped spur nationwide strikes, boycotts, and demonstrations. These provoked the famous Soweto uprising (16 June 1976), which left upwards of 700 dead and 4000 injured. The movement, which was intended to heighten uprising in neighbourhoods of the so-called African, Coloured, and Asian communities in South Africa, was led by Steve Biko, among others. It also proved successful to some degree in countries like Mozambique, Angola, and Zimbabwe. By 1973, Black Consciousness had become so popular that it became "a quasi-political focal point for the black population."[23] It played a big role in restructuring the social and economic order. This was the Black Consciousness hype that caught on in other parts of Africa, the United States, and the Caribbean. It was the context of the revolutionary philosophy of President Thomas Sankara (1949–87) of Burkina Faso to "decolonize minds" in Burkina Faso and in the whole of Africa. It was also the context of the late Bob Marley's 1980 hit song, "Uprising," in which he urged Black people, "Emancipate yourselves from mental slavery. None but ourselves can free our minds." The point here is that "consciousness" as used in Black Theology at this time is not what Lonergan means by data of consciousness. But it is hard to dismiss the fact that the Black Consciousness Movement called attention to the cognitive-psychological aspect of oppression, the awareness of which contributed to liberation and self-determination. Perhaps it is fair to say that the Black Consciousness Movement, in its various hints at the cognitive-psychological trauma of oppression, anticipated what Lonergan will make a central concern of inquiry, i.e., that we pay attention to the data of consciousness.

Understandably, Black Theology contented itself with the data of sense to the neglect of the data of consciousness. The human drive to know, to understand, to see why, to discover the reason for something, and to be able to explain that thing further, which Lonergan calls a basic human orientation, begins with the data of sense.[24] But sense experience (collecting data) is only the first of multi-layered levels of this innate human orientation. There is a further important level of theory that follows, followed still by the critical level of interiority. The thinking mind must advert to all three levels and know what it is doing when and why it is doing what it is doing. Understandably, Black Theology knows, from the data of sense, that prejudice has been raised to an art-form in the United States and that Black people are on the receiving end of this artistry. But it has not paid proper attention to the mind behind the artistry (prejudice), i.e., what induces in a person acts of prejudice and the conditions for their manifestation. This is the part of the data of consciousness that needs to be recovered in Black Theology. The first condition of hermeneutics or interpretation, according to Hans-Georg Gadamer (1900–2002), is that understanding begins when something addresses us. It therefore requires what he (Gadamer) calls suspension of all prejudices,[25] including one's own. It is not clear, however, how one can suspend one's own prejudices, nor did Gadamer explain how to achieve this. But if prejudice is, in its negative sense (and I believe it is) a false belief, then behind the false belief is a false believer.[26] "One has to look into the manner in which one happened to have accepted erroneous beliefs, and one has to try to discover and correct the carelessness, the credulity, the bias that led one to mistake the false for the true."[27] This is the trajectory this chapter takes – to help Black Theology be more attentive to the data of consciousness.

The data of consciousness helps us to understand what it is in a human person's cognitive acts that induces in the person prejudices and hostility towards members of another group. Allport's *The Nature of Prejudice* defined the field of intergroup relations for social psychologists interested in the study of prejudice in human dialectic community.[28] Allport organized existing research on group relations and the nature of prejudice in a way that suggested new directions for research.[29] Thus, Allport's work is the beginning, not the end, of the process of grappling with the role of consciousness in acts of prejudice. I shall now explore a new direction mediated by the philosophical thoughts of Lonergan and I will identify its resonances in new studies in neuroscience and social psychology. Lonergan employs the technical term "bias" – a flight from understanding – to stand for and go beyond what Allport and modern psychologists call prejudice, incorporating their treatment of prejudice as a phenomenon of cognitive functioning. He explains its motivational underpinnings and locates its affective resonance in a person's psyche. Before turning to Lonergan's treatment of this flight from understanding, I explore the definitional meaning of prejudice as a context of understanding.

Prejudice: A Provisional Judgment?

The term "prejudice" derives from the Latin *praejudicium*, denoting a pre-judgment. It is used to designate a favourable or unfavourable feeling towards another based on their social group or associations. Gadamer noted "that all understanding inevitably involves some prejudice."[30] Gadamer also tells us that it was not until the European Enlightenment (1715–89) that the concept of prejudice acquired the negative connotation that it has today.[31] The Enlightenment's critical theory of prejudices, i.e., their "prejudice against prejudices," was a well-calibrated attack against the Bible and Church authority. A well-known principle of the Enlightenment was that authority is a source of prejudice. That, at least, was what Immanuel Kant intended when he formulated his famous Enlightenment motto: Have the courage to make use of your own understanding.[32] But what Kant failed to realize was that human reason too can be loaded with prejudice. Trying to give a positive value to the Enlightenment "prejudice against prejudices," Gadamer distinguishes between the prejudice that is due to human authority and the prejudice that is due to overhastiness in oneself. "Overhastiness is the source of errors that arise in the use of one's own reason. Authority, however, is responsible for one's not using one's own reason at all."[33] The Enlightenment critique of religion tries to make prejudice seem like an "unfounded judgment." But the only thing that gives a judgment dignity, Gadamer insists, "is its having a basis, a methodological justification (and not the fact that it may actually be correct)."[34] Attempting to rehabilitate the pre-Enlightenment notion, which the Enlightenment critique distorted, Gadamer recalibrates prejudice as "a judgment that is rendered before all the elements that determine a situation have finally been examined."[35] In German legal terminology, he argues, a prejudice is "a provisional legal verdict before the final verdict is reached."[36] Harking back to the Latin *praejudicium*, denoting "adverse effect," "disadvantage," or "harm," Gadamer insists that this negative sense is only derivative and "depends precisely on the positive validity, the value of the provisional decision as a prejudgment, like that of any precedent."[37] It would seem, therefore, that for Gadamer, what we need to avoid is "the tyranny of hidden prejudices that makes us deaf to what speaks to us in tradition."[38]

Although Allport does not make the kind of philosophical distinction Gadamer makes, his notion of prejudice comes close to that of Gadamer. Allport does not consider a prejudgment to be necessarily a prejudice. For him, a prejudgment only becomes a prejudice when one wilfully refuses or is unable to reverse the judgment. But he offers an affect-laden and cognitive-based definition of prejudice not offered by Gadamer, i.e., that prejudice is a felt or expressed "antipathy based upon a faulty and inflexible generalization."[39] Thus, prejudice, for Allport, has a plural causation. It is a serious error, he argues, "to ascribe prejudice and discrimination to any single taproot, reaching into the economic exploitation, social structure, the mores, fear, aggression, sex conflict, or any other favored soil."[40] Allport does not deny that prejudice and discrimination "may draw nourishment from all these conditions,"[41] particularly since economic and social influences are always determinants of a person's choices and decisions, but that there are other causes of prejudice beyond these, some of which may have historical explanations. To understand why a person chooses to be prejudiced against one group, we must go "beyond the fact that the individual perceives a certain group in an oversimplified way, and understand why he sees them as he does."[42]

What we gather from both Gadamer and Allport is that prejudice is a prejudgment or provisional knowledge, which can be either negative or positive. For Lonergan, a prejudgment is an unreasonable judgment. In its common usage, prejudgment usually has a negative connotation. A correlate or common cognitive component of prejudice is stereotype. Stereotypes are beliefs, attributes, and behaviours a person or members of a group ascribe to other people or members of a different group.[43]

Like prejudice, which in its pristine meaning before the Enlightenment construct is not necessarily negative, socially shared generalizations about members of other groups (stereotypes) are not necessarily negative and can be positive, though they are developed and maintained through social roles and are often expressed in negative terms. An example of positive prejudice can be found in romanticizing, as in when Africans in the diaspora romanticize Africa the mother land or when Irish-Americans romanticize their homeland in Ireland. The romanticizing can become a stereotype. The net effect of stereotypes is that they lead to negative judgments and discriminatory behaviours towards members of other groups. The most common stereotypes are those pertaining to race, gender, sexuality, and culture. At times, people engaged in discriminatory behaviours may not even be aware of their actions. African Americans suffer from age-old stereotypes. There is a continuum between stereotypes and more severe forms of racism. The social psychologists Mahzarin Banaji and Anthony Greenwald have provided a persuasive account of how stereotypes can lead to discrimination. They have conducted numerous studies that reveal that while most Americans are not overtly racist, when given the choice between whites and African Americans in a range of contexts, far too many still show preferences for whites over African Americans. They concluded from this and other studies that not only can this lead to discrimination, it can also account for the social and economic disparities between the two groups.[44] For Lonergan, stereotypes reflect a laziness of human intelligence based on group bias. Racial stereotypes, which in Lonergan would be unreasonable judgments of group bias, are often fed by egoism of the group. Lonergan calls egoism an incomplete development of intelligence.[45] It is a deliberate exclusion of correct insight, correct understanding. The deliberate exclusion of correct insight leads the egoist to develop an uneasy conscience. "The egoist's uneasy conscience is his awareness of his sin against the light."[46]

In the United States, the unfolding of racism, to use Lonergan's terms, is rife with the paradoxical known-unknowns and unknown-knowns.[47] The knowns are the common, everyday-life discriminatory practices, such as racial profiling and driving while Black (DWB, i.e., being pulled over while driving black) that African Americans know to expect. The unknowns are better left to the imagination. This is because the systems of racial and social control adapt, morph, rebound, and are reborn.[48] This is why for many people, racism is an ambiguous concept, with opaque and often shifting meanings.[49] In the United States, the history of race and racism is "paradoxical, shameful, and complex, filled with countless examples of legally sanctioned racial oppression."[50] There are even more egregious examples in which "social scientists have been involved, negligently if not intentionally, in stigmatizing populations of color as culturally deprived or inferior and, by implication, not worthy of the effort to fully understand and address their injuries and oppression."[51] Racism remains a potent force with deleterious consequences. A more nuanced theological analysis of the root cause of this peculiar form of prejudice is, therefore, needed. As indicated already, Lonergan provides an analysis he technically calls "bias." This theological analysis is steeped in Christian scripture, while still not neglecting the useful insights of the social sciences. The analysis he offers meets the imperative to distinguish, as some social scientists have insisted must be done, the prejudice that informs racism as a conscious belief system and ideology from individual prejudice that can arise from personal feelings or other causes.[52] This analysis will be considered next, but only after clarifying the role of critical theory in the matter.

How Applying Lonergan's Notion of Common Sense to Critical Race Theory Enhances Race Discourse

Lonergan is unique among Christian theologians in the sense that he is the only one who has made the term "common sense" a philosophical category. This philosophical category has very rich theological implications. The term quite often has a technical meaning in his theological parlance. When he uses the term common sense, it is his own way of distinguishing the knowledge derived from it from the knowledge derived from science – knowledge of fact. Simply put, what Lonergan calls common sense stands in opposition to the method of valid reasoning. Common sense is the specialization of intelligence in the particular and the concrete. It has no use for theory. Common sense has biases that people may know, but to which they may not be attentive. What Lonergan does is help us identify what these biases are and how they operate. For example, it was long taken for granted in U.S. jurisprudence that there is only one law and that this law is universal and applicable to everyone in the same way. But more recently, some legal minds working out of critical race theory are beginning to question why the education they received in their training did not address such concerns as group inequality, sexual differences, and cultural identities. This is because they are now realizing that the law makes it pertinent that whites hold social and institutional power over people of colour. They are now questioning what was thought to be "only one Law, a law that in its universal majesty applied to everyone without regard to race, color, gender, or creed,"[53] and wondering whether this might not be the very essence of racism. The impetus for this critique began in the 1960s with the invention of a theoretical framework, critical race theory. It was a framework that helped to challenge and question "the very foundations of the liberal order, including equality theory, legal reasoning, Enlightenment rationalism, and neutral principles of constitutional law."[54] In effect, critical race theory is a recognition that the legal system of the United States can no longer be conducted on the level of what Lonergan calls common sense because common sense consists in a set of insights that remains incomplete. It is common without being general.[55] This incompleteness of the insight of common sense has been teased out by Shawn Copeland in her application of Lonergan's work to both social construction of gender and race and the Christian teaching about the human person. "Christian teaching about the human person faltered," she writes, "and the consequences for black women were grave."[56] Christian teaching even helped to dig Black women further into "the crossroads of two of the most well-developed ideologies in America, that regarding women and that regarding race."[57]

Even though common sense can be improved, it always "reverts to its normal state of incompleteness."[58] Some white subjects who benefit from the system of white privilege and institutional racism sometimes appeal to the law to exonerate themselves from culpability. They are quick to remind critics that they did not enact the laws of the past – that the past is detached from and has nothing to do with the present.[59] What they are doing is espousing one of the many flaws of common sense that Lonergan has brought to light. In her beautiful essay on "White Fragility," the white feminist whose work has become important for critical race theory, Robin DiAngelo, writes that white people in North America live in a social environment that protects and insulates them from race-based stress. "Whiteness accrues privilege and status; gets itself surrounded by protective pillows of resources and/or benefits of the doubt; how Whiteness repels gossip and voyeurism and instead demands dignity."[60] She points out that whites are rarely without these "protective pillows," and on rare occasions when they are without the protective pillows, it is usually temporary and by choice.[61] Lonergan tells us that common sense does not have to be articulate and that it always appeals to an incomplete set of insights. Racism is "the exercise of power against a racial group defined as inferior by individuals and institutions with the intentional and unintentional support of the entire (race or) culture,"[62] Critical race theory exposes the common tendency to acknowledge race as something central to the law and policy of the United States and goes beyond the common-sense popular belief "that getting rid of racism means simply getting rid of ignorance, or encouraging everyone to 'get along.'"[63]

Lonergan tells us that common sense likes to argue from analogy, even though its analogies defy logical formulation.[64] The law has played a role in the practice of exclusion and structured disadvantage of Black people in the United States. It was only in the 1970s that activists and legal scholars, working out of critical race theory, began to recognize that the systemic racism that is institutionalized in American society needs to have the beliefs and attitudes that make it flourish, upended. They began to understand that it is not all about understanding the American social situation, but also about changing it; not all about ascertaining how society organizes itself along racial lines and hierarchies, but also about transforming it for the better.[65]

According to Lonergan, common sense likes to generalize, but it generalizes in ways different from science. A generalization of common sense has a "quite different meaning from a generalization proposed by science. The scientific generalization aims to offer a premise from which correct deductions can be drawn. But the generalizations issued by common sense are not meant to be premises for deductions. Rather they would communicate pointers that ordinarily it is well to bear in mind."[66] They can function like proverbs, adages, or aphorisms. Apart from differing from science in logic and in the meaning it attaches to analogies and generalizations, common sense "operates from a distinctive viewpoint and pursues an ideal of its own."[67] In racial terms, this generalization and ideal of common sense has resulted in a system of domination that the race critic, Zeus Leonardo, explains as being "quite simple: set up a system that benefits the group, mystify the system, remove the agents of actions from discourse, and when interrogated about it, stifle the discussion with inane comments about the 'reality' of the charges being made."[68] Common sense does not aspire to universally valid knowledge and because of ambiguity in its communication (terms are not clearly defined and postulates are not clearly stated, it has no use for technical language, and no inclination towards a formal mode of speech) it does not exactly mean what it says. Since it is only concerned with the concrete and particular, its procedure is ad hoc – aspiring to master each situation as it arises.[69] Deriving from this common-sense notion, racism is a form of prejudice "that involves the use of group power through organizations and institutions as well as the imposition of the cultural preferences of the racial group in power."[70]

Christian theology is not done at the level of common sense. This has been the critique of Black Theology against white theology. Good policy-making is not done at the level of common sense. This has always been the insistence of the civil rights movement. Race constructs cannot be done at the level of common sense, as the Enlightenment-inspired race construction has done. This is what application of Lonergan's critical realism to common sense reveals. Just because people with common ancestry share certain physical traits or attributes, like skin colour, shape of their nose, colour of their eyes, physique, and hair texture, does not mean common sense now has the licence to exercise omnipotence and determine who they are and regulate how they should be treated. No one denies that these are genetic endowments. But common sense needs adequate theory to move toward a comprehensive viewpoint. However, common sense, as Lonergan tells us, does not like theory and does not want to work with theory (science). Thus, the one factor of a people's genetic endowment, which common sense singlehandedly engineers to arrive at "race," not only dwarfs what we all have in common as human beings, but also has "little or nothing to do with distinctly human, higher-order traits, such as personality, intelligence, and moral behavior,"[71] which we know by theory (science). It is because common sense "chooses to ignore these scientific facts, creates races, and endows them with pseudo-permanent characteristics"[72] that Lonergan's critical realist approach should be a conceived as contributing to a new form of critical race theory. Black Theology needs to resist the othering of Black bodies. Womanists, like Copeland, decry the fact that for centuries, "black female bodies have been defiled, used, and discarded, quite literally, as refuse – simply because they are female and black, black and female."[73] Black Theology needs Lonergan's critical realist approach to counter the bias of common sense in all its ramifications. The emphasis on Black experience is a common-sense starting point and often follows the procedures of common sense. Consequently, some of the criticisms of common sense, particularly its tendency to generalize, its tendency to revert to a state of incompleteness, and its tendency to be descriptive as opposed to being explanatory, can ground a legitimate criticism of Black Theology. There are psychological sensitivities in Lonergan's account of human propensity for evil and the negation of the good. But he transposes them into philosophical and theological language that goes beyond the limitations of common sense. Race construction based on common sense alone has no biological or genetic reality.[74] Sadly, in the United States, decisions about race have far too often followed a common-sense procedure, not science. It is, therefore, not surprising that throughout its history, decisions about race in the United States and the consequent racism these decisions have birthed have been made to promote the interest of white subjects.[75]

In the next section, I advance the argument that the biases of common sense, in Lonergan's technical usage, are what social scientists collectively refer to as prejudice. Prejudice, I will show, is a provisional knowledge that is incomplete. Bias, similarly, is a blind spot, a block or distortion of intellectual development.[76] The spectrum of what constitutes the blind spot is vast, including fear, resentment, apathy, ignorance, naivety, and hatred.[77] What Lonergan helps us see, which many social scientists have neglected, is that biases (prejudice in the language of social science) belong in the realm of common sense. Lonergan tells us that in the logic of common sense, "the only interpreter of common-sense utterance is common sense."[78] I take this key statement to mean he is referring to the dictatorship of prejudice, as well as the tyranny of prejudice. Just like the tyranny of prejudice can make a person deaf and resentful of true knowledge, the tyranny of common sense can leave a person isolated. "Where the scientist seeks the relations of things to one another, common sense is concerned with the relations of things to us."[79] While science seeks to move inquiry from the familiar to the unfamiliar, from the obvious to the recondite, and "attend to things as related to us, in the manner that leads to things as related to one another,"[80] common sense nurses no such aspirations. Rather, "it clings to the immediate and practical, the concrete and particular. It remains in the familiar world of things for us."[81]

The Multilayered Faces of Bias

The Cognitive Bias Codex lists upwards of 180 biases, including Group attribution error, Ultimate attribution error, Authority bias, Automation bias, Confirmation bias, and Anchoring bias. They all, in varying degrees, affect human cognition.[82] What these terms mean is not the same as what Lonergan means by "bias," although aspects of their meanings interpenetrate our current quest to envision "racism as both a disease and a crime."[83] Lonergan's thought on "bias," which pertains to the human tendency to be irrational and irresponsible, can also elucidate how these terms can be appropriated in the current conversations on racial prejudice.

From a scientific point of view, the work of the African American psychologist, Jennifer Eberhardt, sheds light on human cognition that Lonergan brings to bear in his discussion of bias. Eberhardt's essential argument in her helpful work, *Biased*, is that bias or racism inhabits in the brain of the person and that cognitive science can play an important role in uncovering and naming the problem. Cognitive science supports the notion that many of our discriminatory behaviours stem from stereotypes that operate in our brain outside of our conscious awareness. Prejudicial acts are triggered when our brain processes errors, irrespective of motive or intent. I will use Eberhardt's work and those of other cognitive psychologists to elucidate what Lonergan means by bias. For nearly fifty years, Eberhardt tells us, scientists have been documenting a universal phenomenon in the brain that they have dubbed the "other-race effect" – that people are better at recognizing faces of their own rather than faces of other races and that this race-selective response intensifies and hardens over time.[84] Over time our brain builds a preference for faces we see every day "at the expense of skills needed to recognize others."[85] This is because the brain has a neuroplasticity – "the brain is not a hardwired machine. It's a malleable organ that responds to the environments we are placed in and the challenges we face."[86] Scientists conclude from this other-race effect that "our perceptive powers are shaped by what we see" and that this is a function of biology and exposure.[87] "Our experiences in the world seep into our brain over time, and without our awareness they conspire to reshape the workings of our mind."[88] Eberhardt goes to on to suggest that the question of how race shapes who we are and how we experience the world is "the starting point of bigger questions about identity, power, and privilege that have molded our country and roiled the world for centuries."[89] Eberhardt argues further that racial stereotypes and implicit bias stem from this normal and universal phenomenon of other-race effect. They occur when the brain makes errors in an otherwise efficient mechanism of sorting out information. We all have stereotypes and prejudices because all human brains do make errors. But we can learn to correct them because the brain has a neuroplasticity that makes it malleable and adaptable. To the extent that we fail to take measures to correct our errors, we bear responsibility and culpability for our stereotypes and biases. The concept of stereotype itself goes back to Plato who explored whether a person's perceptions correspond to the way things really are. In popular discourse, it is a concept used to capture "preconceived notions," "pictures in our heads" and subjective impressions we mistake for objective reality.[90] Not only is stereotype a precursor to prejudice, it has the practical function of serving the powerful and tainting certain groups to protect the status quo.[91] Eberhardt's work, along with other research works in psychology, not only shed light on what Lonergan calls bias (a term that can have, among other things, the inclusive meaning of prejudice and stereotype), they also help us to understand better the distinction Lonergan makes between the four different kinds of common-sense bias: dramatic, individual, group, and general bias. Grasping how these biases work helps our understanding of both the human capacity for inhumanity (racism) and the human capacity to appreciate divine love.[92]

(a) Dramatic Bias

James Baldwin, speaking as a poet and a political writer, remarked that as a child he used to watch the Cowboy vs Indian films and that he always rooted for Gary Cooper beating up on the Indian, but that little did he know that he was the Indian. What Baldwin was referencing is the operational process of what Lonergan calls dramatic bias. Another name for it is the bias of unconscious motivation.[93] This bias can spontaneously and unconsciously make a person act against his or her own interest. It was the same bias the African American psychologist, Eberhardt, was attempting to convey with the story of her five-year-old son who boarded an airplane with her and upon seeing a black man whom he thought looked like his daddy, remarked that he hoped "that man doesn't rob the airplane." Eberhardt tells us that in truth, in height, skin colour, and facial features, the man does not look like the boy's daddy. The boy's daddy is bald and the man in question had dreadlocks. When asked why he thought the man may rob the airplane, the boy replied that he did not know why he thought that. The experience made Eberhardt realize that we live in a bewildering and frightening world that can influence us "so profoundly, so insidiously, and so unconsciously."[94] The scotosis that underlies this bias is at the root of self-hatred. It is at the root of Black-on-Black violence. Both Baldwin and Eberhardt poignantly used their own experiences to pinpoint a scotosis that Lonergan dissects and shows works preconsciously.[95] The European Enlightenment project of "turn to the subject," which resulted in the dialectic of exploitation and colonization of non-Europeans, was a process that was set in motion preconsciously by the scotosis of the dramatic subject. Thus, when the European colonialists went to Africa with their "civilizing" project, their widely held belief that the natives were inferior or non-beings was not something from rote memorization. It was a preconscious act that manifested when they set foot on African soil. It stemmed from years of assimilated ideas of inferiority of native peoples.

The cognitive approach to prejudice in social psychology tells us that prejudice is a function of the cognitive process in intergroup relations, i.e., that members of one group store up information or stereotypes about members of the other group, which in turn affects their judgment towards members of that group. In her study, Eberhardt reveals that categorization – whether of people, animals, or things – is a fundamental tool our brains are wired to use. When we categorize we fill it with information, beliefs, and feelings and these direct our actions toward it. The beliefs we have about the groups can become stereotypes and the attitudes we have about them can become prejudice.[96] "Whether bad or good, whether justified or unjustified, our beliefs and attitudes can become so strongly associated with this category that they are automatically triggered, affecting our behavior and decision making."[97] Suggesting that this behaviour works "dramatically" and preconsciously, Lonergan begins discussion of dramatic bias with the cryptic statement, "Besides the love of light, there can be a love of darkness."[98] Freud's depth psychology had characterized what Lonergan calls dramatic bias as something that leads to a suspension of understanding. Going beyond Freud to provide a more nuanced perspective, Lonergan suggests that this prejudice vitiates theoretical investigations.[99] Dramatic bias can make one exclude insights that can move investigations forward. To exclude an insight "is also to exclude the further questions that would arise from it, and the complementary insights that would carry it towards a rounded and balanced viewpoint."[100] Lonergan calls the further blind spot that results from these a scotoma.[101] Such scotoma are at the root of mass incarceration in the United States that disproportionately affects African Americans. A study (14 June 2016) on mass incarceration of African Americans in the United States confirms a bias African Americans have been decrying for years. The study found disparities in most states, i.e., that African Americans are incarcerated at more than five times the rate of whites in most of the United States and ten times the rate of whites in at least five states. The study documents how "incarceration creates a host of collateral consequences that include restricted employment prospects, housing instability, family disruption, stigma, and disenfranchisement."[102] A similar study conducted in Portugal found that in several cultural contexts across the globe, the penal system imprisons more Black than white, including Blacks from upper class social status. Both the United States study and the Portugal study found that Black people are disproportionately convicted of crimes for which judges assign longer sentences. The Portugal study is significant because Portugal is a country with a small Black population. Even in this country with no sizeable Black population, Black people are more than five times more likely to be incarcerated, compared to whites. Another interesting finding about the study is that people from the lower class are incarcerated far more than people from the upper class. "The disparity becomes more pronounced when the two categories are combined, revealing a racially based class disparity in imprisonment: black Americans from the low social classes are much more frequently incarcerated than white people from any social class."[103] In sum, these studies that show racism as the underbelly of the criminal justice system[104] support Lonergan's assertion that the scotosis in dramatic bias arises "not in conscious acts, but in the censorship that governs the emergence of psychic contents."[105] It is significant that Lonergan calls the exclusion of insight a "censorship." He says it represses from the conscious mind any scheme that would suggest the excluded insight. The censorship, repression, and inhibition undergirding the refusal to understand have a series of consequences – they weaken the development of common sense,[106] set the stage for psychic trouble,[107] and set in motion psychogenic disorder.[108] In other words, dramatic bias results from the trauma of psychological wounds.[109] John Dadosky has elaborated on how the trauma can prevent a person from being attentive to relevant data when that person feels that the data will arouse feelings or evoke memories that will remind him or her of the wounds.[110] Dadosky has also suggested that psychological wounds are "related to the extent to which one feels threatened by another person, and this includes the challenges to intersubjective relations (that flow, for example, from mimetic rivalry as expounded by René Girard)."[111]

Finally, Lonergan points out that dramatic bias is at the root of aberrations of religion and morality.[112] Some practical examples bear him out on how dramatic bias distorts religion and morality. A study done in England by the Equality and Human Rights group (2016),[113] finds that ethnic minorities are three times as likely to be excluded from school, to be unemployed, live in poverty, be restrained by the police, and be prosecuted and sentenced to jail.[114] Baldwin was alluding to dramatic bias when he deplored the white subject's response to a statement that will win approval, if it is uttered by a white person, but will be met with disapproval, if the statement were to be uttered by a Black person: "When any white man in the world picks up a gun and says; give me liberty or give me death, the entire white world applauds. But when a black man says exactly same thing, word for word, he's judged as a criminal (by whites) and treated as one. And everything possible is done to make an example of him to ensure there wouldn't be any more like him."[115] A more familiar example would be the bias that some whites have that make them fear Black people. It is an instance of dramatic bias. The fear of Black people is a preconscious act. In Freudian psychology, it can be explained as a theory of unconscious motivation. In Jungian psychology, it is the personal unconscious, i.e., the thoughts, feelings, and images that were once conscious in a person that were for one reason or another repressed. At a future event they will manifest preconsciously. Some people are concerned about the movement towards emphasis on unconscious bias. They "fear that the focus on bias from an unconscious standpoint may provide cover for people who can easily deny their prejudice by claiming it is unconscious."[116] This is why dramatic bias is a better term. How dramatic bias aligns with individual and group bias (as will be shown later) takes care of this concern.

(b) Individual Bias

When Lonergan discusses individual bias, it is almost always in negative terms. This does not mean that he does not acknowledge that there are some positive biases or value-neutral individual biases that can be put to constructive use. His primary concern is to show how negative individual bias aligns with the other three biases to distort the good of order. In a dialogue with the African American womanist poet, Nikki Giovanni, Baldwin made this memorably sad remark: "You know when you're called a nigger you look at your father because you think your father can rule the world – every kid thinks that – and then you discover that your father cannot do anything about it. So, you begin to despise your father and you realize, Oh, that's what a nigger is.' But it's not your father's fault and it's not your fault."[117] What Baldwin was referencing is a good instance of how dramatic wound interpenetrates individual bias. A person almost always carries with him or her dramatic wounds of the past and these affect actions.

Personality approaches to prejudice in social psychology tell us that prejudice is a function of individual personality and that prejudice is rooted in stereotypes. A stereotype is a socially shared set of beliefs about traits that are characteristic of members of another social group. It is, as it were, a fixed impression that conforms very little to the fact it pretends to represent.[118] "Stereotypes guide judgment and action to the extent that a person acts toward another as if the other possesses traits included in the stereotypes."[119] Lonergan acknowledges what personality approach to prejudice in social psychology says about stereotypes and begins his treatment of individual bias with the cryptic statement that animals are led by their instincts, but human beings are led by their intersubjectivity. An animal kills its prey, but is not considered egoistic. It is simply following its animal instinct, i.e., to secure a biological end. But when it comes to human subjects, the intersubjective nature of human life demands a different kind of spontaneity – that one satisfies both his or her own appetite, as well as helps his or her fellow human subjects attain their satisfaction.[120] But individual bias or egoism can distort this basic human spontaneity. Not only is egoistic individual bias in conflict with the good of order,[121] it leads to violation of the Golden Rule: Do unto others as you would want them to do unto you (Matthew 7:12).

Whereas the scotosis and bias of the dramatic subject is preconscious, the bias of individual egoism is neither preconscious nor spontaneous.[122] Psychologists tell us that "people may be willing to acknowledge the possibility of unconscious bias within them, even as they would vigorously deny harboring conscious bias."[123] For this reason, Lonergan emphasizes that the egoist is not unaware or his or her deceptions.[124] Psychologists who have studied consequences of people's behaviour, regardless of intent, also tell us that people tend to see intended harms as worse than unintended harms, even when the two harms are identical.[125] People who claim to be colour-blind deceptively do so because they want to appear preconsciously unprejudiced. Clinical research exploring how white subjects behave in situations in which the desire to appear unprejudiced is put front and centre found that it is those subjects who tried the hardest to appear colour-blind by avoiding the use of race who were the same ones that were least friendly when interacting with Black subjects.[126] Again for this reason, Lonergan emphasizes that individual bias works in concert with group bias. The fatal shooting of Trayvon Martin, which ignited national debates about race and racial profiling in 2012, was a case of individual bias (the killer's own personal biases) working in concert with group prejudice (white perception of Black men). Trayvon was an unarmed seventeen-year-old African American boy who was killed on 26 February 2012 by a white neighbourhood watch volunteer in Sanford, Florida. The neighbourhood watch volunteer said he thought Trayvon looked like "a suspicious person," even though Trayvon was only walking home from a trip to a convenience store. The same confluence of individual and group bias was responsible for the death of Ahmaud Arbery in 2020 – another case that stoked race debate in the United States. Arbery was an unarmed twenty-five-year-old African American man who was pursued by two white men in a pickup truck and fatally shot on 23 February 2020 while jogging near Brunswick, in Glynn County, Georgia. Even though there was no evidence to chase down Arbery, unless you consider the colour of his skin an evidence, the two men, who turned out to be father and son, claimed that Arbery "resembled a suspect who had committed burglaries in the area." The incident validates Gadamer's claim: "The prejudices of the individual, far more than his judgments, constitute the historical reality of his being."[127] Thus, individual bias rarely works in isolation from group bias. The prejudices that group egoism confers "are legitimized by the person who presents them."[128] Take housing discrimination as an example. A white landlord may share a group bias against Black tenants in general, but may have an additional individual bias that makes him gouge his Black tenants.

(c) Group Bias

Baldwin was adamant that the word "nigger" was an invention of an exploitative system that needed to scapegoat Black people as a way of avoiding guilt, responsibility, and blame for social inequality. White people and the ruling elites, he submits, invented the nigger to keep whites and Blacks divided. Baldwin understood the idea of a "nigger" to "be a longstanding American idea to make one group feel superior to another, to maintain divide and rule for the powerful."[129]

Although not all group memberships are inimical to the other and not all group bias is aimed at oppressing or suppressing the other, the social-psychological approach to prejudice states that group membership and association can induce in people prejudicial acts towards members of other groups. Lonergan fleshes it out in terms of ideologies that corrupt minds.[130] He agrees with Gadamer's idea that "Long before we understand ourselves through the process of self-examination, we understand ourselves in a self-evident way in the family, society, and state in which we live. The focus of subjectivity is a distorting mirror. The self-awareness of the individual is only a flickering in the closed circuits of historical life."[131] What Lonergan calls group bias has resonances in social psychology, particularly social dominance theory (SDT) that speaks of hierarchy-legitimizing myths in intergroup relations. Hierarchy-legitimizing myths are used to advance and sustain group inequalities. The theory posits three main types of intergroup behaviours: institutional discrimination, individual discrimination, and behavioural asymmetry. These three are inseparable and interpenetrate. They collectively account for group inequalities. According to the theory, when there are inequalities, legitimizing myths are constructed and used as the moral and intellectual justification for the inequalities. Legitimizing myths often take one of two forms: it can be an enhancing-myth (when it is used to show the superiority of one group over the other) or it can be hierarchy-attenuating, say discrimination against minorities (when it is used as a basis to justify the so-called inferiority of one group).[132] SDT links institutional discrimination with individual discrimination and behavioural asymmetry, in much the same way that Lonergan links group bias with individual and dramatic bias. Lonergan speaks of these biases as resting "on an interference with the development of practical common sense."[133] He writes, "But while individual bias has to overcome normal intersubjective feeling, group bias finds itself supported by such feeling. Again, while individual bias leads to attitudes that conflict with ordinary common sense, group bias operates in the very genesis of common-sense views."[134] Simply put, the egoism that informs group bias works in almost the same fashion as the egoism that informs individual bias. The one difference may be that group egoism is geared towards serving the interest of the group, not that of a particular individual. But it still does it in ways that are inimical to the interest of the members of other groups. Policies that become structural and inform systemic inequality emerge from the same kind of group egoism. This is why Lonergan calls the egoism that informs group bias an incomplete development of intelligence. "Just as the individual egoist puts further questions up to a point, but desists before reaching conclusions incompatible with his egoism, so also the group is prone to have a blind spot for the insights that reveal its well-being to be excessive or its usefulness at an end."[135] He drops a hint that even group bias can be "dramatic," i.e., preconscious (like dramatic bias). Group-based prejudice, after all, is ubiquitous. It is pervasive in human affairs. It can find expression in various disguised ways. It is at the root of the Crusades of the medieval period (1095–1492). It is at the root of the French Wars of Religion between the Catholics and the Huguenots (1562–98) and the wars of religion in Europe between Catholics and Protestants (1524–1697). Nationalism, like patriotism, in its worst expression, can degenerate into a group-based bias and can lead to chauvinism. Nationalism, degenerating into group-based bias, is at the root of the ancient European persecution of the Jews and the new forms of anti-Semitism unfolding in Europe and North America. It is at the root of the ethnic conflicts in Africa, particularly the Rwanda genocide (1994) and the "Land Cruiser War" in Darfur (2003). It is at the root of the ethnic cleansing in the former Yugoslavia (1991–2001) and the balkanization of the region – Serbia, Montenegro, Kosovo, Slovenia, Macedonia, Croatia and Bosnia and Herzegovina. Patriotism, degenerating into group bias, is at the root of genetic and cultural theories of in-group superiority that breeds sentiments and resentments.[136]

What Lonergan means by "group" here should be understood along the lines of an autonomous strong cluster of identities, as opposed to fluid identities where one can cross over from one group to another. It can fuel social stratification and identification along the lines of race, religion, and class. Social psychologists tell us that groupings with strong group identities have an uncanny way of making their positions appear as self-apparent truths. It is built on "hierarchy-legitimizing myths"[137] and motivated by the desire for group dominance, which often culminates in oppression of other social groups. Development guided by group bias is bound to be one-sided because group bias directs development to its own aggrandizement and "provides a market for opinions, doctrines, theories that will justify its ways and, at the same time, reveal the misfortunes of other groups to be due to their depravity."[138] Thus, group bias or hierarchy-legitimizing myths lead to horizontal inequalities (differences between groups) as opposed to vertical inequalities (differences between individuals). This is what social psychology tells us helps to stabilize oppression.[139] The privileging of one group over another can lead to milder forms of distortion, such as stereotyping the other, and to more severe forms of aberrations of morality, such as racism.[140] When society perpetuates myths that some people are "good" and should be allocated resources and others are "bad" or not as good and should be allotted less positive social value, just because some European Enlightenment philosophers, like David Hume, Immanuel Kant, and the American political thinker Thomas Jefferson, perpetuated the myth of a correlation between skin colour, intellectual limits, ability, and beauty,[141] the myths become instantiated in personal acts of discrimination and also in institutional discrimination.[142] In the United States, this plays out in different forms of racism that deny Black people jobs, bank loans, and decent health care, etc. Group-based bias finds expression in cultural elitism. The United Kingdom and the United States, for example, have elitist ideologies that are built on the cultured v. non-cultured polarity. In this binary, the elites are considered cultured and deserving of the goods of society and the working class and poor are considered non-cultured and undeserving of the goods.[143] This problematic binary could be understood along the lines of group conflict theory in sociology.

Group conflict theory refers to the individual-level irrational pathology model of prejudice, a pathology that reminds us that racial policies are about the allocation of resources, and that prejudice, therefore, "should be thought of as a sociological phenomenon growing out of unequal intergroup outcomes."[144] According to this theory, there are three variants of group conflict: defense of dominant group interests, social dominance theory, and group interest.[145] From these we learn that racial policy attitudes do not derive from personal prejudice or individual bias, but are a product of institutions and inequalities stemming from the group bias that exacerbates and tries to defend group ideologies and interests. The dominant group usually creatively modifies "the important myths (dominant ideology) in society to justify and maintain existing inequalities (including race, class, and gender-based inequality)."[146] The causal force behind group conflict, sociologists tell us, is the irrational drive for group domination. This is why "classes become distinguished, not merely by social function, but also by social success; and the new differentiation finds expression not only in conceptual labels but also in deep feelings of frustration, resentment, bitterness, and hatred."[147] In this legitimizing myth of cultural elitism,[148] "the advantage of one group commonly is disadvantageous to another, and so some part of the energies of all groups is diverted to the supererogatory activity of devising and implementing offensive and defensive mechanisms."[149] In the end, group bias leads to decline of the social order. In reinforcing each other's hierarchy-enhancing tendencies, individuals and groups make their discriminatory behaviours powerful and difficult to change.[150] "Now to a great extent the attitude of the dominant groups determines the attitude of the depressed groups. Reactionaries are opposed by revolutionaries. Progressives are met by liberals."[151]

(d) General Bias of Common Sense

Baldwin was dismayed about the psychological hazards of being Black in America, and believed that a great psychological hazard is that of all the images and standards the Black person sees, none of them applies to him or her. Baldwin thinks that all images and standards are really metaphors for the oppression of the Black man or woman. Regarding the decision the Black person has to make with respect to the images, he writes, "You have to decide who you are. The image of you is that which the white man has created. What white people see when they look at you is what they have invested: the agony, the pain, the demoralized; you represent a level of experience that America denies."[152] What Baldwin was alluding to is what Lonergan refers to as the general bias of common sense.

General bias of common sense is so-called because of its tendency to privilege the animal passions. Although all humans are rational animals, Lonergan argues, "a full development of their animality is both more common and much more rapid than a full development of their intelligence and reasonableness."[153] In *Superior*, the science writer Angela Saini suggests the possibility that science may inform prejudice or can even be recruited to service prejudice. She cites the example of Homo sapiens, which according to widely accepted scientific theory made its first appearance in the African savannah about 195 000 years ago. There are, however, some scientists with ideological motives in places like China, India, and Russia and some parts of Europe who dispute that Homo sapiens first appeared in Africa and now make a case that it first appeared in their own respective regions. This leads Saini to conclude that science, after all, is not as neutral as we thought and that theory among scientists may be driven more by personal motivation than by data.[154] The idea of using science as an intellectual justification for race or racism speaks to the larger issue of what Lonergan calls general bias of common sense. It is a resistance to theoretical knowledge. This bias concerns itself with the concrete and particular. It also prefers common sense to theory and has no aspirations for abstract and universal laws.[155] In opposing questions that will lead to theory and dismissing them, general bias thinks of theory as an impediment to practicality.[156] Dadosky has helped to explain that Lonergan thought of general bias along the lines of Eric Voegelin's "pneumopathology" – a kind of disease of the human spirit. It escalates into what Lonergan calls the "longer cycle of decline."[157] In social psychology, evidence continues to mount about how white people view racism as a zero-sum game (zero-sum bias). For example, there were many who conveniently thought that Barack Obama's presidency (2009–17) ushered in a "post-racial" America. But researchers studying racial attitudes in the so-called post-racial America found something different – a disturbing trend. They located a new general mindset among white people in America; they thought that whites had replaced Blacks as the primary victims of discrimination. This is in spite of the fact that nearly all metrics – from employment to police treatment, loan rates to education – continue to indicate drastically poorer outcomes for Black than white Americans. Even with the much-vaunted rapid improvement of African American socio-political life, the median income for Blacks in America is $31 000, compared to $48 500 for white Americans. The African American poverty rate remains twice that of whites.[158] Not to mention the system of mass incarceration that cages millions of people of colour and relegates them to a "permanent second class status," something Michelle Alexander calls America's own "caste system."[159] A lot of white Americans "perceive increases in racial equality as threatening their dominant position in American society, with Whites likely to perceive that actions taken to improve the welfare of minority groups must come at their expense."[160] In philosophical terms, this perceived threat or fear is a product of general bias of common sense. Lonergan says general bias is easily "led to rationalize its limitations by engendering a conviction that other forms of human knowledge are useless or doubtfully valid."[161] The rationalization is at the root of Cain's obtuse retort to the maker of the universe, "Am I my brother's keeper?" (Gen. 4:9), in effect telling the God who desires that all should love thy neighbour as thyself, "My brother is not my problem."

All the four biases work in concert. Let me illustrate this with the residential, racially explicit policies of the federal, state, and local governments in the United States prior to the mid-twentieth century that are still operative today, despite the best efforts of the U.S. courts to do away with them. The racially explicit policies of the government at the time defined where whites and African Americans should live.[162] This systematic and forceful policy feeds many other racially charged individual prejudices, such as white flight, real estate steering, bank redlining, and income differences.[163] The individual discriminatory practices in turn give support to unjust government policies. In the end, what plays out is group bias, in this case the government's *de jure* segregation by law and public policy,[164] giving expression to individual biases that probably would have existed in isolated cases, and individual discriminatory practices providing justification for *de jure* segregation. Of the four biases, general bias is the most serious (for the reasons enumerated earlier about common sense) and for the reason that the damage done by this bias to the dialectic of community can have long-lasting effects. "Preference scales become distorted. Feelings soured. Bias creeps into one's outlook, rationalization into one's morals, ideology into one's thought. So one may come to hate the truly good and love the really evil."[165] To use Lonergan's own expression, "such is the monster that has stood forth in our day."[166]

The privileged who benefit from the system are often the first to resist change and may even castigate those questioning the system and demanding change. It is probably why Lonergan says of general bias that it generates a significant empirical residue, which becomes a "social surd."[167] Empirical residue is Lonergan's technical term for that which remains after abstraction that is incidental but nonetheless has the potential for further insight. In subsequent chapters I will speak of racism as having an empirical residue. When I speak of racism as having an empirical residue, I mean that in every racial act, there is always that which remains and that which remains always has potential to do further harm. It accounts for why racism and white privilege (the other side of racism) remain cyclic and systemic, in spite of the rhetoric of doing something about it. To return to the matter of the privileged who benefit from the system and for that reason resist change, in resisting change what they want is for the system to remain as it is. They will regard any talk of change as "starry-eyed idealism" and resist meaningful proposals as silly and impracticable.[168] These same people who resist change "would lay the axe to the root of the social surd."[169] A surd is based on an irrational assumption, which confers "dominance because of one's race or sex."[170] The "dominance" is at the root of the refusal to rethink systemic racism. If systemic racism is an "organized system premised on the categorization and ranking of social groups into races that devalues, disempowers, and differentially allocates desirable societal opportunities and resources to racial groups regarded as inferior,"[171] the dominance is at the root of the refusal to undo institutional inequalities. This gives further credence to

Lonergan's argument that when combined with group bias, general bias accounts "for certain features of the distorted dialectic of community."[172] Group bias leads to a shorter cycle of decline. General bias leads to a longer cycle of decline. General bias also involves sins of refusal to advance in knowledge, as well as sins of omission.[173]

The Structures of Sin

Lonergan's analysis of bias vis-à-vis social surd helps put in context what Black Theology has laboured, sometimes unsuccessfully, to explain as the problem of the colour line. "Racism originates in domination and provides the social rationale and philosophical justification for debasing, degrading, and doing violence to people on the basis of color."[174] The American society and its Protestant ethic is built on the belief that human beings are in fact good by nature. This belief about the unmitigated goodness of the human person runs counter to the Christian idea of our inherited fallen human nature. The problem of racism in both Church and society cannot be adequately addressed without a renewed appreciation of how bias works and how it further deepens the wound of our fallen human nature (original sin).[175] Lonergan's enumeration of the ways bias distorts the dialectic of community also gives legitimacy to the Catholic way of speaking of the structure of sin. Sin is a theological concept. It is embodied in individuals. The Catholic Church recognizes two variants of personal sin: venial and mortal. Although sin is embodied in individuals, the Church also recognizes that sin has a social dimension. Racism typifies the class of sin that is sustained by both personal attitudes and structural forces.[176] John Paul II went as far as teaching that social sin is the embodiment of personal sin and injustice in social structures.[177] Social sin, "understood in terms of structures of sin and sinful social mechanisms,"[178] is an acknowledgement of "the blindness produced in persons by the dominant culture, blindness that prevents them from recognizing the evil dimensions of their social reality."[179]

The term "structures of sin" was first used in the 1960s by Liberation theologians who wanted to draw attention to societal culpability of sins committed by individuals. When John Paul II appropriated the term in *Reconciliatio et Paenitentia* [Reconciliation and Penance] (2 December 1984)[180] and *Sollicitudo rei Socialis* [On Social Concern] (30 December 1987),[181] he was not unaware of the Marxist origin of the term and how it can be misused to deflect individual responsibility. In addition to reaffirming collective responsibility, the pontiff wanted to heighten awareness that structures of sin are ultimately structures built by collective individuals for the purpose of sinning.[182] Racism is a proto-structural sin and needs reconciliation and penance. It is rooted in complex networks of interlocking relationships of dramatic, individual, group, and general bias. "In the United States, the original purpose of racism was to justify slavery and its enormous economic benefit. The particular form of racism, inherited from the English to justify their own slave trade, was especially venal, for it defined the slave not merely as an unfortunate victim of bad circumstances, war, or social dislocation but rather as less than human, as a thing, an animal, a piece of property to be bought and sold, used and abused."[183] There are two other quintessential structures of sin that ought to be of "social concern" for Christians – white privilege (discussed in chapter 4) and implicit bias (discussed in chapter 5). "White privilege is invisible, structural, and systemic," writes the American Catholic ethicist, Charles Curran. "White privilege is a structural sin that has to be made visible if it is to be removed."[184] Lonergan's extrapolation of counterpositions in common sense has helped us see that in the United States, as in Great Britain, race has been socially constructed to identity people by the colour of their skin, their physical features, and language, and how the same people are classified and ranked into distinct socio-political groups, so as to provide each group with different degrees of social access and opportunity.[185] We see more clearly how, in this racial classification, one group is considered superior (white) and another particular group is considered inferior (Black). From a Christian perspective, this racial classification (racism) "negates the reason for which Christ died – the reconciling work of the cross. It denies the purpose of the church: to bring together, in Christ, those who have been divided from one another, particularly in the early church's case, Jew and Gentile – a division based on race."[186]

How Black Theology Might Appropriate and Use Lonergan's Notion of Bias

I have alluded to the fact that Black Theology, in its first stage of meaning, missed an opportunity in not appropriating the work of cognitive psychologists like Allport. In the door that has opened for a new stage of meaning, Lonergan's notion of bias, which is alert to the data of consciousness, can help Black Theology appropriate the newly emerging research in social psychology on the complexity of the human mind and how the various biases emerging from the mind affect human conscious behaviour. As Lonergan expressly makes clear, the conditions for using mental acts as experienced and systematically conceived as a logical first in the search for interiority are numerous.[187] I further suggest that many (not all) of the over 180 kinds of biases on the Cognitive Bias Codex can be harmonized under the four structures of bias Lonergan provides in order to better understand and systematically conceive the operations of the mind. Appropriating and harmonizing these biases will also help Black Theology develop a heuristic for action.

In the decades following the pioneering work of Cone, Roberts, and Cannon, in the United States at least, society seems to be showing a trend towards inclusivity: the Civil Rights movement, the women's movement, the expansion and acceptance of equal rights for other historically marginalized groups, like the lesbian, gay, bisexual, and transgender people, are a few examples. At the conscious level, at least, the standard of behaviour is changing.[188] But we know too well that the so-called progress still remains "quite fragile."[189] More recent tests by cognitive psychologists and neuroscientists continue to point to "a human dynamic that ranges from the curious to the tragic,"[190] – that "human beings are consistently, routinely, and profoundly biased."[191] A theory of human action will require a keen awareness of these studies and how they are illuminated philosophically by Lonergan's notion of bias. The theological implication will result in a theory of action in which the wound or trauma caused by these biases is named and identified. One of Freud's essential insights in his theory of the unconscious, which has proved fruitful when applied in the Truth and Reconciliation Commission in South Africa and in all other reparation movements, is that it is not possible to heal a traumatic psychological injury that is hidden by repression and denial until one uncovers the origins in trauma and until one admits that the injury has happened that the process of healing can begin.[192]

The theory of action that Black Theology needs can take several forms including, but not limited to, the following:

1. An action plan for society's collective cognitive restructuring: We know we all have biases because scientists have shown us that all human brains make errors. But scientists also show us that these errors can be corrected because the brain has neuroplasticity that makes it malleable and adaptable, depending on exposure. Eberhardt's study tells us that since our brains and our minds are remoulded by our experiences and our environments, "We have the power to change our ways of thinking, to scrub away the residue of ancient demons."[193]
2. A program of Lament: We know from the Bible that there is something cathartic and clarifying about righteous anger that is done with a contrite heart.[194] David, Job, and Isaiah all put on sackcloth and ashes and mourned when they had to. The way Rachel wept

for her children "with lamentation and bitter weeping" (Jeremiah 31:15), also shows that lament can be empowering and enabling. To cite an example of a form of lament, there was an allegation that Canada's residential school system forcibly separated indigenous children in Canada from their families and subjected them to malnourishment and physical and sexual abuse from about 1831 to 1996. The atrocities came to light in 2021 after hundreds of unmarked graves of indigenous children were discovered at the sites of former residential schools across Canada. The country's Truth and Reconciliation Commission called the act "cultural genocide." In September 2021, the Canadian Conference of Catholic Bishops, a part of a global network of conference of bishops in the Catholic Church, formally apologized for their role in the scandal, after refusing to acknowledge it for years. In a statement they put forward, they finally "acknowledge the grave abuses that were committed by some members of our Catholic community; physical, psychological, emotional, spiritual, cultural, and sexual." Continuing, they added, "We also sorrowfully acknowledge the historical and ongoing trauma and the legacy of suffering and challenges faced by Indigenous Peoples that continue to this day."[195] Lament is always a good step on the path to reconciliation.

3. A program of Restorative Justice: In Christian theology sin is a theological concept and is embodied in individuals and social structures. The cry for justice is a Christian principle. The Bible is full of examples of justice restored when there is recognition of the wrong done, repentance for the sin committed, and restitution for what was stolen or taken away (Lev. 6:2 and Num: 5:6).

This theory of action flows from Lonergan's schema. Recognition/cognitive restructuring is at the level of sense experience, lament flows from interiority, and restitution is at the level of conversion because it signals true repentance.

Conclusion

In Shawn Copeland's work, she pointed out how slavery and Christianity forged a dangerous alliance in the United States. "The system of slavery was deeply entwined with Christianity," she writes. "From the monarchs of Portugal, who required the baptism of the captured Africans, to pastors and ministers who were reluctant to baptize the enslaved peoples, from the use of the Bible as a tool for sustaining and sanctifying the submission of the enslaved peoples to segregated seating and distribution of Holy Communion,"[196] the way Christianity was practised imperilled the message of the Gospel and endangered the very soul of Christianity.[197] The legacy of slavery and inhumane treatment of Blacks has been at a huge spiritual, mental, and emotional cost, economics aside. It has left what Joy Deruy Leary has aptly termed a post-traumatic slave syndrome – the effect of multigenerational oppression suffered by enslaved Africans and their descendants.[198]

Towards the end of the last century, Pope John Paul II acknowledged and "denounced the Catholic Church's complicity with racism and the inhumane treatment of blacks."[199] To be clear, John Paul II was not the first pope to condemn in an explicit way the practice of slave trade. The Venice-born Gabriele Condulmer, who became Pope Eugene IV (1431–47), issued a papal bull in 1435, *Sicut Dudum* (Against Enslaving of Black Natives from the Canary Islands), condemning the slave trade and threatening excommunication for offenders.[200] Over a four-hundred-year span, several other popes after him repeated the condemnation, including Gregory XVI (1831–46) whose papal bull, *In Supremo Apostolatus* (1839), denounced the slave trade, particularly in the New World,[201] and forbade "any Catholic cleric or layperson to defend, publish, or teach in public or in private, anything that supported the trade."[202] These explicit condemnations notwithstanding, American Catholics did not end the trading of slaves. Some American bishops, including Bishop John England of Charleston, South Carolina (1820–42), chose to interpret the papal bulls as "a condemnation of slave trading, but not necessarily owning slaves." Even Archbishop Francis Kenrick of Baltimore (1851–63), who served as a bishop of the then diocese of Philadelphia before taking up the See of Baltimore, was also caught in the same equivocation. He upheld the status quo of American slave holding and trading. In spite of the American bishops' refusal to adhere to the Vatican's condemnation of slave trade, subsequent popes, like Pius IX (1866) and Leo XIII (1888 and 1890), at various times further reiterated the Catholic disapproval of slave trade.[203] What was new in what John Paul II did at the end of the last century was that he called for ecclesial repentance for the Church's complicity in this crime. In effect, John Paul II was following a precept Lonergan considers transcendental and inevitable in the search for genuine repentance and peace: "Acknowledge your historicity."[204] The precept implies that one has a duty to acknowledge the historicity of one's moral views as well as a duty to readily admit oversights in one's self-knowledge.[205] But what John Paul II did not do sufficiently was indicate what it means for the Church to repent of the sin of slavery. He also did not address how the victims and their descendants are to cope with the lingering trauma and its vestiges. The recent furore about reparation to the descendants of Jesuit slaves who were sold to fund Jesuit institutions of learning has again brought to the fore the problem of mental health and racism. In 1838, some 272 African American men and women who were slaves owned by the Jesuits of the Maryland Province were sold, along with scores of others, to help fund a Jesuit-owned college, known today as Georgetown University. The slaves were sold to one Henry Johnson, a former governor of Louisiana, and Jesse Batey, a Louisiana landowner, for $115 000. Although more than a dozen other universities in the United States, including Brown, Columbia, University of Virginia, and Harvard have since publicly acknowledged their ties to slavery, the controversy surrounding the 1838 Jesuit sales seems like the one that will not go away anytime soon.[206] This is perhaps because of the sheer size of the Jesuit trade and perhaps also because not enough reparation, spiritual and material, has been done. If the Jesuit trade is a microcosm of the issue of slavery vis-à-vis the call for reparation, the vestiges of post-traumatic slave syndrome in general occupy a wide spectrum, ranging from mental health issues related to the indignity of being considered 3/5 of a person, to mis-education, to abject poverty. The reparation debate is too complex to discuss here. The many issues involved in the debate are a matter for a different research project. For example, how do you determine adequate compensation for the millions of Black people who died in the trade? How do you determine adequate compensation for the suffering endured by the slaves and their descendants? If the target of reparation is not the dead, but the living, as advocates of reparation insist, what issues are at stake in intergenerational responsibility? Who should be charged with correcting the errors and oversights of past generations? How do you address the concerns of some Americans who deny complicity in the slave trade, like the Irish and the Polish, because their forebears came to the United States well after the Civil War? What is the metric for calculating what is owed to African Americans? Is the debt, assuming it can be fairly determined, something society can pay? Does the reparation for African Americans extend to Africans? These complex issues have been discussed extensively by Donald Shriver in *Honest Patriots; Loving a Country Enough to Remember Its Misdeeds* (2005).[207] Ecclesial repentance that acknowledges these matters and their emotional tolls is what Black Theology needs an action plan for. The hope is that a true ecclesial repentance can filter down through osmosis into the human political community. Chapter 6 explores the unique approach suggested by Lonergan for addressing ecclesial repentance – an approach that addresses the reality of sin and its manifestation in systemic and institutional forms of racism, as well as in post-traumatic slave syndrome.

Chapter Four

The Karen Phenomenon and the Conceptualist Problem of White Privilege Discourse

Black Theology is a search for what Lonergan understands as interiorly differentiated consciousness. What Lonergan calls consciousness is the "interior experience of oneself and one's acts."[1] In interiorly differentiated consciousness, "mental acts as experienced and as systematically conceived are a logical first. From them one can proceed to epistemology and metaphysics. From all three one can proceed … to give a systematic account of meaning in its carriers, its elements, its functions, its realms, and its usages."[2] Although what Lonergan means by interiority is much more nuanced than the change of heart and mind that Black Theology has been searching for, Black Theology needs both a methodological clarification and a foundation that involves interiority – a heightening of consciousness that will help one "experiencing one's experiencing, understanding, judging, and deciding."[3] The good that Black Theology seeks, intellectually at least, is "the good of order."[4] But Black Theology has rarely addressed the conceptualist problem that hinders discourse on this good. While conceptualists strongly affirm concepts, they naively disregard insights that can lead to interiorly differentiated consciousness and conversion.[5] Ever since Peggy McIntosh (1989) defined the term and set the parameters for the conversation,[6] discourse on white privilege still basically remains at the level of concept. The categories for understanding it have also remained empty.[7] It does not pay attention to the interior mind or what Lonergan calls the data of consciousness, i.e., that one endeavours to understand one's own experiences and critically scrutinizes and corrects one's understandings of those experiences.[8] It is only when one does this kind of self-scrutiny that the person can gain an ability to resolve a host of life's conundrums, whether they be philosophical or theological.[9] In this chapter, I engage white privilege to make explicit the connection between racism and white privilege. Racism is not a label reserved for a derelict few,[10] but a phenomenon tied to white privilege and the status quo, something that has made its foray into the good of order structurally. There is evidence from cognitive psychology to suggest that the bias (stereotypes and prejudices) that causes it operates at a cognitive level beyond one's conscious awareness. It is when it is triggered that this bias becomes dramatic or automatic. The racism that results from it is often not caused by bad people with bad motives, but caused by a brain processing error that operates independently of motive and intent.[11]

The binaries of white and Black have formed much of the structural discourse of the United States' race problem. The binaries appear here, despite my best efforts to avoid them. This speaks to the larger issue of the problem at hand. Building on the argument of the last chapter on bias, especially the unfolding of the type that Lonergan calls dramatic bias (unconscious prejudice in social psychology), it is no longer doubtful that unconscious racism exists. The crucial question is how to recognize and label it. This chapter on white privilege is an entry point for understanding and labelling one of the many manifestations of bias. White privilege is a surd of sin and one of the two interlocking empirical residues (by which I mean lingering manifestations) of racism, the other being implicit racism (discussed in chapter 5). Empirical residue (some form of matter left behind) is a term Lonergan introduced to theology and used many times in *Insight*. Empirical residue is what is left over after abstract inquiry. The fact that Newton was hit in the head by an apple as it occasioned his insight into gravity is an empirical residue – irrelevant to the theory he developed. What Lonergan calls empirical residue can be grasped through inverse insight.[12] An inverse insight occurs when I realize I have been asking the wrong question in terms of the line of inquiry. My use of the term empirical residue here is metaphoric. I use it to designate a form of something left behind in connection to racism, the United State of America's own original sin,[13] since racism is always evolving and leaving something new behind that later takes on a life of its own. My contention is that a remainder concept (such as white privilege) is an integral part of the phenomenon itself (racism), particularly since racial hierarchies in U.S. society are interlocking. For, in the United States, despite its being a melting pot of different ethnicities and races, racism expresses itself in various forms that include ethnicity and race.

Discourse on white privilege is a tacit acknowledgement that Black and white people live in different worlds, a world that is confined within a specific horizon. That world is also determined by historical, social, and psychological ranges of their interests and knowledge.[14]

Put in simple terms, there are two Americas: one white and the other Black, and they are separate and unequal. This was the conclusion of the National Advisory Commission on Civil Disorders, known as the Kerner Commission in the report it submitted in February 1968 to President Lyndon B. Johnson, in the wake of the 1967 urban riots. The Kerner report alluded to bad policing practices, a flawed justice system, unscrupulous consumer credit practices, poor housing systems, high unemployment, voter suppression, and other culturally embedded forms of racism as factors militating against African American lives.[15] The same culturally embedded forms of racism exist to this day. Half a century after the report, the same culturally embedded forms of racism are manifesting in different ways. Using the Karen phenomenon that emerged in the light of COVID-19 pandemic and lockdown in 2020, I exposit some counterpositions in the myths of "sameness" and "post-racial society" that have gradually crept into the discourse on white privilege. These myths, in philosophical language, wrongly mistake the real for what is given to immediate experience. In practical terms, they are the myths that wrongly mistake the shadow for the real thing. They incorrectly assume that what is apparent, i.e., tokenism, symbolism, and the many gimmicks of racial equity, are realities and the true indicators that society has achieved the much-needed genuine racial justice and reconciliation. Through engagement with Black Theology, particularly with Black women (womanism) who criticize white feminist theology for ignoring racism and white supremacy in church and society, the chapter hopes to take steps towards rescuing the white privilege discourse from the ambiguity (naïve realism) that hinders its effectiveness. What is at stake, to paraphrase Lonergan, is the unity and coherence of Christian teaching on divine grace and divine love.[16]

A Truncated Discourse?

For a long time, I have found the discourse on white privilege to be truncated. I take as paradigmatic Lonergan's statement that the "neglected subject does not know himself."[17] From the perspective of Black Theology, it is still not clear to what extent this discourse, that emerged in the context of white Women's Studies, stems from white women's genuine commitment to end racial inequalities and to what extent the prime motivation was to draw attention to the neglect of white women vis-à-vis the phenomenon of unacknowledged white male privileges that are institutionally protected. What is clear, however, is that it was through thinking of white men's unacknowledged privilege as a phenomenon that McIntosh taught "there was most likely a phenomenon of white privilege which was similarly denied and protected."[18] The term "white privilege" has never been adequately clarified. Many of its definitions have hinged on assumptions regarding what constitutes whiteness, as opposed to Blackness. The definitions have failed to note that whiteness, like Blackness, is not a biological fact, but a social construction with origins in the European Enlightenment project, which sought to show that white Europeans are superior to non-whites. When applied to contemporary human relations, what is considered whiteness acts as an all-encompassing racial template.[19] Whiteness becomes a set of locations historically, socially, politically, and culturally produced.[20] It is intrinsically linked to unfolding relations of domination in which whiteness is part of a larger culture of power. This culture of power produces racial disparities and profits from its perpetuation.[21] Consequently, I have found the discourse on white privilege to be uninviting, for several reasons.

1. It is a discourse that is largely dominated by white subjects.[22] They wear the artefacts of privilege openly. Furthermore, the white subjects are well insulated by privilege. The privilege that insulates them exposes the lack of desire to dismantle the institution of racism of which white privilege is a proto expression. Yet these white subjects seem to relish and take pleasure in intellectual discussions of white privilege. Perhaps for some, taking part in the discourse is part of the "culture of empowerment and empathy" and/or a "culture of redemption and innocence" that is "emblematic of the power of whiteness."[23] By this I mean it is probably an act of sin-offering that represents "a white way of assuring themselves that they are basically 'good' persons."[24] That is as far as it goes. In each case, to borrow a phrase from the title of David Leonard's book, it seems like it is just part of the mechanics of "playing while white."[25] But as Lonergan reminds us, "far more impressive than talking is doing. Deeds excite our admiration and stir us to emulation."[26] As the Letter to the Hebrews puts it, "Do not neglect doing good and sharing, for with such sacrifice God is pleased" (Hebrews 13:16).
2. As with the overall discourse on racism, white privilege is not easy to engage without offending the guilty. Guilt is fragile. Both the fragility of guilt and denials that accompany difficult conversations on race keep Black theologians away from seminars on white privilege dominated mainly by white liberals. From its definition, it is easy to see that not only is white privilege a prickly term, it also tends to elicit a visceral response.[27] Let me be clear, I am not suggesting that it is not helpful for white subjects who choose to

do so to find a space where they can remind other whites who may be unaware (assuming such people really exist) that simply being white provides privilege and at the same time creates barriers for racialized people of colour. It is indeed commendable for whites to remind their fellow whites that their unearned advantages are built into the fabric of society. This is easy to miss because the neglected and truncated subject, as Lonergan writes, "not only does not know himself but also is unaware of his ignorance and so, in one way or another, concludes that what he does not know does not exist."[28] But white confessional statements about their unearned advantages are helpful only "insofar as they represent a discursive strategy to recognize the insidiousness of structural privileges" and in so far as they "articulate an attempt to side with racial minorities through their sympathetic appeal to undo the said privileges."[29] If, as Lonergan says, the good is the object of desire,[30] then merely naming a problem without challenging it does not lead to the good of order.

3. Lonergan differentiates cognitional self-transcendence from real self-transcendence. Cognitional self-transcendence is the first stage in a person's attempt to transcend the shortcomings of his or her existential situation and become a genuine human being who articulates and responds to these shortcomings in a meaningful way. After cognitional self-transcendence comes the real self-transcendence where the person, as it were, moves from asking questions of fact to asking questions of value, and begins to do only what is truly good and worthwhile.[31] The real self-transcendence is moral self-transcendence. Following this distinction, discourse on white privilege ought to be a search for genuine self-transcendence. Unfortunately, it seems to remain only at the level of cognitional self-transcendence. The people who engage in discourse on white privilege have, as it were, surveyed their surroundings, noticed their defects, and are raising questions of fact, i.e., why being white accords privilege. The questions of fact they raise lead to awareness that privilege is something unearned, exclusive, and socially assigned. The implication of this is that there are others that are not privileged; they are even exploited.[32] But rarely does the discourse move from questions of fact to questions of value. Lonergan, speaking of Aristotle's account of virtue and how his own account of virtue is similar to that of Aristotle notes how it presupposes the preexistence of virtuous people and self-transcending subjects. Actions "are called just and temperate when they are such as the just and temperate man would do; but it is not the man who does these that is just and temperate, but the man who also does them as just and temperate men do them."[33]

> How many have stepped back, after looking at policies and attitudes that hold back the disadvantaged Black people or people of colour, and come up with policies for meaningful change? How many have addressed the privileges that lead to invisible discrimination and racism in their own daily lives?

The five pillars of racial prejudice, in the United States at least, are employment, housing, healthcare, education, and Christianity. All these pillars cannot be discussed extensively at the same time, but I have done my best to touch on all five areas, albeit some more extensively than others. The two I have given more attention because of my context are the fourth pillar, education, and the fifth pillar, Christianity. I have discussed the fourth pillar somewhat more extensively in chapter 1 and now return to it again in this chapter. I will also discuss the fifth pillar (Christianity) briefly in this chapter in the discourse on Karen and Systemic Racism and will also offer some more extensive insights in chapter 6. Many of the subjects involved in the discourse on white privilege are academicians and professionals in colleges and universities. Are our schools not hotbeds of white privilege? Are the schools not ironically the products of systemic racism to a greater or lesser degree? Do Black people and people of colour not face torrents of workplace racism in our schools? For all practical purposes, have most not chosen to ignore addressing this issue in their institutions? When they do, is it not often mere tokenism or an exercise in rhetoric – just to give an appearance of doing something? One of the defects of conceptualism (which is an incomplete knowledge), Lonergan says, is its excessive abstractness; it does not know how to relate the intelligible to the sensible, the universal to the particular.[34] This is where the discourse on white privilege is off-putting. It does not take the much-needed reflexive turn.[35] Granted, the white subjects engaged in the discussion did not create the system in which whiteness is treated as the norm, and arguably it is through no fault of their own that they find themselves in a racialized culture that treats whiteness as the ideal, but there still remains the problem of the assumed internalized superiority that is hardly recognized. This brings to mind the other defect of the truncated subject Lonergan eschews – its anti-historical immobilism. Concepts, such as racial binaries of "white is superior" and "Black is inferior," are immobile; they are abstract and remain just what they are defined to mean.[36] But human understanding changes and develops, "and as it develops it expresses itself in ever more precise and accurate concepts, hypotheses, theories, systems. But conceptualism, as it disregards insight, so it cannot account for the development of concepts."[37] It was in the attempt to avoid conceptualism that Robin DiAngelo brutally admitted, "Raised in a culture of white supremacy, I exude a deeply internalized assumption of racial superiority."[38]

4. Herein lies another defect, the discourse on white privilege hardly addresses the complicity of the white subject in perpetuating a structure of domination. Sometimes it seems like the discourse is merely the white subjects' attempt to extricate themselves from culpability. It is like saying, "I know I'm privileged, but I didn't do it. I only inherited it. What more can I do?" But this is just only half of the truth. It makes sense to see why Lonergan locates a third defect of conceptualism in the notion of being. "Conceptualists have no difficulty in discovering a concept of being, indeed, in finding it implicit in every positive concept. But they think of it as an abstraction, as the most abstract of all abstractions, least in connotation and greatest in denotation."[39] People racialized as white not only live a life forged in a system that benefits them; many also help to perpetuate it. If whites enjoy privileges, it is because they have created a system of domination under which they can thrive as a group.[40] What the conceptualist white privilege discourse has failed to grasp is that the notion of being is, as Lonergan says, not abstract, but concrete. "It intends everything about everything. It prescinds from nothing whatever. But to advert to this clearly and distinctly, one must note not only that concepts express acts of understanding but also that both acts of understanding and concepts respond to questions."[41]

Engaging the Normative View of White Privilege

I suggest that a way to gain a better understanding of white privilege and how it is related to particular acts of racism is to deconstruct how proponents have defined the term. I examine some standard definitions of white privilege in order to show the problematic of the concept itself. To help uncover some of the difficulties, I exposit two of the main analogies proponents have employed. The discourse on white privilege, according to these proponents, is best grasped through analogies.[42] But analogies are what Lonergan calls "the technique of implicit definition," which helps fix meaning of fundamental terms and relations.[43] When we examine these analogies, rather than fix the meaning of the fundamental terms and relations, we see a tendency towards their destruction.

- Analogy 1: Analogy of the Biker: This analogy derives from a white pastor in Michigan, an avid bike rider, Jeremy Dowsett. He calls white privilege a form of systemic imbalance.[44] He uses his experience as a bike rider who shares the road with cars and trucks to explain what is meant by white privilege. Like many bikers who experience open hostilities from car and truck drivers, Dowsett recalls many experiences of being yelled at and told to get off the road and how some drivers even intentionally drive through puddles to splash mud at him. Dowsett admits that most of the hostilities he faces on the road are not intentional. Some of the hostilities usually come from drivers who are simply following the rules of the road. But the rules of the road are unintentionally dangerous to bikers. When semis and trucks, for example, speed past him, their wheels spray him with gravel, unintentionally. Dowsett acknowledges not only that these drivers do not intend to spray him with gravel, they also might not even realize they are doing it. Dowsett concludes from it that for people of colour who find themselves in a white-majority context, life may feel a bit like being on a bicycle in the midst of traffic. Though they have the right to be on the road and the laws in the books make it equitable, at least theoretically, it does not change the fact that they are on a bike in a world made for cars.[45] Just like bikers find themselves dominated on the road by motorists, on the highway of life, domination is a relation of power and is forged in the historical process.[46] "It does not form out of random acts of hatred, although these are condemnable, but rather out of a patterned and enduring treatment of social groups. Ultimately, it is secured through a series of actions, the ontological meaning of which is not always transparent to its subjects and objects."[47]

– Analogy 2: Analogy of Walking down the Street: This analogy was offered by a panellist at the 1998 American Educational Research Association. The panellist described being white as akin to walking down the street with money being put into your pocket without your knowledge.[48] Supposing someone questions, how so? Who put the money in the white man's pocket? This is a question that can be answered meaningfully by inverting the analogy, says the panellist. Inverting the analogy captures the experience of being Black in a race-obsessed world. The experience of being Black or racialized as a person of colour is akin to walking down the street and having your money taken from your pocket.[49] "Money" here is not something literal. It represents material and cultural resources. The analogy is intended to capture the utter sense of oblivion that many whites engender toward their privilege. The inversion of the analogy is intended to capture the net effect of racism, i.e., the resources that whites take from Blacks and other people of colour

> to build a case for having earned such resources.[50] To return to the question, who put the money in the white man's pocket? From our inversion, it seems it is those racialized as the people of colour who put the money in the pocket of the white subject.

What do these analogies tell us? On the positive side, the analogies help put in context how white privilege is the other side of racism. The question, what does it mean to be white? cannot be asked in isolation from the question, what does it mean to be Black or Latino or Asian? Racism and white privilege are two sides of the same coin. The one feeds the other. Generally, people who are privileged either take their privilege for granted or pretend they are unaware of it. On the negative side, there are two main problems in the two analogies examined. In the analogy of the bike, the idea that those depriving the biker of the use of the road do so unintentionally makes its application to white privilege problematic. In white privilege, those visible racist acts on people of colour are made by people who know perfectly well what they are doing. It is no longer true to say they are oblivious to what they are doing. In the second analogy, the suggestion that it is people of colour who put the money in the white subject's pocket seems to make the white subject less culpable for their action. It also unfairly distorts historical facts. This is why Zeus Leonardo suggests that the discourse on privilege comes with "the unfortunate consequence of masking history, obfuscating agents of domination, and removing the actions that make it clear who is doing what to whom. Instead of emphasizing the process of appropriation, the discourse of privilege centers the discussion on the advantages that whites receive. It mistakes the symptoms for causes."[51]

The standard definition of white privilege was offered by McIntosh (1989) who described white privilege as "an invisible package of unearned assets which I can count on cashing in each day, but about which I was 'meant' to remain oblivious. White privilege is like an invisible weightless knapsack of special provisions, maps, passports, codebooks, visas, clothes, tools, and blank checks."[52] The tools contained in the knapsack, according to McIntosh, confer special benefits on white people and make it easier for white people to navigate through social space and achieve positive outcomes.[53] McIntosh is credited with helping white people "understand the taken for granted, daily aspects of white privilege: from the convenience of matching one's skin color with bandages, to opening up a textbook to discover one's racial identity affirmed in history, literature, and civilization in general."[54] Other definitions of white privilege do not significantly deviate from McIntosh's own definition. They capture the same idea that we live in a world of race discrimination in which white people are the beneficiaries of the racial disadvantage inflicted on non-whites.[55] The one definition that deviates from McIntosh's definition seems to be rather a radical critique of white privilege. It was offered by Leonardo who suggests "that a critical look at white privilege, or the analysis of white racial hegemony, must be complemented by an equally rigorous examination of white supremacy, or the analysis of white racial domination."[56] Unlike McIntosh who does not link white privilege with white supremacy, Leonardo thinks white privilege and white supremacy are related because it is the conditions of white supremacy that make white privilege possible.[57] "In order for white racial hegemony to saturate everyday life," he writes, "it has to be secured by a process of domination, or those acts, decisions, and policies that white subjects perpetrate on people of color. As such, a critical pedagogy of white racial supremacy revolves less around the issue of unearned advantages, or the state of being dominant, and more around direct processes that secure domination and the privileges associated with it."[58] Ultimately, the common denominator in the definitions of white privilege comes down to this: that white subjects accrue privileges by virtue of being constructed as whites through a valuation process of white skin colour, hair texture, shape of the nose, culture, and language.[59] White privilege not only makes it possible for privilege to be granted without the subject recognizing that life is made a bit easier for them, privilege is also granted "despite the subject's attempt to disidentify with the white race."[60]

In general, the standard definition of white privilege is descriptive, not explanatory. It simply follows and does not deviate from the common-sense analogies that are riddled with counterpositions. We established already (in the previous chapter) that we all have biases because, as humans, our ideas, beliefs, and conscious motivations come in a mixture of true and false information.[61] Granted that one's personal biases can make one blind to the invisible structures, systems, and behaviours that confer privilege and power routinely to one's group, it is a myth that whites who are privileged do not know it. It is even more mystifying when they choose not to acknowledge that they know it, if the goal is to correct the imbalance. James Baldwin once said that it is in the nature of myth that those who are its victims and those who are its perpetrators are unable to examine the myth. The ultimate answers to the hopes and fears that pervade contemporary society rest on the moral fibre, wisdom, and responsibility of those who wish to promote the course of development.[62] It takes moral fibre, wisdom, and responsibility to deconstruct myths in order to direct action towards constructive solution.

The COVID-19 World and the Quest for an Explanatory Definition

The COVID-19 world ushered in a new slang in the lexicon of the United States of America's race relations, "Karen." It is a name used to denote "an obnoxious, angry, entitled, and often racist middle-aged white woman who uses her privilege to have her way or police other people's behaviors."[63] "Karen" emerged as a way of expressing a new racism that pivots towards women.[64] The internet is full of viral videos of middle-aged white women freaking out, displaying outbursts, throwing tantrums, and committing overtly racist acts in public either because they have been denied a privilege or have been dispossessed of an entitlement. These hugely popular memes all go by the name "Karen." Karen is now a ubiquitous term used to describe white women perceived as acting entitled in public. It is also used "for any white woman who's thought to be acting inappropriately, rudely, or in an entitled manner."[65] "Karen" is not just a stand-in for problematic white women, it is a new term for white privilege. It "represents a faction of the population threatened by the prospect of losing its place atop a toxic, racial hierarchy rooted in the original sin of slavery."[66] There are far too many internet examples of Karen. Here I highlight four samples for case study (with their names removed because the goal is to render Karen gender-neutral) to highlight what takes place in the dialectic of community:

- Case 1: In May 2018, a woman in Oakland, CA, called the cops on a group of Black men grilling barbecue in a park.
- Case 2: On 25 May 2020, in Central Park in New York, an African American man was birdwatching when suddenly a white woman walked up to him. The white woman is caught on a video calling cops on the African American man who had asked her to leash her dog. She falsely claimed that the African American man was threatening her life. The viral video generated backlash and accusations of racism.
- Case 3: In May 2020, a viral video shows a woman physically blocking a car from moving in a parking lot to prevent the driver from taking the parking space. The viral video generated a backlash, accusing her of entitlement.
- Case 4: In June 2020, in North Hollywood, CA, a woman at Trader Joe's is caught in a video throwing a tantrum after being asked by Trader Joe's staff to put on a mask in compliance with the store's mask mandate. She yells and responds angrily that she has a breathing problem and that she was being harassed to wear a mask. The viral video generated backlash and accusations of entitlement.

Case 1 and Case 2 have one thing in common: the women calling cops on Black men know the unsavoury history of Black men and cops in the United States. It is a power-play of women who know that cops will most likely take their word against the Black men, irrespective of the facts of the case. Thus, Case 1 and Case 2 show racism that benefits the white subject and disadvantages the Black subjects. Case 3 and Case 4 have one thing in common: showing that entitled white women, who know they are privileged and afraid of losing their unearned privilege, will do anything to maintain it. As will be exposited in the next section, white privilege includes a host of unearned benefits, including an outlook on life and character traits that white people take for granted as part of everyday life, but which non-whites do not have. Long before the Karen phenomenon went viral, social scientists and race theorists concerned with circuits and meanings of whiteness in everyday life have been exposing "the codes of white culture, worldview of the white imaginary, and assumptions of the invisible market that depends on the racial other for its own identity."[67] I have discussed this elaborately (in chapter 3) in terms of what Lonergan technically calls bias. John Dadosky has fleshed it out in terms of what René Girard calls mimetic rivalry between groups.[68] Race theorists who tell us that racism in our day has become subtle, invisible, and more indirect have spoken of it as symbolic racism,[69] modern racism,[70] implicit racism,[71] and aversive racism.[72] Derald Wing Sue speaks of it as the microaggressions that are delivered daily on marginalized groups without the conscious awareness of perpetrators.[73] It is not insignificant that the Karens that have gone viral are white women who feel threatened by the presence of Blacks and people of colour. Womanist theology has frequently charged that white women whom women of colour encounter are oppressive. The positions of privilege and power of Karen reinforce womanist theology's claim that structures of domination are reinforced and reproduced on the basis of race, sex, and class.[74] It validates womanist theologians' quest to separate themselves from white feminists because of the white women's "participation in the perpetuation of white supremacy, which continues to dehumanize black women."[75]

Entitlement and privilege expose a larger issue of systemic racism. "Privilege is the daily cognate of structural domination," writes Leonardo. "Without securing the latter, the former is not activated."[76] Some critics, mostly feminists, have pointed out that the internet's archetype of white privilege is sexist and part of an age-old effort to shame women who speak out. The merit of their argument cannot be dismissed. I am sympathetic to this position and have addressed it squarely in a journal article.[77] That said, it also has to be noted that the real reason why the Karen phenomenon has become an internet sensation is because of white privilege and racism.[78] The blonde woman who yelled to a Native-American woman in a gas station, "You're going back to Mexico" or the white woman who called cops on a Black girl selling bottled water or the famed white woman in Illinois (dubbed the Home Depot Karen) who refused to wear mask and vaunted as her excuse, "Yes I am entitled. I am white. I am a woman" – these are all examples that run counter to the claim that it is about shaming women, i.e., the evidence clearly shows that this is all about racism and white privilege. It is the intrigue of the "modern Prometheus" W.E.B. Dubois decried in "The Souls of White Folk."[79] ´Fessing up to white privilege is not about shaming, blaming, or guilt-tripping, but about being cognizant about how one recreates or perpetuates oppressive and domineering actions willy-nilly at both the individual and institutional levels. Karen, after all, is not just a one-off occurrence about one eccentric white woman. Rather, these events reveal something deeper – a horizon of feelings and "existential scale of value preferences."[80] Karen knows she can use race to her advantage. Karen knows that the race of people who are Black or non-white constitutes for them a disadvantage she can exploit because society has set up its structures that way.

In sum, what I have tried to do is use the Karen phenomenon to point to a larger issue of systemic imbalance that is not restricted to a specific gender or person. The Karen phenomenon points to a system of power in which white women are as culpable as their white male counterparts. To use a neologism made current by the American feminist, Elizabeth Schussler Fiorenza, the Karen phenomenon exposes a system of kyriarchy. Kyriarchy is a term Fiorenza used to explain how ethnicity, class, gender, economics, and education intersect to oppress both men and women. She defines kyriarchy as "a complex pyramidal system of intersecting multiplicative social structures of superordination and subordination, of ruling and oppression."[81] Just like the human person is not a single identity, but a complex web of intersectionalities, human inhumanity to one another is not a single or isolated matter, but complex and multiform. Although Fiorenza meant to use kyriarchy as a substitute for patriarchy, kyriarchy "helps to explain how women themselves can in some cases morph into the supremacist bully."[82]

The Karen phenomenon is associated with a set of meanings and values that are detrimental to the good of order. Although Karen exposes the female side of a historic system of oppression, it is part of a larger system of oppression in which men and women have participated, albeit in different ways. Lonergan says "we are subjects, as it were, by degrees."[83] Karen is a caricature of existential subjects who freely and existentially construct a self by actions and choices. It is undeniable, therefore, that the caricatured Karen is a racist. The caricatured Karen is an existential subject who knows self as a doer who consciously deliberates, evaluates, chooses, and acts. It is also, therefore, undeniable that the caricatured Karen knows that self as racist. The caricatured Karen knows that for many African Americans the "police have come to symbolize white power, white racism, and white repression."[84] We know (by self-affirmation of the knower) that Karen is a racist. The good, Lonergan says, is the object of desire. The inverse is equally true – whatever is contrary to the good is not an object of desire. We know that Karen is a racist because Karen's actions are contrary to the good. Karen creates an atmosphere of hostility and simultaneously tries to use the symbol of white power and repression to extricate self from it. Just like the good subject, the good choice, the good action, are not found in isolation,[85] the bad subject, the bad choice, the bad action, are not found in isolation. The worst part is, Karen may not even care that we know Karen is a racist. After all, Karen is a product of society and society has institutional structures Karen can invoke to support the said actions. Dramatic bias, as shown in chapter 3, can shape what people see and hear to the extent that they lose the affective dimension. The degree of an act of racism in society, like the degrees of consciousness, varies from the lowest level of unconscious acts to a minimal conscious act, to mid-level conscious act, and higher degrees of conscious racist acts. Like the degrees of consciousness, all degrees of racism are arrived at by sublation.[86] Thus, it is in the light of a host of new revelations about Karen that I argue that white privilege needs a redefinition and a re-postulate. Definitions and postulates are part of that formulation of general knowledge that make a discourse credible and imbue it with a technical language.[87] To maintain this specificity, terms must be defined unambiguously and "be employed exactly in that unambiguous meaning."[88] As I show in the next section, Karen exposes further ambiguities in the white privilege discourse and opens up new layers of awareness of systemic racism to which society can no longer pretend to be oblivious.

Karen and Systemic Racism

From our argument thus far, it is clear that Karen is not unaware that whiteness confers privileges and that these privileges are backed by a "culture of power." It is clear that Karen is not unaware that that the privilege, which others who do not look like Karen do not have, is built into the structure of society and maintains the fabric of society. It is clear that Karen is not unaware that Karen is not Black or a person of colour and is quick to tell the coloured person, "go back to Africa" or "go back to Mexico." Simply put, Karen knows that everything tilts to Karen's advantage and that Karen can use the power it gives to dominate. The reason racism continues to persist, in spite of the goodwill of many who have tried to do something about it, is because it is systemic and structural and larger than any one person or group.[89] In the wake of the protest following Floyd's death (May 2020), the United States, as an act of reckoning, has begun the process of tearing down some monuments to historical figures that were complicit in slavery and removing confederate flags hitherto displayed in public institutions. But as commendable as these efforts are, "little scrutiny has been given to the cultural institutions that legitimized the worldview behind these symbols: white Christian churches."[90]

Circumstances, Lonergan reminds us, alter cases.[91] Deconstructing the Karen phenomenon has helped to expose some counter-positions in the way white privilege is framed and understood. The very notion of privilege that Karen embodies suggests it is derived from a mythic notion. Lonergan says a mythic notion fails to differentiate between mythic expression and developed expression.[92] Even Mcintosh, who coined the term "white privilege," admits that the most appropriate term may perhaps be not white privilege but "conferred dominance" that has accrued to white people over time. McIntosh relates how her schooling teaches her, as it does other whites, "to think of their lives as morally neutral, normative, and average, and also ideal, so that when we work to benefit others, this is seen as work which will allow 'them' to be more like 'us.'"[93] This brings us back to the matter of the fifth pillar of racism, Christianity. Christianity can no longer deny complicity in racism. It is no longer Black theologians who are making the charge. White Christian pastors and theologians are now coming to a moment of reckoning on this matter. More recently, Robert Jones has pointed in the direction of complicity of white Christians in sustaining "a project of perpetuating white supremacy that has framed the entire American story."[94] White Christians, i.e., Evangelicals, Protestants, and Catholics, "are consistently more likely than whites who are religiously unaffiliated to deny the existence of structural racism."[95] To determine the depth and breadth of the problem, Jones created a system index, consisting of 15 sets of questions, designed to get beyond personal biases to get to the heart of structural injustice. The questions include the treatment of African Americans in the criminal justice system, the general perception of race and racial discrimination, whether monuments to Confederate soldiers are symbols of Southern pride or racism, and whether Christians agree with the statement, "Generations of slavery and discrimination have created conditions that make it difficult for Blacks to work their way out of the lower class." After collating the data, "the Racism Index reveals a clear distinction. Compared to nonreligious whites, white Christians register higher median scores on the Racism Index, and the differences among white Christian subgroups are largely differences of degree rather than kind."[96]

White privilege, as an idea, is a blind spot rooted in mythic consciousness. Mythic consciousness stands in sharp contrast to self-knowledge that seeks self-transcendence.[97] Lonergan identifies mythic consciousness with the inability or refusal to go beyond description to explanation, and says it lacks or neglects effective criteria for passing judgments on anticipations and acts of understanding.[98] Mythic consciousness can be a nostalgic longing for the idealized past and thinking "you can get right back to it very easily."[99] Mythic consciousness comes in different varieties, in different shapes and forms. It can be crude or subtle. The mythic consciousness of Karen is a nostalgic look at the American past (slavery and Jim Crow era laws) when Black men served white women and Black men dare not look white women in the face. To be clear, it is not only white women who have mythic consciousness. Male racists have it too. In the run up to the 2012 Democratic presidential primaries between Hillary Rodham Clinton and then Senator Barack Obama, a frustrated Bill Clinton, at the prospect of seeing his wife lose the nomination was reported to have remarked, "Back in the day, he (referring to Barack Obama) would be serving us coffee."[100] Mythic consciousness is an infatuation with a glorious past you want to maintain even when your basic instinct tells you it is not sustainable. Lonergan says of mythic consciousness that it experiences and imagines, understands and judges, but does not distinguish between these activities and is therefore unaware of myth and how to go beyond it.[101] In a nutshell, the Karen meme does not exonerate white men from racism. The heteronormative white male and that culture of power remains fundamental. The culture of power in its systemic and institutional forms always reproduces itself. Karen is equally a reproduction of that culture of power, a racism that pivots towards women. White women, compared to white men, may have "lacked power for so long that even while exhibiting racism they aren't taken completely seriously,"[102] but Karen exposes why they now need to be taken seriously. Karen models a systemic racism, a dominant ideology that women know, but pretend to be unaware of. Like patriarchy and misogyny, Karen (a systemic racism women benefit from but pretend not to know much about) is one of the layers of discrimination and bias with a deep history in human social institutions. Karen seems "harmless enough to laugh at yet hateful enough to skewer."[103] She is like "a mascot, of sorts, who bridges the gap between the violent truth of white nationalism and the satisfying reality that she often lacks power to keep people of color 'in their place' and it's freaking her the hell out."[104] Emmett Till (1941–55), the fourteen-year-old African American, was lynched in Mississippi in 1965 after being accused of flirting with a white woman. There was no social media or camera then to refute the allegation. The woman admitted years later that the story was untrue.[105] White domination comes in different shapes and sizes. One of the things Karen exposes is that white domination, whether in the power relation of slavery, colonialism, or Jim Crow, is never settled once and for all. Rather, it is constantly re-established and constructed anew by whites.[106] I suggest, therefore, that a deconstruction of white privilege is necessary because it will help to debunk a host of myths that Black Theology identified long ago, calling for their extermination. For the time being, I will provide only a general outline of the myths in need of debunking and will not concern myself here with how white privilege is operationalized in the academy.[107] The myths that need to be debunked include the following:

1. The Illusion of Colour Blindness: Colour blindness is one of the many excuses people use to deflect questions of race. Social constructs, like race, are so powerful that even seemingly good people can be blind to them.[108] Those who claim not to see colour think by so doing they will appear non-biased and non-racist. Social and behavioural scientists have taken to naming this unwillingness to acknowledge or to admit to seeing a person's race or colour as an instance of microinvalidations, a subset of microaggression. They think microinvalidations are "the most insidious, damaging, and harmful form" of microaggression because they "directly or indirectly deny the experiential realities of socially devalued groups."[109] Studies indicate "that race and gender are two of the most easily identifiable qualities seen by people,"[110] and yet some people are content to play the colour blindness game. The colour blindness game takes many forms and finds many expressions: "When I look at you, I don't see color;" "We are all one human race;" "We are all Americans;" "Regardless of your gender or race, I believe the most qualified person should get the job."[111] Social and behavioural scientists are nearly unanimous that "the denial of differences is really a denial of power and privilege. The denial of power and privilege is really a denial of personal benefits that accrue to certain privileged groups by virtue of inequities."[112] In the next chapter, I will discuss colour blindness and other variants of microaggression more extensively. Lonergan

alludes to the demonic and infantile aspects of mythic consciousness.[113] There are also two aspects of the myth of colour blindness. One follows along the demonic lines of mythic consciousness and the other follows along the infantile path. The demonic line captures those who claim not to be racist because they are colour-blind. The infantile captures those who simulate colour blindness to deflect efforts to address racial imbalance. For the latter, race is a zero-sum game. Interestingly, the Cognitive Bias Codex refers to a zero-sum game as a form of bias. It is a bias that thinks white people will lose something if people of colour gain access. When they say they are colour-blind, they mean that decisions should be made without regard to race, disregarding centuries in which race has been the cornerstone of society and its legal system.[114] When challenged, they are very quick to throw out the charge of reverse racism. A 1969 debate on institutional racism between Baldwin and Prof. Paul Weiss, a renowned scholar and professor of philosophy at Yale, was very revealing on this illusion of colour blindness. It also reveals the demonic aspect of mythic consciousness. Almost everybody knows the state of African American life in the United States in those turbulent times – segregation was still well and alive, to say the least. Prof. Weiss vehemently denied that there is such a thing as systemic racism. His argument was that Blacks, like whites, face obstacles in life. Each of us, he argued, is terribly alone, regardless of race, colour, creed, or religion, and that each one faces obstacles. The problem, according to this armchair dilletante, is to become a man. Prof. Weiss argued that prejudice is not really at the centre of the obstacles we all face as Homo sapiens and that the obstacles are not insuperable, if one knows what one is looking for. He berated Baldwin for "always concentrating on color," instead of other ways of connecting humanity. A Black author, like Baldwin, would not achieve what Baldwin achieved, if there was really systemic racism, he argued. To illustrate how clueless he was on the matter, he asked Baldwin to explain to him how being Black gets in the way of his scholarship (as an author). Baldwin tried to explain the difficulty of what it means be a Black American with no history, i.e., the difficulty of a person whose identity has been systematically destroyed, finding himself confronting a white man with a bible, a gun, and a cross. Prof. Weiss objected immediately, claiming that he was colour-blind – that he does not read Baldwin's book because Baldwin is Black, but that he reads Baldwin's book because Baldwin is an accomplished author. He claimed that if everything Baldwin says about American Black experience were to be true, Baldwin would not have become an accomplished author. Baldwin tried to explain to him the psychological trauma of being Black: that white people have the power to control your life and the power to destroy your life and yet somehow in the face of it you have to decide that you are not going to allow yourself to be controlled by what white people think of you. Baldwin tried to point out that the gap that has been placed between his own assessment of his own experience (as a Black man) and other writers (who are white) is very wide. Prof. Weiss, refusing to give up the comfort of his ivory tower, declaratively retorted, "I don't believe it." Baldwin was not surprised that Prof. Weiss did not believe that systemic racism exists. A Black person, said Baldwin, faces a real social danger in which he or she has to be afraid of every cop, every boss, and everybody in the world around him. Prof. Weiss, in his mythic fantasy, was not only unable to get the point, he also failed to acknowledge Baldwin's own experience – a Black man born in Harlem, New York, who had to flee the United States to live in exile, just to escape racial discrimination and Jim Crow laws. He failed to acknowledge that for every James Baldwin that made it in America as a scholar and writer, there are numerous others who could not because the system is set up for them not to succeed. Blindspot is pervasive. Baldwin's concluding remark is instructive in that it shows how institutional racism is operationalized:

> I don't know what every white person in this country feels, but I can only conclude what they feel from the state of their institution. I don't know whether white Christians hate negroes or not, but I know we have a Christian church, which is white, and a Christian church which is black. I know as Malcolm X once put it, 'the most segregated hour in American life is high noon on Sunday.' That speaks a great deal for me as a Christian nation. That means I can't afford to trust most white Christians because of the Christian church. I don't know whether the labor union and their bosses really hate me, that doesn't matter, but I know that I'm not in their union. I don't know whether real estate lobbyists really hate black people, but I know that the real estate lobbyists keep me in the ghetto. I don't know if the Board of Education really hates black people, but I know the textbooks they give my children to read and the schools that we have to go to. Now this is the evidence. But you want me to make an act of faith on an idealism that you cannot show me is true.[115]

It is easy to think no sane person today will hold the kind of view Prof. Weiss held in the 1960s. But if he held that in the 1960s, it is easy to see why the illusion of colour blindness persists till this day. Many white people are too quick to deny that the benefits accrued to white people are systematically conferred. They claim to be colour-blind and deny the existence of race as a meaningful category and would want people to believe that the benefits they have are earned, not gifted.[116] In this twisted logic, they will point, like Prof. Weiss did, to some examples of white people they know who have not been successful. No one says white privilege necessarily guarantees white people good results or outcomes. White privilege is just a term that captures the unearned advantages that white people have over people of colour by virtue of their race. To pretend to be colour-blind simply means you choose to ignore the experience of Black people in the face of a system that will never allow Black people to succeed.

2. Whitewashing: Whitewashing is related to colour blindness. Research on colour blindness racial ideologies (CBRI) show that these ideologies permeate the attitudes of whites, i.e., Blacks are less likely than whites to embrace these attitudes.[117] But there is evidence that people of colour are equally affected by these ideologies, especially when they find themselves in spaces dominated by whites. Researchers found that these ideologies are "also present within subgroups of the racial minority groups, and that these attitudes are in part patterned by their exposure to whites, and show that some types of CBRI may become more hegemonic over time, if their acceptance by racial minority groups grows."[118] If colour blindness reveals the "demonic" aspect of mythic consciousness, in Lonergan's sense of the term, whitewashing is its infantile manifestation. Whitewashing is a neoliberal idea that pretends that society has evolved and that we live in a post-racial society while in actual fact it privileges whites in economic and social structures. While it pretends to deny race as a meaningful category of measurement, it at the same time promotes and fosters white culture. The magnitude and vehemence of the denial reveals a collective mental block.[119] Whitewashing is very common in schools, businesses, and politics. On her own experience as a British woman, Susan Durber writes:

> I grew up in a world where white was "normal." I was aware of race issues in the American South and in apartheid South Africa, but I had little understanding that my own country had a problematic past or present. My learning of the Christian faith was also defined by white saints (or those I thought of as white) and by a white Jesus, with blond hair and blue eyes. At my confirmation, I was given a book about a white missionary to China, Gladys Aylward. At university, I worshipped in an Oxford college chapel where David Livingstone was portrayed in stained glass and lauded as a hero (though he was part of creating the Victorian construct of "darkest Africa").[120]

What Durber describes is part of the diffusion of privilege when it is normalized and internalized. Unconscious negative attitudes of ethnic minorities promote and enhance white privilege.

3. The Myth of Sameness: Scholars are beginning to unearth a notable absence of racial imagery with respect to how white people view themselves. Racial imageries have long been attributed to Blacks and other native peoples of the world, but racial imagery is hardly ever attributed to white people. White people, in other words, do not see or think of themselves in racial terms. They just know they are white and not like non-whites. White people see themselves, not in terms of ethnicity, but in terms of their cultural origins as, say British, Italian, Polish, German, Catholic, Protestant, and Orthodox. This notable absence of race in white people's self-understanding makes being white seem like the norm of being human. Even white liberals and those who think of themselves as least racist get agitated and angry when attention is drawn to their whiteness and when they are reminded by non-white people that they are white.[121] Ironically, these liberals invest in the myth of sameness, even when their actions "reflect the primacy of whiteness as a sign informing who they are and how they think."[122] The notion that other people are raced and white people are just people, suggests that other people are something else. Critics are beginning to note how this is something "endemic to white culture" and should be countenanced as the other side of racism.[123] In different representations whites are made to seem like the norm, the ordinary standard of being human. "Precisely because of this and their placing as norm they seem not to be represented to themselves as whites but as people who are variously gendered, classed, sexualized and abled. At the level of racial representation, in other words, whites are not of a certain race, they're just the human race."[124] But this neglects the very core principle of race, i.e., that Blackness exists because there is whiteness and vice-versa. "Race itself would be meaningless if it were not a fault line along which power, prestige, and respect are distributed."[125] As long as whiteness is perceived to be the human condition, "then it alone both defines normality and fully inhabits it."[126] The equation of being white with the human condition secures a position of power. Whether done intentionally or otherwise, it is white people who construct the image of others and set the standards by which they (white people) are to succeed and by which others are bound to fail.[127] Embedded in this construction is a privilege that confers a set of advantages on white skin. One of the ways to counter this power imbalance is to end "the conspiracy of silence" that allows white people to accept the unearned advantages of their skin colour.[128] As one writer puts it, "whiteness needs to be made strange."[129]

White Privilege – A Theological Problem for Black Theology

A new body of research supports anecdotal evidence that talking about racism and raising the issue of prejudice and discrimination explicitly can lead to better outcomes and help people be more open-minded and act more fairly. This is because raising the issue openly can and does help people to reflect better on their choices.[130] There is no compelling literature, however, to support any notion that raising the issue of white privilege openly has helped to reduce occurrences of white privilege in the workplace. The ideologies, institutions, and structures that shape white privilege are still very much intact since McIntosh defined the term and set the parameters of the conversation (1989). As a phenomenon that occurs with regularity, white privilege – the other side of racism – is a theological problem. From a theological point of view, the phenomenon is an affront to the justice and mercy of God because it is a perversion of justice (I Samuel 8:3). The Hebrew Bible uses the word *hesed* over 250 times to communicate an essential aspect of God's character – love and faithfulness. As "imitators of Christ" (I Cor. 11:1), understanding God's *hesed* ought to inspire the Christian to love the other mercifully and compassionately as God loves. The words used to describe God's justice or righteousness, *tzedek* and *mishpat* (Micah 6:8 and Amos 5) equally communicate the same ideal. These are terms used to provide societal guidelines for fairness and equity in Israel (Lev. 24:22; Deut. 11; Is. 58). While God loves the poor and the rich equally and does not show any favouritism, the scriptures tell us that God shows a predilection for the needy, the suffering, and the oppressed. Yahweh's message to Moses demonstrates this: "I have seen the affliction of my people who are in Egypt, and have heard their cry because of their taskmasters; I know their sufferings, and I have come down to deliver them out of the hand of the Egyptians" (Exodus 3:7–8). The book of Exodus tells us how the liberation of the poor is at the very heart of God's design (Exodus 6:5–7). Anytime an establishment comes up with plan to "deal shrewdly" (Exodus 1:10) with a minority or oppressed group, God always "hears their groaning" (Exodus 2:24) and their "cry" for help (Exodus 3:7) and always seeks to intervene. The same God who intervened and liberated Israel is incarnate in Jesus Christ. This was what Karl Barth tried to communicate: "God always takes His stand unconditionally and passionately on this side and on this side alone: against the lofty and on behalf of the lonely; against those who already enjoy right and privilege and on behalf of those who are denied it and deprived of it."[131] The gospel's emphasis on God's predilection for the poor and oppressed secures the vocational direction of Black Theology.[132] If Barth is right (and I believe he is right on this matter) that "the command of God is a call for the championing of the weak against every kind of encroachment on the part of the strong,"[133] how Black Theology is to be faithful to this vocation of communicating God's preferential option for the poor, of which the Black subject is the proto-poor, without creating a false dichotomy between the rich and the poor that is not biblical and a false dichotomy between Blacks and non-Blacks, and Blacks and peoples of other races, remains a theological challenge.

The white privilege discourse also poses a theological problem for Black Theology. The problem it poses is analogous to the conceptualist and intellectualist problem Lonergan spent a great deal of time confronting. A context here will be helpful. In his time, Lonergan saw some of the prevailing interpretations of Aquinas to be conceptualist, i.e., they were an abstraction. He found such abstractions to be very troubling. Conceptualists confuse the abstract with the concrete and do not know how to distinguish between the abstract and the concrete. Lonergan critiqued conceptualism much the same way that he critiqued intellectualism. Just as conceptualism is a prevailing temptation to form concepts intuitively, intellectualism is also a prevailing temptation to form concepts prior to acts of understanding. Generally speaking, conceptualism is a problem of intuitionism that is traceable, even if indirectly, to Duns Scotus. Intellectualism is a problem that is traceable, even if indirectly, to Aristotle and from him to Aquinas. Both are aberrations of understanding. In a way, they both confuse genuine knowing with a prior intuitionism or a prior universalism.[134] The net result of the different sets of abstractions is that they conceive of the human person in a static and ahistorical manner. To combat conceptualism and intellectualism, Lonergan had to embark on the important task of clarifying what it means to understand and understand correctly and what it means to know and know correctly. For Lonergan, acts of insight pivot between the abstract and the concrete. "The universal can be thought, but cannot be, without the instance; the limit can be thought, but cannot be without the continuum, the invariant can be considered, but does not exist apart from particular places and times."[135] He goes on further to explain, "Inasmuch as we are understanding, we are grasping the universal apart from its instances, the limit apart from the continuum, the invariant apart from particular places and times, the ideal frequency apart from the nonsystematic divergence of actual frequencies."[136]

What we learn from Lonergan is that incompleteness of knowledge is a philosophical problem and that its ramifications for theology can be dire. The problem the white privilege discourse poses for Black Theology pivots along the two poles of conceptualism (abstractions based on concepts) and intellectualism (abstractions based on intuition). They confuse the abstract person of colour with the concrete Scottie, Willie, Kenyatta, and Shaquana. They do not know how to distinguish between the universal-abstract Black person from the concrete person that works daily in their institutions and in their academies. They claim to understand white privilege, but noble intentions aside, their understanding of race and racism is primarily intellectualist – based on the same intuitionism of the Enlightenment construct that produced race and racism in the first place, i.e., the same intellectualism that foregrounds white privilege. They claim to denounce privilege, but the denunciation is intellectualist and that is why they still remain beneficiaries of privilege, despite the best intentions to talk about it. Their basic terms and relations for grasping "privilege" remain abstract and do not cohere with the realities of the lived-life experiences of people of colour. Lonergan was clear that the intelligible that is grasped in sensible data is the same as the intelligible that is uttered in definition and that the object when grasped is different from the object when defined.[137]

Black Theology more than ever needs cross-cultural interactions. And still more than before, Black Theology needs to attend to bias in this cross-cultural interaction. The German philosopher and cultural critic, Friedrich Nietzsche (1844–1900), together with some late modernity thinkers, like Marx and Freud, cautioned that false consciousness can infect a person's received ideas. Nietzsche worked out the perspectival optics of cognition. What Nietzsche calls perspective or "optics" of knowledge, in his criticism of perspectival objectivity in philosophy, has both a positive and a negative dimension. Without going into detail on Nietzsche's theory, the operation of perspective makes a positive contribution to human cognitive endeavours. If nothing else, it is a reminder that one cannot ignore the perspectival limitations of one's theorizing.[138] While I do not adhere to Nietzsche's extreme idea that all truth claims are contingent on and are a product of a person's cognition, his metaphor of perspectivism can be used as a safeguard to avoid self-referential biases in our theorizing.[139] The philosophical development of this idea was what became a "hermeneutic of suspicion" in Michel Foucault (1964)[140] and in Paul Ricoeur (1965).[141] This idea that all perspectives are shaped by the biases of the subjects and their location in time and space is gaining traction in modern science. Social psychology has been unearthing in the past two decades or more the complexity of the human mind and how it affects human conscious behaviour, regardless of intent. It is a body of research that supports Lonergan's essential argument regarding cognitive prejudice – that none of us is immune from bias and that these biases play out in varying forms, both at the individual and collective levels. Even the best of us is susceptible to bias. No one is immune to it. Even ideas that begin with the best of intentions, if unchecked, can morph into an ideology and become a place of self-interested bias. It is hard to deny that many, if not most, of the subjects in the white privilege conversation group are well-meaning individuals who are passionate about doing something about this other side of racism – their unearned privilege. The problem, however, is that the same intelligent and passionate people discussing the issue of white privilege are perpetuating it. This is not necessarily because they all collectively harbour the intent of maintaining the status quo, but because they have not attended adequately to the role played by human unconscious thoughts in human behaviour. Lonergan's notion of dramatic bias, supported by the explosion of studies on unconscious bias in social psychology, has revealed that the general belief that stereotypes and bias are the purview of bigoted people is no longer tenable.[142] Even good people have blind spots and biases that surface preconsciously.[143] Black Theology leaves to its peril discussion of racial justice to the white privilege group. It may seem counterintuitive, but recognizing your privilege does not mean you are doing something about it. Recognizing your privilege does not mean that the struggle for equity is over or less credible.[144] It is unclear how discussion of white privilege can address on its own what cognitive science has pointed out are discriminatory behaviours based on stereotypes that are outside of our conscious awareness. This will involve a shift to the data of consciousness, a turn or shift that the discussion group has not made and has no reason to make, as far we know. We live in a world that is not colour-blind. A few years ago I attended a conference where one of the sessions was a discussion group on racism. All the presenters were white subjects; none was Black. They presented fine papers and you could not help but marvel at their erudition. During the question and answer session, a white male in the audience asked, "Could any one of you tell me stories? I want stories, not theories. Is there anyone among you who has stories to tell?" The speakers all went dead silent. None of them had any story to tell because none of them has experienced racism. Racism for them is an abstraction and collection of data and artefacts to help formulate fine theories. There are many resources Black Theology can offer to the discourse of white privilege, one of which is stories that stem from lived-life experiences. There is always a tendency to put up resistance when Black people are trying to tell their stories. That resistance is a threat to racial justice. Stories of lived-life experiences of Black people must go hand in hand with the science of implicit bias. For research has shown that stories from particular persons who are threatened are more effective than data or watertight theoretical arguments.[145] Another resource Black Theology can offer the discourse of white privilege is this shift to the data of consciousness (that is advocated here), as a way to help us come to terms with our conscious and unconscious bias. More than ever before, more harm is done by "well-intentioned people, who are strongly motivated by egalitarian values, who believe in their own morality, and who experience themselves as fair-minded and decent people who would never consciously discriminate."[146] These two elements – stories of lived-life experiences and attentiveness to the data of consciousness – must be brought together. This is in line with what Lonergan was trying to convey in his remark that corporeal matter is known separately through the senses, but the quiddity or nature or cause is known separately through the intellect and when defined: "what became known earlier through distinct acts are now brought together into one."[147]

Conclusion

The Karen phenomenon has provided Black Theology with another way of thinking and talking about racial discrimination, a way of understanding its long history, the complexities of its manifestation, and the injury it does to people of colour. Not only has the Karen phenomenon helped us to understand that racism is "a crime and a disease," it has also helped us to understand "that the illness of racism infects almost everyone."[148] The phenomenon shows that our society shares "a common historical and cultural heritage in which racism has played and still plays a dominant role."[149] Lonergan's remark regarding the need to move from cognitional self-transcendence to real self-transcendence must be taken seriously. There is a body of literature that is emerging from social psychology that supports Lonergan's idea that cognitive biases can be overcome through conversion. This body of literature, using the language of cognitive psychology, shows that cognitive biases that operate automatically and cloud a person's judgment can be controlled, corrected, and even eliminated "through careful process of re-engineering."[150] The process of "re-engineering," or conversion in the language of Lonergan, helps in the transition from cognitional to moral self-transcendence. Those white subjects who, to their credit, recognize the problem of white privilege and are talking about it have reached a stage of cognitional self-transcendence. But they need to do more with that knowledge. Knowledge, as one writer puts it, does not consist "in a manipulation of man and nature as opposite forces, nor in the reduction of data to mere statistical order, but is a means of liberating mankind from the destructive power of fear, pointing the way toward the goal of the rehabilitation of the human will and the rebirth of faith and confidence in the human person."[151] The Bible speaks of the fruit of the Spirit as love, joy, forbearance, kindness, goodness, faithfulness, gentleness, and self-control (Galatians 5:22–3). These are the fruits of real self-transcendence as well. They are the markers for knowing when one has transitioned from cognitional self-transcendence to real self-transcendence. The Galatians text, after enumerating the fruits of the Spirit (fruits of real self-transcendence) ends with a quip: "Against such things there is no law" (Galatians 5:23). It is a recognition that even the law, no matter how subtle, can have some pervasive forms of discrimination, particularly in areas like employment, policing, housing, and education.[152]

Black Theology needs to be mindful of "the seductive powers of the ideologies of equal opportunity" in all its forms.[153] In psychological theory of unconscious of motivation or dramatic bias in Lonergan's terminology, there is a view of ideology that is called the "strain theory." The theory explains ideology as a "defense mechanism against the anxiety felt by those who hold power through means and with motives that they cannot comfortably acknowledge."[154] What the ideology does is provide "'a symbolic outlet' for emotional disturbances generated by social disequilibrium; it enables the privileged individuals to continue practices they would otherwise condemn and in which their own complicity would be painful to admit."[155] Understanding how this ideology works will help Black Theology adopt a "hermeneutic of suspicion," which will serve as a safeguard against ideologies that purport to advance its cause, but in actual fact inhibit it.

Chapter Five

Implicit Bias and the Zero-Sum Game Problem

In the quest for liberation, Black Theology must be able to speak, not just to the spiritual hope that is to come, but also to the societal ills that are a stumbling block to the realization of the two natures of the kingdom of God – "the now and the not yet, the promised and the fulfilled."[1] The American culture with its many great, unprecedented achievements, to adapt the words of Bernard Lonergan, "is not just a realm of sweetness and light."[2] It is also a realm of human suffering, human sin, and the destructive power and the sustained blindness that disenchant us with progress and make us suspicious of development and advance.[3] Racism, in both church and society, epitomizes this surd of sin and sustained blindness. In a private conversation in 1990, as recounted by my colleague, Prof. John Dadosky, the African American Benedictine monk, known for his work on the history of African American Catholicism, Cyprian Davis (1930–2015),[4] likened racism to radiation. If you are Black in America, from driving while Black (DWB) to teaching while Black (TWB) to other things you do in your daily living while Black, you will be met with successions of implicit and explicit messages that are meant to remind you that you are the diminutive other. Every Black person receives this racism-radiation. It is just a question of the degree you receive and at what point in time. Social and behavioural scientists speak of these in terms of microaggressions – ways racism and bias can manifest through aggressive and coded behaviours.[5] This line of argument has been developed, to some extent, in chapter 3, where we used the language of Lonergan to hint at the notion that racism is a landscape of the known-unknowns and the unknown-knowns. This is because the systems of racial and social control adapt, morph, rebound, and are reborn. The burden of the present chapter is twofold: to show how the known-unknowns and the unknown-knowns are furthered by implicit bias; and to offer a critique of microaggressions with a view to determining whether the category itself is adequate to capture the magnitude of the surd of sin – racism.

In the previous chapter, we adapted the term empirical residue, a term Lonergan employed to explain how understanding always abstracts;[6] we used it to show the ingenious ability of racism to be subtle. We made clear in that chapter that there are two abstractable empirical residues of racism, *white privilege*, which was thoroughly discussed in that chapter, and *implicit bias*, which is the burden of this chapter. Peggy McIntosh's seminal essay on white privilege lists about fifty different ways a white person can exercise his or her privilege on a daily basis. All fifty ways, McIntosh admits, "confer dominance because of [the white subject's] race or sex."[7] Robin DiAngelo's well-written essay on the subject has corroborated the idea – that white privilege "gets itself surrounded by protective pillows of resources and/or benefits of the doubt."[8] Both McIntosh and DiAngelo also point to the two movements of white privilege or dominance: it "systematically over empowers"[9] the white subject, while at the same time it disempowers and deprivileges people of colour.

This chapter takes the argument of the two previous ones a step further. It draws from statistical evidence to show that women of colour and white women experience largely different realities.[10] The statistical evidence shows that despite the number of white liberal women who pride themselves on being well-meaning, "many women of color see [white women] as the enemy."[11] Moving beyond statistical data to anecdotal evidence, the chapter draws from studies in social psychology, which show how prejudice is revealed in implicit attitudes, to illustrate how implicit bias gives us another category of understanding the mechanics of the privileging and deprivileging and the over-empowering and disempowering that is integral to the phenomenon of racism itself. Social psychology points to implicit attitudes as a promising way to peer more deeply and more accurately into the human mind.[12] The conclusion of the chapter is that the power of white privilege and its correlate, implicit bias or prejudice against people of colour, render the pathway to success for people of colour "on a larger scale next to impossible."[13] A subset of this argument is that what social psychology calls implicit bias, endemic in church and society, may be seen as the prime analogate of what Lonergan calls dramatic bias. Lonergan, however, makes important modifications to the Freudian-derived term implicit bias, which Freud correctly notes works preconsciously.[14] Social psychologists also speak of a zero-sum relationship behind reverse discrimination – that men tend to think that addressing bias against women is associated with increasing bias against men. This perception of a zero-sum relationship makes it seem like men and women are in competition. "So, if things are better for women, things are worse for men," so to speak. Correlating this to race-relations, research in social psychology supports the body of evidence that whites perceive a similar relationship to minority groups – that white subjects tend to think in zero-sum terms.[15] The need to draw from the social sciences was long ago validated by Lonergan who, appealing to Cardinal John Henry Newman's (1801–90) theorem, insisted that theology must cooperate with other disciplines, if theological reflection is to contribute to authentic humanism. According to Newman's theorem, the omission of a significant opportunity to learn from other disciplines leaves "a blind spot, the mutilation of an organic whole, and a distortion of the disciplines that remained and endeavored to meet real human needs."[16]

The Perduring Myth that Blacks Pose a Racial Threat

Theories of racial prejudice have suffered benign neglect,[17] particularly in theology, at least since Gadamer and Lonergan. Psychologists have shown that "Our conscious motivations, ideas, and beliefs are a blend of false information, biases, irrational passions, rationalizations, prejudices, in which morsels of truth swim around and give the reassurance, albeit false, that the whole mixture is real and true. The thinking process attempts to organize this whole cesspool of illusions according to the laws of logic and plausibility."[18] Following this understanding, Gadamer contends that anyone who thinks he or she is "free of prejudices, relying on the objectivity of his procedures and denying that he is himself conditioned by historical circumstances, experiences the power of the prejudices that unconsciously dominate him as a *vis a tergo*. A person who does not admit that he is dominated by prejudices will fail to see what manifests itself by these lights."[19] No one is ever bias-free, but some people let their biases influence their actions more than others. According to the "continuum model of impression formation" of social psychology, bias sways behaviour. According to the model, our reliance on stereotypes in decision-making exists on a continuum and shifts by degrees, rather than operating in absolutes.[20] Overt racism may have declined in the United States, but racism continues to exist in subtle forms. In the United States, social scientists have uncovered how prejudice intersects with politics and public opinion. These three come together in ways that are both subtle and not so subtle.[21] Given the way that the three are connected is complex, and at times controversial, researchers have developed theories of each of these three concepts, explored their connections, and have gone to great lengths to reveal the extent to which public opinion and prejudice play out in politics more generally.[22] In a study carried out by Kinder and Sears (1981) to understand whether prejudice is a political force and a determinant of white people's political behaviour, the researchers found that "whites' resistance to change in the racial status quo are unmistakable."[23] The study developed a formidable hypothesis the researchers termed "racial threat," i.e., white people's resistance to Black people is usually motivated by the perception that Blacks pose real and tangible threats to their personal lives. From the same hypothesis, they concluded that "as blacks increasingly demand a larger share of the Good Life, whites react with predictable hostility."[24] There is an antecedent for this, the researchers found, in the civil rights struggle of the 1960s – "that Northern whites' enthusiasm for the civil rights movement waned when the movement 'moved north,' because they supposedly favored it only when it did not disrupt their own lives."[25]

The study supports existing research on the two approaches to implicit bias in social psychology. The first approach pertains to what social scientists call the racial threat hypothesis, otherwise known as racial group conflict theory.[26] It is the hypothesis that when two groups, say Black and white, compete for the same scarce resources, prejudice inevitably creeps in. "Competitive interdependence produces the perception of threat, which in turn leads to hostility directed at the members of the threatening group, Social attitudes, in short, reflect private interests."[27] As more Blacks demand to move to suburban neighbourhoods which are currently mostly white, and seek better jobs, which would potentially displace white workers, hostilities tend to increase. The second approach is called the socio-cultural learning hypothesis. The socio-cultural hypothesis attributes prejudice to socio-cultural learning. Children and adolescents acquire prejudices that are normative in their social environment alongside other cultural values and attitudes. Even when realistic threats become anachronistic and dissipate, "the solid core of prejudice remains."[28] For a long time in the United States, the content of early learned prejudice was centred on legally sanctioned discrimination and segregation. But as such laws are dismantled, on paper at least, they are gradually being replaced with what social scientists call "symbolic racism," i.e., "a blend of antiblack affect and the kind of traditional American moral values embodied in the Protestant ethic."[29] Symbolic racism is "a form of resistance to change in the racial status quo based on moral feelings that blacks violate such traditional American values as individualism and self-reliance, the work ethic, obedience, and discipline."[30] The theory of symbolic racism developed out of the theory of symbolic politics. The two main components of symbolic racism are anti-Black sentiment and the drive to maintain traditional American moral values.[31] Social scientists have uncovered data that reveals that "as the size of the black population increases, whites respond with increasingly negative racial attitudes."[32] This is consistent with group threat theory – that white racial attitudes respond to the proportion of Blacks in the local community.[33] Politically, symbolic racism is the most potent element of racial prejudice because in the end it has little to do with any tangible and direct impact on the white person's private life, but is rooted instead in early learned racial fears and stereotypes.[34] Symbolic racism continues to drive inequalities between racial groups through policy preferences with racial implications. There is a suggestion that the prejudice is motivated by fear – that "white people are threatened by having to accept growing numbers of people of color as their equals."[35] It is the zero-sum game problem. Although it has no basis in fact, many whites are coming to believe that "whites are the 'new losers' in a playing field that they believe has been leveled now that the United States is a supposedly basically egalitarian, color-blind society."[36] This means, for them, that whites can now claim the status of victim. The implication of this way of thinking is politically and culturally profound. One visible consequence is the opposition by whites to policies, such as affirmative action, that have been put in place to help ethnic minorities.[37] This zero-sum game problem and the idea whites are new losers in the quest for racial justice have morphed into myths that engender fear. They are barriers to social equality. They stunt equal opportunity. Most egregious of all, they feed implicit racism. "In a white supremacist context, white identity in large part rests upon a foundation of (superficial) racial toleration and acceptance," writes Robin DiAngelo. "Whites who position themselves as liberal often opt to protect what they perceive as their moral reputations, rather than recognize or change their participation in systems of inequity and domination. In so responding, whites invoke the power to choose when, how, and how much to address or challenge racism."[38]

The Recurring Problem of Dramatic Bias

It is easy to think that racism is something of the distant past, that it takes place in remote places, and that it is perpetrated only by white supremacists and persons with radical ideologies. As difficult it is to admit, "racism is not a practice engaged in solely by White supremacists or radical individuals and groups. It is part of our national culture and identity. That is, race and racism are part of our national 'genetic makeup' – (see U.S. Constitution, pre-13th Amendment) and are embedded into our institutions and traditions."[39] In her seminal essay on "White Fragility,"

Robin DiAngelo points to a large body of research about children and race demonstrating "that children start to construct ideas about race very early; a sense of white superiority and knowledge of racial power codes appears to develop as early as pre-school."[40] The American pioneer of psychometrics and psychophysics and a revered experimental psychologist, Louis Leone Thurstone (1887–1955), stunned the world in 1928 when he declared what was previously unthinkable – that attitudes are measurable. Like-minded experimental psychologists soon followed and "began to make significant contributions to attitude assessment."[41] These experimental psychologists "took the ephemeral mental quality of favoring and disfavoring and rendered it the subject of scientific study," making attitude a keystone in American social psychology.[42] Their fundamental presupposition was "that attitudes (or their mental manifestations) were accessible to introspection."[43] Several notable research projects in social psychology have since confirmed that attitudes exist in implicit and explicit forms.[44] "Attitudes are mental states of readiness, propelling us toward those things we like and away from those things we dislike. As such, attitudes are fundamental to the human enterprise, both in the immediate present and the evolutionary past. In their absence, the individual is confused and baffled."[45] Social psychologists admit that although it is not easy to categorize, generically, implicit attitudes belong to intuition (they are automatic). In philosophical-psychological terms, the negative expression of implicit attitude is what Lonergan calls dramatic bias, also known as the bias of unconscious motivation, which was discussed at length in chapter 3. Explicit attitudes, according to social psychologists, belong to reason (they are controlled). In philosophical terms, adherence to what Lonergan calls transcendental precepts – be attentive, be intelligent, be reasonable, and be responsible – leads to a positive attitude. But the violation of these precepts through a biased and egoistic disregard for others because of unhinged loyalty to one's group, leading to hostility to other groups, as well as concentration on short-term benefits that overlook long-term costs, lead to a negative explicit attitude.[46] The effects can be worse than just attitude. They can bring about societal decline (see discussion of individual, group, and general bias in chapter 3).

Social psychology tells us that unlike explicit attitudes that are slow, intentional, and consciously activated, "implicit attitudes are more likely to exist outside conscious awareness; easier to activate; and harder to control."[47] Perhaps that is why Lonergan warns against violating the transcendental precepts – because "such aberrations are easier to maintain and difficult to correct."[48] Social psychology teaches that in general, the relationship between implicit and explicit attitudes might vary, depending on the context in which the attitudes are measured, say politics or race. But these psychologists are unanimous that the distinction between implicit and explicit attitudes has to do with the measure or trigger of the prejudice. This is why, in Lonergan's theological analysis of the biases, he makes it clear that one may have the bias of unconscious motivation and still have a well-developed egoism that stems from individual, group, and general bias.[49] Explicit prejudice is usually easy to control and slow to activate because the subject who is prejudiced is conscious of his or her prejudices and may choose to dissemble. It is of this human ability to dissemble so well that the Lord remarked, "You hypocrites! You are like whitewashed tombs, which look beautiful on the outside but on the inside are full of the bones of the dead and everything unclean" (Matthew 23: 27–8). But implicit prejudice, on the contrary, is easier to activate because the subject unconsciously expresses his or her prejudices, even when he or she does not intend to do so. "Every good tree bringeth forth good fruit; but a corrupt tree bringeth forth evil fruit. A good tree cannot bring forth evil fruit, neither can a corrupt tree bring forth good fruit" (Matthew 7:17–18). Although easier to activate, implicit racial prejudices are usually quite subtle. The reason, according to social psychologists, is because "implicit attitudes represent a reflexive gut reaction, [while] explicit attitudes reflect a subsequent stage of processing that is 'corrective' in nature."[50] Lonergan's own cryptic statement regarding egoists in general, "egoists do not turn into altruists overnight,"[51] underscores this point. Lonergan likewise explains dramatic bias as due to psychological conditioning often beyond a person's control. "It is responsible for an orientation of the dramatic pattern of our everyday lives against the emergence into consciousness of images that would be material for insights we do not want [and it] displays many of the features that Freud highlighted in his notion of the repressive censor."[52]

In 1998, Anthony Greenwald et al. developed a technique they called the Implicit Association Test (IAT).[53] When the procedure was used to measure racial attitudes, participants were asked to categorize a variety of clearly valanced words, such as poison/gift as pleasant or unpleasant and black/white as pleasant or unpleasant. The test reveals that "participants were overwhelmingly faster at responding when black was paired with unpleasant than when black was paired with pleasant. On average, then, the participants found it much easier to associate the target concept black with the attribute unpleasant than with the attribute pleasant."[54] To this day, researchers use the IAT to measure implicit bias. As recently as 2007, Brian Nosek, a professor at the University of Virginia, working together with Anthony Greenwald, his colleague at the University of Washington, created the IAT for Americans, to expose subconscious racial prejudice that might be lurking beneath what on the surface looks anti-racist. The two research projects summed up their findings on implicit bias this way: "There's stuff in my mind that exists there without my permission, without necessarily my desiring it and without my necessarily being able to control it. And so what that introduces is that I may be behaving in ways that are inconsistent with my values without even really recognizing it."[55] Implicit bias and its effects play out in three key component and interrelated processes: Priming (a psychological phenomenon in which word, image, sound, and other stimuli are used to elicit an associated response); Associations (a phenomenon that associates a group of people with certain tendencies and reinforces them through priming; it occurs without conscious guidance or intention); and Assumptions (prejudices we hold about other people). These three processes are usually used to justify systemic racism.[56] I will illustrate how the processes play out with some real-life examples in the next section. The illustrations will show why Lonergan treats dramatic bias in a way that points to the reorientation in psychoanalysis.[57] Thus, bias or prejudice will be shown to be a multidimensional construct. It can be expressed through negative beliefs or acts toward members of the discriminated group or revealed through biased thoughts or feelings that are implicitly expressed.[58]

It Is Not Microaggression but Dramatic Bias

It is hard to deny that the United States has come a long way since the days of Jim Crow laws. It is no longer legal to discriminate against people on the basis of race, sex, gender or religion. It is also considered socially unacceptable to be overtly biased and discriminatory, especially when it comes to inflicting physical hurt or pain on racial and ethnic minorities.[59] In general, society has become more "politically correct," so to speak. Most people are aware of what is socially acceptable to say or do, especially when it comes to issues related to race, sex, gender, and religion. But while many continue to claim that they do not hold biases against Black people or people of colour, social psychology continues to unearth a wealth of evidence that biases and prejudices still manifest in subtle and unconscious ways. These studies "reveal that many white people still subconsciously hold negative feelings toward people of color or maintain implicit biases about these groups."[60] The old-fashioned or more blatant forms of discrimination may no longer exist because society has evolved, but new, subtle forms of discrimination continue to emerge.[61] "Hostile groups," Lonergan writes, "do not easily forget their grievances, drop their resentments, overcome their fears and suspicions."[62] As we noted in the previous chapter, researchers have used numerous terms, such as modern racism, aversive racism, and covert racism, to describe these new phenomena. More recently, the most commonly used term to conceptualize these new, subtle forms of racism is microaggression. The term "microaggression," which is often used in a racial context, goes back to the Harvard psychiatrist, Chester M. Pierce, who coined the term in the 1970s. The concept, however, is deep-rooted in the work of Jack Dovidio, Ph.D. (Yale University) and his colleague Samuel Gaertner, Ph.D. (University of Delaware) in their formulation of aversive racism – "many well-intentioned whites consciously believe in and profess equality, but unconsciously act in a racist manner, particularly in ambiguous situations."[63] The concept has been further developed by Derald Wing Sue, a professor of counselling psychology at Columbia University. Sue defines microaggressions as the everyday slights, indignities, put-downs and insults that members of marginalized groups experience in their daily interactions with people who quite often may not be aware that they have engaged in an offensive or demeaning manner.[64] "People of color do not just occasionally experience racial microaggressions. Rather, it is a constant, continuing, and cumulative experience,"[65] he writes. In other words, what researchers call microaggressions are "verbal, behavioral, and environmental manifestations of bias; although they are often unintentional or unconscious, they communicate a spectrum of negative messages, primarily to people of historically marginalized groups."[66] Sue uses a real-life example to illustrate occurrences of this new form of racism that he thinks can be best described as microaggression:

> Not too long ago, I (Asian American) boarded a small plane with an African American colleague in the early hours of the morning. As there were few passengers, the flight attendant told us to sit anywhere, so we chose seats near the front of the plane and across the aisle from one another. At the last minute, three white men entered the plane and took seats in front of us. Just before takeoff, the flight attendant, who is white, asked if we would mind moving to the back of the aircraft to better balance the plane's weight.
>
> We grudgingly complied but felt singled out as passengers of color in being told to "move to the back of the bus." When we expressed these feelings to the attendant, she indignantly denied the charge, became defensive, stated that her intent was to ensure the flight's safety, and wanted to give us some privacy. Since we had entered the plane first, I asked why she did not ask the white men to move instead of us. She became indignant, stated that we had misunderstood her intentions, claimed she did not

see "color," suggested that we were being "oversensitive," and refused to talk about the matter any further. Were we being overly sensitive, or was the flight attendant being racist? That is a question that people of color are constantly faced with in their day-to-day interactions with well-intentioned white folks who experience themselves as good, moral and decent human beings.[67]

The consequences of microaggression on the physical and mental health of victims are grave.[68] Perpetrators of microaggressions also suffer cognitive, affective, behavioural, and moral costs of oppression. Sue's research, and those of other leading proponents in the field, document "how African Americans, Asian Americans, American Indians and Latina(o) Americans who receive these everyday psychological slings and arrows experience an erosion of their mental health, job performance, classroom learning, the quality of social experience, and ultimately their standard of living."[69] Sue offers a threefold classification of incidents of microaggression:

1). Microassaults: refers to conscious and intentional discriminatory actions, such as using racial epithets and displaying symbols historically associated with hate, e.g., swastika.
2). Microinsults: refers to verbal and non-verbal communications that are used to convey, even if subtly, rudeness and insensitivity to a person's racial, ethnic, gender, sexual, or religious identity.
3). Microinvalidations: refers to messages that subtly exclude or nullify the thoughts, feelings or experiences of a marginalized group, that subtly exclude or negate one's experiential reality, e.g., a white person asking an immigrant of colour where they are born to convey the message that they are foreign and do not belong or suggesting there is no such thing as ethnic or racial differences.

Sue points out two important cofactors which he says we must not take for granted. The first is that the denials by the perpetrators are usually not conscious attempts to deceive; that they honestly believe they have done no wrong. "For White Americans to acknowledge that they harbor antiminority feelings and have acted in ways that oppress others shatters their self-concept as good and moral human beings."[70] Second, "microaggressions hold their power because they are invisible, and therefore they don't allow whites to see that their actions and attitudes may be discriminatory."[71] In these lie the dilemma. "The person of color is left to question what actually happened. The result is confusion, anger, and an overall draining of energy."[72]

Earlier (in chapter 3) when we applied Lonergan's critical realism to critical race theory, we exposed some of the counterpositions of common sense. We saw, as Lonergan says, that common sense "commonly feels itself omnicompetent in practical affairs, commonly is blind to long-term consequences of policies and courses of action, commonly is unaware of the admixture of common nonsense in its more cherished convictions and slogans."[73] We are now back to where we must expose again a common nonsense of common sense's cherished slogans. The assertion by the perpetrators of microaggressions that they have done no wrong belongs to the waste basket of common nonsense. Not only do members of the privileged group deny their microaggressions, they at times even hit back with negative affective and behavioural responses when the disadvantaged group raises the issue of their prejudice.[74] Since in theology an acknowledgement of guilt is the *sine qua non* condition for reconciliation, I suggest that we need a better term for envisioning what behavioural psychologists have now labelled microaggressions, a concept that has been appropriated by many schools in the United States and beyond as part of their diversity education training. This does not in any way, shape or form undercut the best intentions of professionals and educators who are using it to address racism on their campuses. From a philosophical and theological point of view, dramatic bias is a better category for speaking of what Sue and other behavioural psychologists call microaggressions. Professionals and educators, in Christian schools especially, will be better served by the concept of dramatic bias for the following seven reasons:

1) Microaggressions are the products of structural or systemic injustice. "Many microaggressions originate from the myth of meritocracy and the failure to consider powerful external forces that affect outcomes."[75] What makes the aggressions "micro," as Sue and others acknowledge, is not their power to harm, but the fact that the privileged members of the community who are the perpetrators regard them as trivial. Irrespective of whether they are intended, microaggressions do inflict a serious harm on the victim, many of which are long-lasting and cannot be undone. Christian theology speaks of sins of omission (not doing what is right, even if inadvertently) and commission (wilfully doing what is wrong) as carrying equal weight: "Therefore, to one who knows the right thing to do and does not do it, to him it is sin" (James 4:17).
2) Some forms of microaggressions have been found to be "more toxic to the target than overt forms of discrimination."[76] This further strengthens the argument that the "micro" in this so-called

microaggression does not mean some of these acts do not have a life of their own and cannot have big life-changing impacts, even if people who commit the "microaggressions" might not be aware of them. The acts can and usually do.[77] All the leading researchers in the field agree that microaggressions have long-lasting effects on the psychological health of their victims, especially historically oppressed groups and communities. They are also unanimous that microaggressions "lead to psychological trauma, notably for people who encounter discriminatory incidents regularly and intensely throughout their lives."[78] Christian theology considers any harm done to one's neighbour, particularly harm as grave as damaging the well-being, self-esteem, group identity, and lifestyle of another for whom Christ died, as a scandal: "If anyone causes one of these little ones – those who believe in me – to stumble, it would be better for them if a large millstone were hung around their neck and they were thrown into the sea" (Mark 9:42).

3) Racism, in its structural nature, is not fluid in the United States, i.e., it does not go back and forth, say one day benefiting whites and another day or another era benefiting Blacks. Rather, racism is a one-directional movement that serves only the interest of white people over people of colour.[79] "The direction of power between whites and people of color is historic, traditional, normalized, and deeply embedded in the fabric of U.S. society."[80] Thus, it is inappropriate to reduce what reifies power imbalance between the privileged group and disadvantaged group and what is done preconsciously to "micro." From a philosophical point of view, this lack of fluidity that insulates and protects the privileged from race-based stress means that it is inadequate to speak of stereotyping as microaggression. It can negate the reality of racism Black people face.[81]
4) There are certain events that occur on a daily basis: a child raises her hand to answer questions in class, the teacher sees her, but refuses to acknowledge her. A woman politely greets her boss at the beginning of her shift, but the boss refuses to acknowledge her and walks away in a hurry. Ordinarily, there are varied ways these actions can be explained away, especially when they have nothing to do with race – indifference, inattention, a cavalier attitude or rudeness.[82] But when race has something to do with it [say a white teacher continuously refuses to acknowledge a Black student who raises his hand to answer questions in class or a white boss walks away and refuses to return the greetings of his Black subordinate], people of common sense can no longer classify these events as "micro."[83] Kimber Shelton and Edward A. Delgado-Romero, who

consider microinvalidations to be the most dangerous kind of microaggressions, point out that microinvalidations are so-called because the perpetrators deny the reality of the experience of the marginalized person or group and even impose an oppressive experience on the person or group on the assumption that this is the true reality.[84] Scripture speaks of this as a hardening of heart (Ps. 95: 8–9; Mt. 19:8; Heb 3: 7–11). In truth, we are all susceptible to hardness of heart. The scriptural antidote for hardness of heart is conversion.[85] It has a sense of anticipatory suffering with those who suffer.[86]

5) Based on the weight of the preceding four reasons, and given that all people are susceptible to prejudice and bias, which manifest preconsciously, "the everyday, subtle, intentional – and often times unintentional – interactions or behaviors that communicate some sort of bias toward historically marginalized groups"[87] should more properly be called dramatic bias. This is because dramatic bias does not work in isolation. It works together with general bias of common sense, individual bias, and group bias, for which one is held responsible. For this reason, unlike the concept microaggression, dramatic bias cannot be swept away by the politics of personal exoneration. From a theological point of view, these thinly veiled everyday experiences of racism (including homophobia and sexism), because they are so common that people take them for granted and dismiss them as trivial (as in the Catholic understanding of venial or slight sin that does not necessitate complete separation from God), can hamper discussions on structural racism, if they are not named dramatic bias (as in serious and harmful sin that can fracture one's relationship with God and community). What is conceived under the term microaggression, therefore, can become part of racially coded language that reproduces racist images and perspectives, while simultaneously reproducing "the comfortable illusion that race and its problems are what 'they' have, not us."[88] This is surely not what Sue and other leading researchers intended in devising the term.
6) Theologically, calling some impactful and long-term consequential acts "micro" may seem to make light of their consequences and diminish culpability. It is the error of common sense to trivialize the impact of every unintended behaviour. Some people are readier to accept a classification of their racial acts as "microaggressions" than they are to call them racist. This is because, in their mistaken notion, "microaggressions" suggest something trivial and less impactful. They may even rationalize them as isolated acts. According to a

recent PRRI American values survey (2018),[89] "White Christians – including evangelical Protestants, mainline Protestants and Catholics – are nearly twice as likely as religiously unaffiliated whites to say the killings of Black men by police are isolated incidents rather than part of a pattern of how police treat African Americans."[90] In the same survey, "White Christians are also about 20 percentage points more likely to disagree with this statement: 'Generations of slavery and discrimination have created conditions that make it difficult for Blacks to work their way out of the lower class.'" To make matters worse, these trends have persisted even in the wake of the recent protests for racial justice.[91] This is the kind of thought pattern microaggressions-thinking generates. Theologically, what is revealed under the garb of microaggressions, in the true sense of the word, are the many ways in which God is absent both in the superstructure and on the day-to-day level of our culture.[92]

7) The psychological solution to evil is not the same as the theological solution to evil. Psychological solutions cannot replace a theological solution. The former can only serve the latter. Sue and all the leading researchers on microaggressions discuss microaggressions with an eye on the consequences of these incidents and ways members of targeted groups can address them. They offer an action-oriented perspective against bias, bigotry, and discrimination they call microinterventions. Their solutions for disrupting, dismantling, and disarming the constant onslaught of micro- and macroaggressions faced by marginalized groups are based on strategies that "make the invisible visible," "disarm" the aggressor, "educate" the aggressor, and "seek external reinforcement or support."[93] These four strategies are their conceptual framework for combating microaggressions in the workplace, in group situations, and in individual interactions. The strategies, although some are group-based actions, are mainly individual actions that individuals can take on their own to voice disapproval, educate others and pressure authorities to make changes.[94] In nearly all cases, the strategies, as valuable as they are, are psychological solutions to the problem of evil. They are not theological. They are anchored in "social justice and social advocacy,"[95] not in a contrite spirit (Isaiah 57:15; 66:2). As we will see in the next chapter, a theological solution to the problem of evil in all its forms – selfishness, prejudice, favouritism, structural injustice, etc., – begins with contrition and true repentance. This biblical term repentance, in Greek *metanoia*, is far deeper than the "re-engineering" of social psychology. It is a turning away from idolatry, from sin, to a turning to a deep faith, hope, and trust in God that leads to conversion.

Is Microaggression a Cloak for Non-existent Ontology of Meaning?

The world we live in is dynamic and so are the forces that divide us as humans. Therefore, we need a calculus that can help us better understand the forces of division that put people down and denigrate them. A necessary first step before a prescription for the malady can be made is access to a good tool for understanding these forces. On the basis of theological arguments offered in the preceding section, microaggression falls short of the calculus needed for conceptualizing the bias that governs intersubjective spontaneities, i.e., implicit acts of racism. Some acts are just plain prejudicial acts that are implicitly revealed. They are habitual orientations against insight in that domain of the person's life. It is repressive censorship that blocks images through which insights could emerge.[96] To tell a Black person, by merely looking at his last name, that he speaks good English, assuming that he was born in a country that does not speak English, when the same person was born in the United Kingdom and spoke English all his life, is an example of implicit bias. The white person who feels threatened in the hallway upon sighting two Black people chatting, presuming they are planning evil, might be an instance of microaggression, but could also be more. Or to offer examples of common experiences Black people routinely face: being followed and monitored in stores or seeing a white person grab her purse to secure it tightly upon sighting a Black male. There is no denying that these might be examples of microaggression,[97] but they are far more than that. They are racism-inspired acts that are done by reflex that those who do them may not even be aware of. The fact that they are unaware of their immediate acts does not make those acts any less prejudicial – they are implicit racism. The repressive censorship that blocks or resists insight, which in turn informs these acts, is a function of psychic underdevelopment.[98] As an umbrella term for a new form of racism, "microaggression" at times mischaracterizes some acts of racism that are consciously or unconsciously perpetrated. Such mischaracterization stems from what Lonergan considers a mistaken cognitional theory or faculty or non-existent ontology of meaning for grasping one's conscious intentional operations.[99] This is why the term Lonergan introduces, *dramatic bias*, is more fitting, for the reasons outlined already. "It is one thing to do something occasionally, by fits and starts. It is another to do it regularly, easily spontaneously."[100] Dramatic bias captures better the erroneous beliefs, the carelessness, and the credulity that inform implicit acts of racism, regardless of intention. To simply call these acts microaggression unfortunately supports "the assumptions about racial matters most of us absorb from the cultural heritage in which we come of age in the United States. It is these assumptions that in turn continue to inform our public civic institutions – government, schools, churches – and our private, personal, and corporate lives."[101] Consider the following impactful real-life cases based on experiences of people of colour:

- Scenario 1: A minority, left alone and ignored for a long time at a car dealership eventually gets the attention of a salesperson. "They negotiate, and she buys a car. Later she learns that she paid almost a thousand dollars more than what the average white male pays for that same car."[102]
- Scenario 2: A minority employed for a teaching position at a "good" university performs her duties creditably well. Several years into her appointment, she is tenured and promoted to the rank of Associate Professor, though not without the agonies that go with being Black and female in the academy. But she soon learns to her dismay that a white colleague in the same department who was hired at the rank of Assistant Professor in the same department four years after her, is making a net salary that is 6 per cent higher, not including other perks the white colleague received that were not offered to her.
- Scenario 3: A highly trained Black woman serving as an organizational development consultant and management coach at a higher institution of learning is overlooked for promotion and awards for years, despite the recognition her group receives as a result of her work. "Meanwhile, the Black woman's white female boss gave a promotion, a raise, and recognition for outstanding work to a white woman with less education who has played a role with no visibility or interaction with client groups."[103]
- Scenario 4: A Starbucks' manager calls police on two African American males waiting to meet a friend of theirs because she thought they were dangerous. The association she made between their race and danger they pose resulted in their arrest.
- Scenario 5: A white woman on a tour of the campus at Colorado State University calls security on two Native American school-aged men who drove from New Mexico to Colorado for the same campus tour of Colorado State University because she thought "they were quiet and creepy and really stand out." By the time security came and questioned the young men and confirmed they were registered for the campus tour, the tour had finished.[104]

Overt racism is inextricably intertwined in American history from the time America was a loose collection of colonies to the present day.[105] The scenarios described above are either overt racism or implicit bias.

Implicit bias, sometimes called societal racism, is based on actual social relations, i.e., how one group in society treats another.[106] Implicit or societal racism is not a modern American phenomenon. Implicit or societal racism is as ancient as human history itself. However, it was only at the dawn of the modern era that societal racism was supported by an elaborate ideological justification. In the United States, racial bias has evolved from a socially accepted version of systemic racism to subtler forms of bias because of the civil rights legislations of the 1950s–70s that supposedly dismantled the elaborate system of legally justified racial segregation.[107] In this evolution, over time, overt and legally sanctioned racism became covert and socially acceptable. Racism "became less obvious and shifted from blatant exclusion and racial hostility to systems and interpersonal mechanisms of exclusion, denial, and blocked opportunity."[108] The acts of aggression in all five scenarios described above are anything but micro. When acts are lumped under the umbrella of microaggression, the subliminal message is that they are overt or covert individual behaviours. The implication then is that they are harmless and excusable. Explaining them away in this fashion can become "a cloak of immunity from scrutiny."[109] Immunity comes with a certain power; it means "not having to be mindful of that from which one is exempt."[110] On 26 February 2012, Trayvon Martin, a young African American man who was walking home from a convenience store, which he had visited to pick up some candies, was fatally shot by a neighbourhood watch volunteer patrolling the townhouse community in Sanford, Florida. Trayvon Martin was killed, not because of microaggression, but because he was reduced to a stereotype.[111] The killing of Trayvon and the subsequent events that unfolded in the trial of his accused murderer, show that people of colour do not "suffer from invisibility but from how they are seen, how they are silenced, and how they are unheard: Trayvon seen (and reduced) as black male, thus necessarily a thug, a threat, and then Trayvon, the hoodie, the icon of the disposable African American male."[112] In a piece in The New York Times titled, "This is the Casual Racism that I Face at My Elite High School" 24 September 2020), an African American student, Rainer Harris, recounts his bouts with casual racism and other kinds of racism Black students like him experience on a daily basis. He tells how his classmates make "numerous comments over the years about how affirmative action puts them at a disadvantage from getting into top schools."[113] The young man wondered whether such insinuations were meant to diminish his own academic achievement and self-worth. My point here is simple – that the questions surrounding racial stereotypes should not be about how true the stereotypes are, but more about "how the truth claims they offer are a part of a larger worldview that authorizes and normalizes forms of domination and control."[114]

To return to the scenarios in our case study, in what way does any of the scenarios deviate from the architecture of white supremacy? In what way does any of the scenarios deviate from the racial dynamics in America that are built on power, privilege, and access, or the lack thereof for racial minorities?[115] Take scenario 1, for example: it is too simplistic to explain it away as part of the system of "market negotiation." It is equally too simplistic to dismiss scenario 2 as integral to the system of "contract negotiation" at the time of employment. These excuses are mere simplistic platitudes.[116] The fact is that the so-called "contract negotiation" is part of a system of employment strategies that lowball and underpay people of colour. There are far too many examples to cite. All five scenarios are but a few examples of the implicit bias that plays out with regularity in the day-to-day life of people of colour. It plays out in racial inequalities of income and wealth, education, health, and safety and well-being in everyday life in American society. "Prejudice both justifies such inequalities and provides an excuse for inaction."[117] Scenario 3 supports the claim people of colour (Black people and Latinos especially) have been making over the years "that white women are their greatest barrier to success."[118] It is the ideological racism of white fragility – a self-perpetuating sense of entitlement deriving from the belief that the white subject's "financial and professional successes are the result of their own efforts while ignoring the fact of white privilege."[119] In her well-researched work, *Understanding White Privilege*, Frances Kendall accurately documents what "many women of color, particularly African Americans and Latinas," have told her over years – "that white women are their greatest barriers to success."[120] Kendall, a white woman herself, notes with dismay that "most white women are shocked when I tell them that many women of color see us as the enemy."[121] Kendall uses our schools and colleges as a good example. In most of these schools and colleges, she argues, "white women have a high percentage of middle management jobs – assistant professors, assistant vice presidents, vice chancellors, assistant deans, and so on. While white men hold the ultimate power, women of color have to move through the white women to get to the senior positions, and, most often, white women hire other white women or white men to fill mid-level positions, rather than promoting the women of color."[122] Sadly, "in many instances," Kendall continues, "women of color are the ones who trained the white woman or man who eventually gets the job."[123] Kendall's example is a testament to the claim of Black women that they are the group on which the triple oppression of race (racial violence), class (economic exploitation), and gender (sexual violence) converge. That said, Kendall's remark about how women of colour see white women as the "enemy" needs a little explanation and nuance. Following the election of Donald Trump as president of the United States in 2016, at one Catholic University (as in many places where there were pockets of protests against the election of Trump either on ideological grounds or because of some of his rhetoric, which some perceived as divisive), a group of white liberals, mostly women, organized a protest, denouncing Mr. Trump as a "racist" and "bigot." Very shortly after the protest ended, a handful of minority faculty at the same university who were due for promotion and well-qualified applied for their promotion. The promotion committee at the school was comprised mainly of white women, many of whom were in the protest march that denounced Mr. Trump. Nearly all of the minority faculty were denied their hard-earned promotions by these same anti-Trump protesters, despite the fact that the minority applicants have better dossiers than some of the white women occupying the same positions. To make matters worse, the people of colour who were denied promotion were denied on frivolous grounds – a hallmark of implicit racism. Considering that the perpetrators were some of the same white subjects who think of themselves as "liberal" and are quick to label Mr. Trump as a racist and a bigot, it raises questions not so much about implicit racism, but also to what extent the benign is really harmless. Some white subjects are adept at using their "benign" race-laced responses to maintain racial inequality in the academy.[124] It is these kinds of situations, which people of colour face with regularity, that Kendall draws attention to as contributing factors to the reason people of colour see white women as the "enemy." Ecclesial repentance, which the Church needs (see chapter 6), must include all aspects of the Church's life, including its colleges and universities. Thus, what scenario 3 in our illustrations above illustrates vividly can be summarized thus: "Although some Whites fight white supremacy and do not endorse 'white common sense' [i.e., that Whites are superior to others], most subscribe to substantial portions of it in a casual, uncritical fashion that helps sustain the prevailing racial order."[125] It also illustrates the interconnection of unconscious bias and systemic and structural racism. Systemic and structural racism are what allow biases (unfair policies, lack of opportunities, and inequitable treatment of ethnic minorities)[126] to persist in the workplace. "Socio-economic status and wealth tend to be disproportionate for people of color and women."[127] A study conducted in 2010 found that white families are 6 times as wealthy as non-white families and white families earn, on average, about $2 for every $1 that people of colour earn. A 2014 study, corroborated by the U.S. Department of Labor, Bureau of Labor Statistics in 2015, found that white women's median weekly full-time earnings were 82.5% of white men's weekly full-time earnings and "Black and Latina women's weekly earnings were disproportionately lower [at] 68.6% and 61.2%, respectively."[128]

Implicit Bias and the Cycles of Decline – Structural Injustice

Lonergan painstakingly discusses the evolution of dramatic bias: from its refusal to understand, which results in a scotosis in the mind (a weakening of the development of common sense), to its aligning with group bias to produce dire consequences, yielding a cycle of decline. A blind spot is the fruit of a complex that prevents people from attending to certain data in their perceptual field. Lonergan's characterization of how the conflict generated by the egoism of group bias "admits a variety of forms"[129] provides new insight into understanding how racial codes appear and develop and how they can prolong the cycle of decline. "Whites often confuse comfort with safety," writes DiAngelo. When they say "we don't feel safe," what they really mean is "we don't feel comfortable."[130] When they say they live in a good neighbourhood or attend a good school, what defines their schools as "good schools" and neighbourhoods as "good neighbourhoods" is a coded language for "the absence of people of color."[131] It is what people with privilege do so well. They create hard circles around themselves to protect themselves from people who are not like them.[132] This insistence on "racial comfort ensures that racism will not be faced,"[133] thereby exacerbating ideologies that corrupt minds and distort progress.[134]

In American society today, group egoism expresses itself in four principal forms that are systemic (ongoing racial inequalities that society continues to maintain), institutional (discriminatory practices and policies that organizations and societal institutions practice), interpersonal (acts of bigotry individuals espouse), and internalized (race-based beliefs that fuel bigotry, systemic, and institutional racism).[135] Decline arises principally because group egoism, in both its implicit and explicit forms, directs development to its own aggrandizement and "provides a market for opinion, doctrines, theories, that will justify its ways and, at the same time, reveal the misfortunes of other groups to be due to their depravity."[136] Because dramatic bias is fundamentally nonconscious and also "ingenious" and "resourceful" enough to adapt itself to new situations,[137] it often manifests in a subtle or implicit manner. When Lonergan speaks of decline resulting from this social surd, he also takes the time to make a distinction between two variants of decline:

a shorter cycle and a longer cycle. This helpful distinction is relevant here because racism produces both shorter and longer cycles of decline: shorter cycles for the deprivileged and longer cycles of decline for society at large. The heart of racism has always been economic, though its roots and results are also deeply cultural, psychological, sexual, even religious, and, of course, political.[138] The most visible and painful sign of racism's continuation is the economic inequality between Blacks and whites. All the major social indices and numerous statistics show the situation to be only slowly improving.[139] For these Blacks, this is their endless shorter cycle of decline.

What Lonergan means by longer cycle of decline should be understood here in terms of structures that violate right-ordered relationships and distort the dialectic of community. Systemic racism leads to inequalities in wealth, education, housing, and to inequalities in leadership representation, to name a few. For people of colour on the receiving end, these are their shorter cycles of decline. This systemic racism creates an unstable equilibrium and disharmony in society, in spite of the state's many attempts to create equilibrium through laws and legislations.[140] This is the longer cycle of decline. Historically, this longer cycle of decline has eaten deep into the fibre of society.

> The U.S. Constitution was written to explicitly and arithmetically devalue Blacks (and other racial groups who were slaves), calculating their worth as 3/5ths of a person (Art. I, sec. 2) and mandating that slaves who escaped must be returned to their owners (Art. IV, sec. 2). The 13th Amendment (ratified in 1865) has a caveat clause that actually permits slavery "as punishment for crime." And the rights guaranteed by the U.S. Constitutional Amendments 14th and 15th (ratified in 1868 and 1870, respectively) – including the right of emancipated slaves to not be discriminated against by race; and equal rights, and "the power to vote" – have been under nearly constant attack and dilution from the time of Reconstruction until the present.[141]

It is this kind of unremitting distortion that Lonergan had in mind when he spoke about how bias can accelerate the cumulative deterioration of the social situation. In *Evangelii Gaudium*, Pope Francis pointed out that since every action has its consequences, an evil embedded in the structures of a society has a constant potential for disintegration and death.[142] When inequities are not reversed, according to the pontiff, it becomes "impossible to eliminate violence" because "inequality provokes a violent reaction from those excluded from the system."[143] The lasting impact of the violence may be irreparable: "Culture retreats into an ivory tower. Religion becomes an inward affair of the heart. Philosophy glitters like a gem with endless facets and no practical purpose."[144] When dramatic bias aligns with group egoism, the group "feels itself the child of destiny."[145] This is so because dramatic bias feeds structural racism and the two together "create barriers that impede access to opportunity across many critical life domains such as housing, education, health, and criminal justice."[146]

What is called microaggression is not only incapable of capturing this dimension of the cycle of decline, it also cannot address the problem of impact versus intent in racial bias, another reason why it is theologically deficient. Implicit bias, understood as akin to dramatic bias, captures the attitudes or stereotypes that affect a person's understanding, his or her actions, and decisions in an unconscious manner. Like the very term "dramatic" suggests, dramatic or implicit bias is activated involuntarily and without an individual's self-conscious awareness or intentional control. It is also dramatic because it evokes strong affectivity. Residing deep in the subconscious, the bias is different from known biases that a person may choose to conceal for the purposes of social and/or political correctness.[147] Implicit or dramatic bias is not accessible through introspection. "The implicit associations we harbor in our subconscious cause us to have feelings and attitudes about other people based on characteristics such as race, ethnicity, age, and appearance. These associations develop over the course of a lifetime beginning at a very early age through exposure to direct and indirect messages."[148] Implicit bias predicts human behaviour and outcomes, most of which are negative, paving the way for cycles of decline. "Common sense commonly feels itself omnicompetent in practical affairs, commonly is blind to long-term consequences of policies and course of action, commonly is unaware of the admixture of common nonsense in its more cherished convictions and slogans."[149] The sins of group bias, though, stem from a secret and unconscious act, so that with time, what was a neglected possibility "becomes a grotesquely distorted reality."[150]

Theologically, microaggression is also incapable of addressing the racism in Christian theology which is subtle and overt. Acknowledging the failure to recognize and deal with the problem of racism in society and the church is only the first step toward a recognition of white privilege and implicit bias.[151] There would be no need for Black Theology, if mainstream theology had not implicitly excluded the experiences of Black people from theological narratives. This, at least, was the reason why some of the early pioneers, such as James Cone and Deotis Roberts, went to great lengths to construct a Black Theology – one that calls racism out for what it is. Cone particularly notes that Christian theology has failed miserably in relating its work to the oppressed in society by refusing to confront the structures and evils of racism. "When it has tried to speak for the poor, it has been so cool and calm in its analysis of human evil that it implicitly disclosed whose side it was on."[152] Cone, for whom "American theology is racist,"[153] indicts American Christian theology for its silence during the period of lynching. If Cone indicts the Christian Church in general for implicit racism, Shawn Copeland brings that indictment specifically to the Catholic Church. Copeland draws attention to the "metaphysical violence" done to Black people and people of colour all over the world by the Catholic Church.[154] She decries the racialization and commodification of flesh attached to the Black body. This commodification, according to her well-honed critique, makes the very meaning of being human anti-Black. The anti-Blackness in turn spawns "'anti-black logics,' that took root in cognition, language, meanings, and values, thereby reshaping nearly all practices of human encounter and engagement."[155] This normative denotation of who is human, according to Copeland, thus refers exclusively to white human beings, more concretely white males.[156] The net effect of this, that is, in American Catholicism, is that there is a subtle "contempt for black human creatures who share in the glory, beauty, and image of the Divine."[157] This is the subtlety of implicit bias in American Catholicism. Lonergan could not have said it any better: "Blind traditionalism is not the essence of religion."[158]

Conclusion

There is a body of statistical evidence, supported by research in social psychology, that implicit bias exists in various sectors of American society. But how does one talk about racial justice in a world that, on the one hand, is obsessed with race constructs, and on the other hand, fakes color blindness – suggesting that race does not matter? Race constructs, after all, are never "theory neutral 'descriptors' but theory-laden constructs inseparable from systems of injustice."[159] White superiority, writes Robin DiAngelo, is ubiquitous and at the same time "unnamed and explicitly denied by most whites."[160] Racism creates for Black people economic disadvantage – the shorter cycle of decline that Lonergan talks about. But it also creates for white people "reduced psychosocial stamina that racial insulation inculcates" – white fragility.[161] All who live within a racist system are enmeshed in its relations, i.e., all are responsible for either perpetuating racism or transforming the system.[162] No doubt, there are some white subjects who think that being treated better than people of colour is somehow normal. This kind of attitude ignores or denies the daily benefits (white privilege) and costs of racism – the longer cycle of decline Lonergan talks about. The solution to the race-problem must begin with eliminating all "forms of resistance to the challenge of internalized dominance."[163] DiAngelo has identified "white fragility" as a resistance. She calls white fragility "a state in which even a minimum amount of racial stress becomes intolerable, triggering a range of defensive moves. These moves include the outward display of emotions such as anger, fear, and guilt, and behaviors such as argumentation, silence, and leaving the stress-inducing situation. These behaviors, in turn, function to reinstate white racial equilibrium."[164] If DiAngelo is correct (and I believe she is correct), then "white fragility," though less acknowledged, is another serious threat to racial justice. "Although all individuals play a role in keeping the system active, the responsibility for change is not equally shared. White racism is ultimately a white problem and the burden for interrupting it belongs to white people."[165] Black people are not asking for anything more. They just want to receive a fair shake. "What is sauce for the goose is sauce for the gander,"[166] Lonergan writes.

The import of studies in social attitudes in social psychology for our understanding of bias or prejudice is that they help us to understand how "implicit and explicit measures capture different aspects of underlying predispositions."[167] Implicit bias, like explicit prejudice, plays different roles in American social, political, and religious life. We cannot privilege one over the other as if only the privileged one represents attitudes people actually manifest. A solution to the problem of bias in its implicit and explicit forms requires human agency – by drawing on human experience, human judgment, and human decision. Irrespective of those things that divide us as humans, we are still bound together by "a common humanity more fundamental than any unity of dogma."[168] The solution has to be sought with a profound religious sense, following the advice of St. Ignatius of Loyola: "Act as though results depended exclusively on you, but await the results as though results depended entirely on God."[169] I argued earlier (chapter 2) that one of the problems Black Theology needs to address is the lack of attention to the data of consciousness. Such recovery is important, if Black Theology is to help Christian theology move beyond cognitional self-transcendence to real self-transcendence. Real self-transcendence pursues values and "moves towards the elimination of the biases that spring from unconscious motivation, individual or group egoism, and the rashly assumed omnicompetence of common sense."[170] Black Theology can play a prophetic role in Christian self-understanding. It can use the experience of Black people to remind the church that it is "not a conventicle of saints."[171] Jesus used the parable of the fish net to describe the church – a net cast into the sea that catches all sorts of fish (Matthew 13:47–52). The prophetic role of Black Theology is to remind the church that there is always "a gap between the ideal and the real, between religion as it strives to be and religion as it is in fact."[172] The gap between the ideal and the real, "apart from cases of self-deception or insincerity," does not imply that Christianity is phony or that Christian people say one thing and do another. "The very being of man is not static but dynamic; it never is a state of achieved perfection; it always is at best striving."[173] Hence, the need for ongoing ecclesial repentance because the "centrifugal force which has scattered and atomized mankind must be replaced by an integrating structure and process capable of bestowing meaning and purpose on existence."[174]

Chapter Six

Overcoming Racism and Conversion

We have now reached a high point with the present chapter that seeks to help Black Theology be more attentive to overcoming racism. It is the high point of our effort to rally the ecumenical power of the mind and heart to enable "man through his mysterious greatness to re-create his life."[1] More importantly, it is the high point of how Bernard Lonergan's thought contributes to Black Theology's quest for racial justice. While legislation can mitigate racism and its effect, passing new laws and symbolic acts of racial charity are not the theological solution to racism. As has been made clear in the previous chapters, Black Theology is a search for interiorly differentiated consciousness. Interiorly differentiated consciousness operates on two levels – the realms of common sense and interiority.[2] Unfortunately, Black Theology has not distinguished properly between the data of sense and the data of consciousness. This inability to differentiate appropriately has not only been a stumbling block but it has also mired Black Theology in the first stage of meaning – the level of experience. Interiorly differentiated consciousness must begin with sense experience, but it need not remain there. It must go beyond experience to determine its basic terms and relations, adverting to human conscious operations – the dynamic structure that shows things in their relations to one another.[3]

In this chapter, I offer a Five-Dimensional Conversion Process (5D-C Process) derived from Lonergan as a schematic solution to the problem of racial bias. Centuries of *de jure* segregation have created in the American social imagination a caste system or a system of domination that exploits and marginalizes African Americans. While most of the policies that created the system of domination may no longer be on the books, they have never been really remedied and their effects continue to endure and multiply.[4] The 5D-C Process offered here can be a starting point for the much-needed remedy.

Racism perpetuates itself where conversion is non-existent. Racism is a stressor. Apart from denying its victims their civil and God-given rights, racism affects the mental and physical health of its targets.[5] Stress is a negative emotional experience. It is often accompanied by "predictable biochemical, physiological, cognitive, and behavioral changes that are directed either toward altering the stressful event or accommodating to its effects."[6] Any solution offered for combating racism must be one that is capable of dealing with multi-layered stressors. Apart from the legal rulings of the courts in the United States that have helped to make some appreciable gains in racial justice, the problem with many of the solutions that have been proffered for racism by both the ecclesial and civic community is that they are mostly a quick fix. Many remain at the level of common sense and never surpass it. A common-sense solution, as shall be made clear in this chapter, is different from a self-transcendent solution. The difference between the two lies in "a more effective control of belief."[7] Even the much vaunted legal victories of the courts have often been met with hindrances and barriers of unimaginable proportions, largely because of the absence of self-transcendence. Quick-fix solutions are a temptation to the undifferentiated consciousness – the most common type of consciousness, which is far too common.[8] An undifferentiated consciousness is marked by the absence of intellectual, moral, and religious conversion. The paucity of proposed solutions to the racial problem is itself indicative of the absence of conversion in these domains.[9]

Absence of self-transcendent knowledge aside, one of the main reasons for the failure of so many of the solutions that have been tried by society is that they are based on a false premise and a faulty way of framing the problem. The African American journalist and op-ed columnist for the New York Times, Charles Blow, has faulted the United States for always framing race around unity, rather than equality. In addition to robbing the oppressed of their legitimate grievances, framing race around unity, rather than equality, suggests "a false premise: that white people and nonwhite ones are operating from equal positions of power in this society and are simply not getting along or agreeing on issues."[10] Framing the problem this way, by implication, makes people of colour equally at fault for the racial impasse in America when both history and social science demonstrate, unequivocally, that this is not true.[11] It is a historical gaslighting and a sinister way of denying racism and minimizing its trauma. But more importantly, the false way of framing the problem reveals the unreconciled oppositions on religious, moral, intellectual, and affective issues between the perpetrators and their victims. *Pax Americana*, like the *Pax Romana* which was "founded on the twin pillars of lies and violence,"[12] is experienced differently by people of different races and classes. Who we are in our intersubjective relations, particularly our racial group and social status, significantly contributes to how we react to stressors and process stressful experiences.[13] What the stressor does to the victim, James Baldwin tells us, is destroy their sense of reality. "When people face discrimination in their lives that is (a) intense, (b) extensive and enduring, (c) threatening to one's sense of safety, and (d) causal of symptoms that are aligned with PTSD (e.g., avoidance, dissociation), their experiences might be labeled as traumatic discrimination."[14] The trauma of racism can induce a range of mental problems, "such as post-traumatic stress disorder and depression; physical health problems; negative health behaviors, such as smoking and excessive alcohol consumption; impaired social and occupational functioning; and overall lower quality of life."[15] Despite the far-ranging consequences of trauma and the high rates of exposure, at least in African American communities, Black Theology has rarely addressed how to educate or help African Americans deal with the trauma.

This chapter asserts that the remedy for racism cannot be located at the level of common sense but must be found in an intelligibility that has as its intelligent ground the question of God. One of Lonergan's best illustrations of the attainment of this long process is that of the religious, moral, and intellectual strivings of St. Augustine. Before his conversion, Augustine was a man of extraordinary intelligence, but he was also a materialist.[16] Because he knew he was a materialist, when he changed (conversion), he wanted to talk about the real, what is really so.[17] Lonergan surmises that "the history of Augustine's thought is the history of the discovery of the limitations of the infantile apprehension of reality and the history of the shift to the true."[18] Thus, I use what Lonergan calls conversion as a heuristic for developing a template for the shift to the true, hoping that such a shift will be beneficial in resolving the moral impotence of racism – because it will be based on an adequate conception of truth and reality. The choice to follow Lonergan's approach is significant for two reasons. First, conversion, in the way Lonergan conceives of it, involves a new understanding in oneself and brings about a new self to be understood.[19] Second, conversion is multi-dimensional, such that conversion in any one of the dimensions leads to conversion in the others, just as relapse from one prepares for relapse in the others.[20]

Conversion – A Resistance against Resistance

Black Theology has been right all along in turning to experience to show that an authentic Christian theology must be autobiographical. It is logical that the coming together of stories of oppression of people of colour, coupled with the Christian awareness of history and the solid philosophical foundation used to moor this historical consciousness, will together lead to a transformation of consciousness. Lonergan's technical term for this transformation is conversion. It is a term derived from scripture and indispensable for Christian self-understanding. It is a term Jesus used in the New Testament to demand a radical change of heart from his followers. In other words, it is a call to repentance and a way of embracing a new beginning (Luke 9:57–62). It is to this change that comes with a new beginning that the apostle Paul refers when he says: "When I was a child, I spoke like a child, I understood like a child, I thought like a child; but when I became a man, I put away childish things" (I Corinthians 13:11). The Christian idea of "conversion" is related to the Hebrew *shuv* (also spelled *shubh*), meaning "to turn back" or "to return" or "to bring back" or "to restore." When used in the Hebrew scriptures it is always in reference to turning away from evil and returning to the Lord God.[21] Both individual Jews and the nation of Israel are called to turn away from evil or idols and to return to God (Jer. 2:27; 11:10; Hosea 6:1; 14:1). The Christian Old Testament idea of conversion has a dual aspect: God "turning" people and people "turning" to God (Jer. 31:18).[22] The covenant context between Yahweh and the people of Israel is crucial for understanding the significance of *shuv*.[23]

The Septuagint (LXX) translates the Hebrew *shuv* as *epistrepho* (to turn towards God) and *metanoeo* (to repent). *Epistrepho* also has the dual element of "turning from" something to "turning to" something. Each of these elements has its own vocabulary in the New Testament.[24] The turning from something to turning towards God always includes an element of faith.[25] Although the New Testament used *epistrepho* to indicate "the return to Christ" of a Christian who has lapsed in faith (Luke 22:32), the New Testament's preferred term, at least in LXX, is the noun *metanoia*, rendered in English as "repentance." It is used to connote the idea of a change of heart (Matthew 3:2; Mark 1:15). As in *epistrepho*, there is also an element of faith in the biblical notion of *metanoia*. Whereas in *epistrepho* the emphasis is on turning toward the new, in *metanoia* the emphasis is on turning away from the old. But that is not to say that both senses (turning away from the old and turning toward the new) are not implied in the meaning of the two terms. One just emphasizes one dimension more strongly than the other.[26]

The English theologian, evangelist, and a leader of the revivalist movement within the Church of England also known as the Methodist movement, John Wesley (1703–91), made every effort to be faithful to the scriptural meaning of conversion. He spoke of "new birth" as a thorough change of heart and life and a turning away from sin to holiness. In his soteriological teachings, he taught that the two fundamental doctrines of Christianity are the doctrine of justification and that of "new birth.[27] Although it is not clear whether conversion is what Wesley meant by new birth, conversion is sometimes spoken of as a "new birth" in the Methodist tradition. The Reformed Churches that follow the Heidelberg Catechism equate true repentance with conversion. The Heidelberg Catechism (1563), a teaching and preaching manual and a symbol of confessional unity among the many Protestant groups in the Palatinate, was composed in Heidelberg, Germany, at the request of Elector Frederick III (ruled 1559–76). It was approved by the Synod of Dort in 1619. The Catechism asks, "In how many things does true repentance or conversion consist?" and answers, "In two things: The dying of the old man and the making alive of the new" (Heidelberg Catechism, 88).[28] Some Protestant theologians speak of conversion and regeneration as two sides of the same coin. "Regeneration is God's sovereign activity by the Holy Spirit in the soul of one who is spiritually dead in sin. Regeneration is the implantation of new life in the soul. Regeneration gives the gifts of repentance and faith. On the other side of the coin, conversion is the response of the one who is regenerated."[29]

It is not only the churches that are struggling to come to terms with the biblical meaning of conversion, society at large is equally struggling to come to terms with this biblical notion. In *The Call to Conversion*, Jim Wallis offers an analysis of this struggle, with respect to the United States. He argues that the United States' understanding of conversion is one of its greatest weaknesses. "Neither evangelicals nor liberals have adequately grasped the meaning of conversion for these times. Both movements are floundering without an understanding of discipleship that is historically relevant. It has been said that evangelicals are strong on evangelism and weak on social action, while for liberals the reverse is true."[30] The problem is endemic everywhere – Catholics, Protestants, Evangelicals, Pentecostals, etc. "The betrayal of the biblical call to conversion has occurred across the theological spectrum."[31] There is always a segment that is strong in evangelism and weak in social action and a segment that is strong in social action and weak in evangelism. The solution to this schizophrenic mentality where one segment has a half loaf and the other has the other half is not to put the two halves together, Wallis cautions. "A pasted-together solution compromises the essential unity of the Gospel" because it is not steeped in faith.[32]

I agree with Wallis that Christian "conversion understood apart from or outside history must be reappropriated and understood in direct relationship to that history."[33] Those familiar with Lonergan's work know how committed he is to preserving the good of order and re-appropriating the Christian notion of conversion in a historically relevant way. He shows how the good of order is realized in authentic self-transcendence and goes to great lengths to identify the disastrous effects of the negation of this value. In chapter nineteen of *Insight* where he discusses general transcendent knowledge, Lonergan distinguishes between three kinds of inhibitions to self-transcendence: physical evil, moral evil, and basic sin. What he calls basic sin, "the failure of free will to choose a morally obligatory course of action or its failure to reject a morally reprehensible course of action"[34] aptly characterizes racial acts in all their forms, i.e., implicit or explicit forms. Following this technical sense, racial attitudes amount to basic sin. Basic sin is at the root of the irrational in human rational self-consciousness. Its consequence, in turn, is a host of moral evils that play out in society, such as unfair housing, job discrimination, and stereotyping of the ethnic other. As Lonergan explains it, "From the basic sin of not willing what one ought to will, there follows moral evils of omission and a heightening of the temptation in oneself or others to further basic sin."[35] The remedy for basic sin is conversion, since racism is a distortion of divine love and a negation of the redemptive suffering of Christ. Conversion must not be frivolous or esoteric. It must manifest in words and deeds and be committed to transforming the situation. Before detailing what is involved in this conversion process, I need to set the parameters for understanding this key notion, which Lonergan conceives as an entry into a new horizon and a shift from arbitrariness or unauthenticity to authenticity. The two key components of this entry into a new horizon are (i) the dynamic falling in love and (ii) the acceptance of suffering.

Falling in love is the basis of Lonergan's notion of self-transcendence and its cognate conversion. Self-transcendence is neither arbitrary nor something to be taken for granted. It is a long and painful achievement. Once it is achieved, it liberates a person from blunders and aberrations of human living, like the naïve realist, empiricist, and idealist blunders or habits of thought that think knowing is like looking.[36] There can be resistance to the self transcending, the same way there can be resistance to understanding and resistance to love. Such resistance can truncate human affectivity. What Lonergan calls conversion is a resistance to this resistance (i.e., an overcoming of this resistance). Conversion is a pull away from these resistances, i.e., a pull "toward a new way of life in which one's sensitive desires begin to reach out toward a condition in which they will match and support the self-transcendence of the pure desire that is the spirit of inquiring consciousness itself."[37] It is precisely for this reason that Lonergan locates conversion as occurring on the fourth level of human consciousness – the level of deliberation, evaluation, and decision.[38] It is a level in which one decides whom and what he or she stands for and whom and what he or she is against. It is meant to be a fully conscious decision about one's horizon, one's outlook, and one's worldview.[39] A person's decisions determine his or her genuineness and the extent to which he or she is absorbed in the dynamism of love. Lonergan takes time to distinguish several kinds of love, drawing particular attention to these three: (1) the love of intimacy, such as the one between husband-wife and parents-children (2) the love of humanity, such as the pursuit of human welfare locally, nationally, or globally and (3) other-worldly love, which admits no conditions or qualifications or restrictions or reservations.[40] Admittedly, falling in love with God and falling in love with people are of two different orders. God is in the order of grace. Nevertheless, it is the third kind of love that is significant (falling in love with God) because it underpins all others. From it proceed not only the acts that constitute methodical theology or sanctifying grace (in the scholastic sense of the term),[41] it is also the only other-worldly love that can be transformational. It is the only love that can undo the basic sin of racism.

Falling in love with God and remaining in that dynamic state of love is not something, technically speaking, we achieve on our own. Rather, it is a gift that we receive, accept, and ratify.[42] This means that the dynamism of love must include an acceptance of suffering because suffering gives love a new significance. "The redemption in Christ Jesus does not change the fundamental fact that sin continues to head for suffering and death. However, the suffering and death that follow from sin attain a new significance in Christ Jesus. They are no longer the sad, disastrous end to the differential of sin, but also the means towards transfiguration and resurrection."[43] The apostle Paul was modelling this acceptance of suffering in expressing that nothing, not even affliction or hardship, can separate one whose heart God has flooded with love: "I am convinced that there is nothing in death or life, in the realm of spirits or supernatural powers, in the world as it is or the world as it should be, in the forces of the universe, in heights or depths, nothing in all creation that can separate us from the love of God in Christ Jesus our Lord" (Romans 8:35, 38–9).[44] Although Lonergan does not explicitly make this distinction, when he speaks of acceptance of suffering, what he has in mind is redemptive suffering (as against destructive suffering).[45] Clearly, racial acts engender destructive suffering. They create a situation in which victims have to be heroic to resist the pressures of the continuing cycle of violence. Destructive suffering breeds negative fruits, such as apathy and sado-masochistic dispositions. But redemptive or transformative suffering stems from *lex crucis* (the law of the cross).[46] Its fruits include endurance, compassion, hope, and even charity towards one's enemies. The Rev. Dr. Martin Luther King

Jr. made this redemptive suffering a centrepiece of his nonviolent movement. James Baldwin spoke similarly about how this redemptive suffering entails the difficult task of loving the enemy.

The Five-Dimensional Conversion Process (5D-C Process)

"Conversion" is Lonergan's technical way of describing how to generate a new self and a new understanding of oneself, one's neighbours, and one's world. It begins with a shift in horizon. Literally, horizon denotes a bounding circle, i.e., the limit of one's field of vision.[47] This Greek-derived term *horizōn (kuklos* = limiting circle*)* captures the scope of one's knowledge and the range and bounds of one's interests. It means that whatever lies within one's horizon is an object of one's interest and knowledge and whatever lies beyond one's horizon is outside of one's range of knowledge and scope of interest.[48] Lonergan considers differences in horizon to be either complementary (when they include one another), genetic (when later stages build on earlier stages, presuppose them, and transform them), or dialectal (when they are in irreconcilable opposition to each other). "What in one is found intelligible in another is unintelligible. What for one is true for another is false. What for one is good for another is evil."[49] Racism stems from a dialectical opposition of horizons. To explain what he means by conversion, Lonergan draws from the French philosopher, Joseph de Finance (1904–2000), who distinguished between a horizontal and a vertical exercise of freedom. According to this distinction, a horizontal exercise of freedom is a "decision or choice that occurs within an established horizon"[50] and a vertical exercise of freedom is "the set of judgments and decisions by which we move from one horizon to another."[51] Lonergan admits that it is possible to have "a sequence of such vertical exercises of freedom, and in each case the new horizon, though notably deeper and broader and richer, nonetheless is consonant with the old and a development out of its potentialities."[52] But he also leaves open the possibility that "the movement into a new horizon involves an about-face; it comes out of the old by repudiating characteristic features; it begins a new sequence that can keep revealing ever greater depth and breadth and wealth."[53] Such an about-face and a new beginning are essentially what Lonergan means by conversion.[54] It is just such an about-face – a change in direction – that can arrest racism. As Lonergan writes:

> So conversion is a change of direction and, indeed, a change for the better. One frees oneself from the unauthentic. One grows in authenticity. Harmful, dangerous, misleading satisfactions are dropped. Fears of discomfort,

> pain, privation have less power to deflect one from one's course. Values are apprehended where before they were overlooked. Scales of preference shift. Errors, rationalizations, ideologies fall and shatter to leave one open to things as they are and to man as he should be.[55]

Conversion, because it involves a set of judgments and decisions, can be intensely personal and utterly intimate.[56] It is the kind of personal and intimate shift Saul experienced when he became Paul after encountering the risen Lord. It is an about-face that made him abandon his pharisaic extremism for a new identity – that of an apostle (Christian). He was always religious as an observant Jew but his interpretation was too legalistic. He became religious in a different way as a Christian. "If anyone is in Christ Jesus, he is a new creation. The old has gone, the new has come" (2 Cor. 5:17). Lonergan emphasizes both the personal and communal dimension of conversion. "It can happen to many, and they can form a community to sustain one another in their self-transformation and to help one another in working out the implications and fulfilling the promise of their new life."[57] The personal and the communal dimensions of conversion are interlocking, in the same way individual and communal dimensions of bias or prejudice are interlocking. Just as prejudice is intensely personal, but not so private, so conversion is intensely personal, but not purely private. "While individuals contribute elements to horizons, it is only within the social group that the elements accumulate, and it is only with century-old traditions that notable developments occur."[58] This is to say, the personal and communal dimensions of conversion work in a process which is the reverse of personal and communal prejudices. In other words, individuals infected with prejudice strengthen the biases of their social groups, helping to make those biases systemic and institutional, while converted individuals can become steeped in their conversion when they are strengthened by a converted community. In the same way that racial attitudes can spread from one generation to another and become historical, conversion can spread from one cultural milieu to another and from one generation to another. "It can adapt to changing circumstances, confront new situations, survive into a different age, flourish in another period or epoch."[59] It is because conversion is intensely personal, yet still communal that we are required to start conversations about arresting racism at the micro level (individual) and from there move to the macro (interpersonal, societal, and institutional).[60] Simply put, multilateral cooperation is required to make a dent in racism. Although conversion involves a change in horizon, it involves more than a change in horizon. "It can mean that one begins to belong to a different social group or, if one's group remains the same that one begins to belong to it in a new way."[61] The Evangelical tradition emphasizes this idea of belonging to one's social group or religion in a new way, in a refreshing way. All religious traditions often use the word "conversion" to mean a "change of religion," as in a Muslim becoming a Christian or a Protestant becoming a Catholic. The Evangelical tradition takes this a step further. The tradition also understands conversion process to mean that people, say nominal Christians, can undergo a radical transformation such that, while there has been no "change of religion" in the sense of repudiating one religion and embracing another, "they now regard themselves as 'true Christians' in a way that they previously were not."[62] In his poem, "As Kingfishers Catch Fire," Gerald Manley Hopkins (1844–89) expresses the lovely sentiment of the transformation that comes with embracing one's religion in way that one previously had not:

> I say móre: the just man justices;
> Keeps grace: thát keeps all his goings graces;
> Acts in God's eye what in God's eye he is –
> Chríst – for Christ plays in ten thousand places,
> Lovely in limbs, and lovely in eyes not his
> To the Father through the features of men's faces.[63]

(a) Religious Conversion

Lonergan speaks of religious conversion as the fruit of God's gift of grace.[64] Because of a contemporary tendency to mistake what Lonergan calls religious conversion for religious allegiances or affiliations, a lengthy quotation of what Lonergan means by this special modality of love is necessary:

> Religious conversion is being grasped by ultimate concern. It is otherworldly falling in love. It is total and permanent self-surrender without conditions, qualifications, reservations. But it is such a surrender, not as act, but as a dynamic state that is prior to and principle of subsequent acts. It is revealed in retrospect as an undertow of existential consciousness, as a fated acceptance of a vocation of holiness, as perhaps an increasing simplicity and passivity in prayer. It is interpreted differently in the context of different religious traditions. For Christians it is God's love flooding our hearts through the Holy Spirit given to us. It is the gift of grace, and since the days of Augustine a distinction has been drawn between operative and cooperative grace. Operative grace is the replacement of the heart of stone by a heart of flesh, a replacement beyond the horizon of

> the heart of stone. Cooperative grace is the heart of flesh becoming effective in good works through human freedom. Operative grace is religious conversion. Cooperative grace is the effectiveness of conversion, the gradual movement towards a full and complete transformation of the whole of one's living and feeling, one's thoughts, words, deeds, and omissions.[65]

It is significant that Lonergan describes religious conversion, not only as loving without conditions, qualifications, reservations, but he also uses the image Jesus employed in the Gospel to describe this special modality of self-transcendence: "Love the Lord your God with all your heart and with all your soul and with all your mind and with all your strength" (Matthew 22:37; Luke 10:27).[66] If the passage Jesus quoted is "the first and greatest" of the commandments (Matthew 22:37), this means for Lonergan that it is religious conversion that sets the stage for moral conversion by transforming the subject and radicalizing him or her in love. The transformation establishes in the existential subject a new basis for loving, valuing, and doing the good. It also establishes the basis for accepting the suffering and pain involved in undoing the wrong that has been meted out to oneself and one's own community.[67] Again, this is because religious conversion is the efficacious ground of all self-transcendence and pursuit of truth, including God who is the Supreme Truth.

For Lonergan, as noted above, conversion is an existential reality that is intensely personal and utterly intimate and it is not so private as to be solitary.[68] Richard Liddy, following an idea developed by the sociologist Peter Berger, has noted that it is possible for a person to attain religious conversion before becoming affiliated with a faith-community. But at the same time, it is only within the faith-community, the *ecclesia*, that religious conversion is effectively maintained.[69] It is the faith-community that helps the person maintain the plausibility of the conversion as well as provide the indispensable structure needed to maintain the new reality.[70] "Saul may have become Paul in the aloneness of religious ecstasy, but he would remain Paul only in the context of the Christian community that recognized him as such and confirmed the new 'new being' in which he now located this identity."[71] How is religious conversion related to moral and intellectual conversion? Lonergan describes the relationship in terms of sublation.

> Though religious conversion sublates moral, and moral conversion sublates intellectual, one is not to infer that intellectual comes first and then moral and finally religious. On the contrary, from a causal viewpoint, one would say that there is God's gift of his love. Next, the eye of this love reveals values in their splendor, while the strength of this love brings

> about their realization, and that is moral conversion. Finally, among the values discerned by the eye of love is the value of believing the truths taught by the religious tradition, and in such tradition and belief are the seeds of intellectual conversion.[72]

Doran has explained this further to mean that religious conversion proximately affects a dimension of consciousness Lonergan at times calls a fifth level – the level of pure openness and reception to grace.[73] This openness to graces receives great emphasis in the Evangelical tradition as well. Jim Wallis, speaking as an Evangelical, relates how he was "saved" at a young age because conversion was key in his evangelical upbringing.[74] But his Evangelical conversion "was rarely related to any concrete historical realities. It remained private and abstract, focused primarily on a few personal habits and practices." It was not until he was "confronted with the brutal realities of racism" in his hometown of Detroit, by his own account, that he began to have a "deeper conversion."[75] Wallis writes,

> I didn't know it then, however, because I had been taught to expect conversion in well-lit churches, not in dark ghetto streets. The more I learned from my black friends and co-workers in inner-city Detroit, the more I felt disillusioned, hurt, angry, betrayed, and rejected by the church. I became separated from the church and, in the process, I felt I had lost my faith. I found my home instead in the civil rights and antiwar movements of the late sixties. The church had convinced me that religion was unrelated to present historical realities. Racism was not a religious issue of broken fellowship; it was merely a social issue that had no place in the church … In retrospect, I see that I was being confronted with racism and war as crucial steps in deepening and concretizing my conversion.[76]

What Wallis describes so well using his own life-experience is an instance of the dimension of consciousness Lonergan at times refers to as the fifth level. On the fifth level, Wallis, so to speak, realizes that the biblical call to conversion is never made in a vacuum and that the call is always grounded in history and is directed to an actual situation in which people find themselves.[77] This level of consciousness helps people to realize that one is called to turn to God in the midst of their concrete historical events, dilemmas, and choices and that that turning, though always deeply personal, as Lonergan describes it, is never private. As Wallis found out, the call to conversion is never an abstract or theoretical concern, but always practical because conversion is always a practical issue.[78]

(b) Moral Conversion

From a psychological perspective, moral development is a long and arduous process. The moral judgment of a principled conscience requires a complex level of cognitive and affective development.[79] Although moral sense is not a given, it can be developed and cultivated. Numerous studies in psychology support the fact that incentives and communal pressures can change a person's attitude and hierarchy of needs.[80] For example, various bodies and institutions in the United States, like the appellate and supreme courts, from the mid-twentieth century at least, have made concerted efforts to limit racially explicit policies created by the federal, state, and local governments in centuries prior, using a carrot and stick approach. While some of these efforts have worked, in general, people have not always been willing participants or partners in them to confront and reduce racism and its effects on different sectors of society.[81] In spite of the courts' efforts to reduce prejudice, real estate agents will still steer whites away from Black neighbourhoods and Blacks from white neighbourhoods.[82] Shrewd federal agencies and private sectors will continue to employ the discriminatory practices of redlining to deny mortgages and loans to poor African Americans and hit them with ridiculously high subprime loans.[83] These show that the cajoling, persuading, ordering, and compelling of a person to do what is right do not necessarily amount to moral development. They are also far from meeting the criteria for what Lonergan calls moral conversion. "Human sensitivity is not human intelligence," Lonergan writes.[84] Without a well-formed cognitive and affective development, a person can be given all the necessary incentives and still exhibit racial bias and fail to make the correct decision. This is why Black people meet "enormous, sometimes violent, resistance at every turn."[85] From a psychological point of view, it is utterly impossible to eliminate all biases and prejudices from the mind because the biases resurface unconsciously – implicit bias. Given that self-development is a long and arduous process, "During that process one has to live and make decisions in the light of one's undeveloped intelligence and under the guidance of one's incomplete willingness. And the less developed one is, the less one appreciates the need of development and the less one is willing to take time out for one's intellectual and moral education."[86]

Although the realm of moral conversion is not the realm of psychology, moral development (as articulated by Jean Piaget and Lawrence Kohlberg in their stages of moral development) can be an aid to moral conversion. The psychological development required for making a moral judgment is a precursor for moral conversion.[87] Lonergan speaks of it as "the context of growth, in which one's knowledge of human living and operating is increasing in extent, precision, refinement, and in which one's responses are advancing from the agreeable to vital values, from vital to social, from social to cultural, from cultural to personal, from personal to religious."[88] Moral conversion is a special instance of cognitional self-transcendence. It is the affirmation of oneself as an empirically, intelligently, and rationally conscious subject.[89] It does not require the persuading, the cajoling, the ordering, and the compelling that less developed subjects need in order to do the right thing. This is why Lonergan differentiates the world of immediacy, which he says is the world of the infant, from the adult world mediated by meaning. "As our knowledge of human reality increases, as our responses to human values are strengthened and refined, our mentors more and more leave us to ourselves so that our freedom may exercise its ever advancing thrust toward authenticity."[90] Normally, moral conversion is the fruit of religious conversion.[91] It changes the criteria of a person's decisions and choices from those of satisfactions to values.[92] It is that "existential moment when we discover for ourselves that our choosing affects ourselves no less than the chosen or rejected objects, and that is up to each of us to decide for himself what he is to make of himself."[93] In other words, moral conversion deepens love among peoples. "People made hard and cynical after years of frustration and discouragement can become gentle. Those who once knew fear now know trust. People bound to the materialism of the world discover the freedom of simplicity ... Whites reared in cultures of racism become hard workers alongside low-income Black tenants. Many people schooled in the ways of competing and winning learn how to devote their energies to active peacemaking."[94]

Moral conversion makes one respond to human values with vigour and strength. As mentioned earlier, a morally converted person does not need incentives, cajoling, or persuading to do what is right. Rather, he or she exercises his or her vertical freedom, opting for the truly good when value and satisfaction conflict.[95] In the wake of the unrest that followed the death of George Floyd in 2020, the New York Times ran a story of a young Black man, named Harris, who had had to endure racist abuse at his Catholic high school in New York. There was a particular racist incident which Harris encountered at the end of his sophomore year at this Catholic high school. It involved some white students who were fond of using the N-word and making racist jokes towards Harris. The protocol for such behaviour at this Catholic high school, at least on paper, was to remove the one "bad apple," under the assumption that removing the one bad apple would root out the racism. But Harris did not want his tormentors in this case to be expelled. He felt that expulsions would do little to change the behaviours of these kids and would also have adverse effects on their lives and those of their families. Rather than consenting to their expulsion, Harris agreed with the school on a different approach – one that will repair the bond between the victim and the offender. The school agreed and adopted an approach it called "restorative justice." They set up meetings with Harris and his tormentors and facilitated dialogue between them. All the parties talked it over and the offenders, having now realized the extent of the pain their racist behaviours were causing their victim, apologized to the victim. The true significance of the story is not in the apology offered by the offenders, but in the transformation it brought about in both the victim and the offenders. "I would have likely not had the chance to positively interact with him again, had he been kicked out of school, and he would no doubt have been embittered,"[96] recounted the victim. What Harris demonstrated throughout the process is an instance of moral self-transcendence, i.e., the recognition and choice of self as a free and responsible originator of value.[97] His approach to dealing with his racist abusers, i.e., not wanting them to be expelled from the school because of the difficulties it would bring their families, illustrates how moral conversion goes beyond individual value and truth to value in its generality. It is an illustration that a person becomes self-transcendent morally when he or she begins to seek only what is worthwhile, what is truly good, thereby becoming a principle of benevolence and beneficence.[98]

Moral conversion affects the fourth level of intentional consciousness – the level of deliberation, evaluation, and choice.[99] This is well illustrated in the decisions made by Harris' tormentors when they realized how much pain they were causing the victim. It illustrates Lonergan's essential argument that moral conversion "promotes the subject from cognitional to moral self-transcendence. It sets him on a new, existential level of consciousness and establishes him as an originating value."[100] Moral conversion according to Lonergan, sublates intellectual conversion.[101] It also sublates cognitive and affective development of a person. In sublating intellectual conversion and a person's cognitive and affective development, moral conversion becomes "the beginning of a deliberate movement toward an ever more complete authenticity."[102] Among public and revered figures of our time, Nelson Mandela (1918–2013) stands as one who has exhibited this kind of authenticity. At his trial in Pretoria (20 April 1964), in which four charges that carry the death sentence were brought against him by the Supreme Court of South Africa under the security legislation, Mandela memorably remarked: "During my lifetime I have dedicated myself to the struggle of the African people. I have fought against white domination, and I have fought against Black domination. I have cherished the ideal of a democratic and free society in which all persons live together in harmony and with equal opportunities. It is an ideal which I hope to live for and to achieve. But if needs be, it is an ideal for which I am prepared to die."[103]

(c) Intellectual Conversion

Driven by a myriad of factors, and in particular by the recent events that exposed the racial fault lines in the United States, experts from different fields often gather to engage tactics and propose solutions based on research that can help reduce incidents of racial volatility. Some interventions, like making people aware of the automatic associations of stereotypes about certain groups of people, such as the perennial associations between African Americans and crime or being Black with inferiority, have been promising and seem to be helping people become conscious of their subconscious racial biases. Even the Bell Curve has been used incorrectly to make connections between race and intelligence. The psychologist Richard Herrnstein and the political theorist Charles Murray in their widely read but controversial 1994 book thought that human intelligence was influenced by genetic makeup and environmental factors, which they also thought was a good predictor of a person's life outcomes.[104] A misapplication of the Bell Curve has contributed to subconscious bias, particularly by virtue of what it does say about IQ.[105] "Nowhere does the book address *why* it investigates racial differences in IQ. By never spelling out a reason for reporting on these differences in the first place, the authors transmit an unspoken yet unequivocal conclusion: Race is a helpful indicator as to whether a person is likely to hold certain capabilities."[106] In a speech he gave to a predominantly Black audience at Howard University in 1963, James Baldwin warned the students of "the many derogatory, degrading, and reductive definitions that this society has ready for you"[107] and made the students promise "that they would never believe the lies the country told about them."[108] Baldwin's intervention is a hint at what Lonergan calls intellectual conversion. Intellectual conversion is a shift or a radical clarification and elimination of an exceedingly stubborn and misleading myth concerning reality, objectivity, and human knowledge.[109] A person is self-transcendent intellectually by the achievement of knowledge.[110] The two key phrases in Lonergan's definition of intellectual conversion are (1) clarification of misleading myth about reality and (2) elimination of the stubborn myth about objectivity. Both suggest that intellectual conversion is a development in one's self-knowledge.

Lonergan begins his illustration of intellectual conversion by distinguishing between the infant world of immediacy and the adult world mediated by meaning. The world of immediacy is a world structured around feelings and perceptions, sights and sounds, and tastes and touches of an individual. But unlike the infant's world of immediacy where the criteria of objectivity are based on ocular vision, the world motivated by meaning is "a world known not by the sense experience of an individual but by the external and internal experience of a cultural community, by the cumulatively developed understanding of the community, and by the continuously checked and rechecked judgments of the community."[111] Here the reality known is not just by seeing, but by understanding, judging, and believing.[112]

Lonergan correctly states that knowing is understanding correctly. Myths about knowing the raced other (stereotypes) further vindicate him. In racial attitudes there is a whole range of issues that are loaded with myths about reality. One long-standing myth used to justify racial segregation in housing has been that a purchase by an African American in a white neighbourhood and the mere presence of African Americans in and near white residential neighbourhoods would bring down the property value of that neighbourhood. This myth has been perpetuated for centuries even when statistical evidence suggests the contrary – that integration causes property values to increase.[113] These types of myths need to be clarified and subsequently eliminated, if racial justice is to be achieved. We noted Lonergan's idea that an adequate account of human knowing, if it is to remain objective, must not be confined to the world of immediacy, but must take into account the complex process of the world mediated by meaning. The movement into the world mediated by meaning begins with willingness to adjust one's views about reality when those views are at odds with the really real. In the field of health care, for example, a large body of literature is unearthing how (implicit) bias is impacting a host of issues concerning African Americans, such as patient-provider interactions, treatment decisions, treatment adherence, and patient health outcomes. A 2015 study found that racial/ethnic minorities (including individuals with lower levels of education) are twice as likely as white patients to spend a longer time waiting for medical care or see a doctor. More and more of these studies show how physicians spend less time interacting with Black patients than they do with white patients and how Black patients are more likely than white patients to die in the ICU receiving life-sustaining treatment than in hospice receiving comfort care.[114] These alone expose the misleading myth about the reality of African American lives. Turning to the stubborn matter of mythic consciousness, which we argued earlier undergirds racial bias, this can be mitigated by intellectual conversion. It is intertwined with the stubborn myth that pretends we live in post-racial America. Both myths use the analogy of ocular vision as the criteria of objectivity. They are the myth of *the world-out-there-now real* – a myth that thinks objectivity is merely taking a look to see what is there to be seen. Many of the counterpositions to which Lonergan contrasts his own position underlie, in different ways and forms, contemporary attitudes underpinning racism. The subjects with naïve realist tendencies, upon seeing Barack Obama become the first Black president of the United States, mistake knowing for looking and conclude that racism no longer exists. The subjects with empiricist mindset see some successful Black professionals in the entertainment industry and other successful Black entrepreneurs and in their world of immediacy (a world of perception and images) restrict objective racial justice to these symbolic experiences. Even some of the liberals who have been in the forefront of civil rights struggles have many times been caught in the idealist and empiricist thoughts about the reality of African American lives today. In thinking that Black people have arrived, they pose the age-old annoying question: what else do the Black people want? It is only when misleading myths about reality are clarified and eliminated that one can take possession of oneself as a knower and then can lay claim to knowing the real. The criterion for the really real is the virtually unconditioned of one's own judgment. The affirmation of oneself as a knower is not a judgment made out of necessity, but a judgment of fact. This is why intellectual conversion affects the second and third levels of intentional consciousness.[115] According to Lonergan, "Normally it is intellectual conversion as the fruit of both religious and moral conversion."[116]

(d) Affective Conversion

Just as Lonergan uses the metaphor of the heart in discussing intellectual, moral, and religious self-transcendence, he does likewise to show how reaching affective self-transcendence is like falling in love. Although Lonergan does not speak specifically about affective conversion very early on, it is nonetheless implicit in much of his earlier work. His recognition of and explicit references to affective conversion as a distinct dimension of the long and arduous process of personal transformation appear rather late in his writings.[117] The key texts in his works that speak to affective conversion all centre around what he says about self-transcendence and the dynamic falling in love with God, which is expressed in changed attitudes. Whereas it was axiomatic in earlier times that *Nihil amatum nisi praecognitum* [knowledge precedes love], "in religious matters love precedes knowledge,"[118] he writes. For a person grasped by ultimate concerns, the supreme value is God and other values are but expressions of God's love for the world. "In the measure that one's love for God is complete, then values are whatever one loves and evils are whatever one hates so that, in Augustine's phrase, if one loves God, one may do as one pleases, *Amat Deum et fac quod vis*. The affectivity is of a single piece."[119] When one is affectively self-transcendent, the isolation of the individual is broken and the person functions spontaneously, not just for self, but for others as well.[120]

Such affectivity can be illustrated by what happened at an IHOP restaurant in Maine a few years ago. A group of Black teens were having a meal and the restaurant requested prepayment before the teens could be served. A white customer who overhead the request stepped in and questioned the reason for the request. At the customer's intervention, the restaurant apologized to the teens.[121] In citing this example as an instance of affective conversion, I am by no means implying that one good instance of virtue equals affective self-transcendence. What Lonergan calls affective self-transcendence, if it is to become affective conversion, must characterize a person's habitual state, i.e., the person's intentional self-transcendence is regular, easy, spontaneous, and sustained as a way of life.[122] It does not mean that the person may no longer err. Although an affectively converted person may err, "lapses from grace are rarer and more quickly amended."[123]

Doran has explained that what Lonergan calls affective conversion is the movement away from felt resistance to insight, i.e., a movement away from a resistance to flee from understanding. It is also a movement away from the psychic resistance against deciding and acting and "the movement away from this resistance toward a new way of life in which one's sensitive desires begin to reach out toward a condition in which they will match and support the self-transcendence of the pure desire that is the spirit of inquiring consciousness itself."[124] We are now left with the important matter of specifying, as precisely as possible, what this inquiring consciousness that participates regularly and habitually in the life of the intelligent, reasonable, responsible, and loving human spirit is. In other words, what is the inner constitution of affective integrity?[125] As in the IHOP example cited earlier, for race-based relations the inner constitution of affective integrity is in the development of empathy. The development of empathy is a learned virtue and can be developed early on through cross-race contacts and friendships. Several psychological studies support the idea that cross-race friendships can help decrease racial bias. One study of intergroup relations among school-age students found that students with higher levels of cross-race contacts or friendships are more likely to view social exclusion of ethnic minorities negatively. They are also more likely to develop a higher degree of empathy.[126] More and more psychological studies are showing that promoting contacts among children of different races and ethnicities "is likely to enhance young people's sense of moral transgression in the face of race-based exclusion during interracial peer interactions."[127] Although he does not speak specifically about race, what Dietrich Bonhoeffer (1906–45) decried as "cheap grace" (i.e., the tendency of the churches to preach forgiveness without repentance) resonates here. Bonhoeffer insists that the truth of God's call to discipleship, when preached by the Protestant churches, must be matched by human action or else justification and sanctification become disjointed. "Cheap grace is grace without discipleship, grace without the cross, grace without Jesus Christ, living and incarnate."[128] In the context of racial justice, asking for forgiveness must be preceded by a true repentance (a turning away from the things that lead to racism, especially those things that make it institutional and systemic). For without true repentance and a change of heart we are left with nothing but cheap grace.

What Lonergan calls affective conversion also entails acceptance of suffering. "Against sin as self-perpetuating, as a chain reaction, there is love of one's enemies and the acceptance of suffering. Sin as a chain reaction has two bases. It has a basis first in the hearts of human beings, where sin leads to ever further sin insofar as hatred arises. But Christ teaches us, 'Love your enemies, do good to them that hate you.' Secondly, there is a chain reaction of sin in the logic of the objective situation, and against that aspect Christianity teaches the acceptance of suffering."[129] The reason Lonergan puts a premium on acceptance of suffering is that the acceptance of suffering puts an end "to the chain reaction of sin that spreads throughout society. When everyone is dodging suffering, when no one accepts it, the burden is passed ever further on."[130] An affectively converted person understands that sin and suffering will remain, "but in Christ they have become transition points to an ever fuller life on this earth with God the Father and the Son and the Holy Ghost, with whom we aspire to live in eternal life."[131] To be clear, acceptance of suffering involves both victims and perpetrators alike. It presupposes that perpetrators are contrite and are ready to repent and victims are willing to forgive and let go. This line of argument is well illustrated in Donald Shriver's *An Ethic for Enemies: Forgiveness in Politics* (1995). Shriver makes a good point about how forgiveness must be both personal and corporate. Considering the history of our inhumanity to one another and all the atrocities committed over the years that have led to people retaining long memories of wrongs done to them, Shriver suggests that the world would be a better place if people practiced forgiveness. One of his main contentions is that to live peacefully, we must learn to forgive each other corporately. He blamed the Middle Ages for moving forgiveness from the congregation (corporate) to the individual. Although his main concern is the practice of forgiveness among nations, he also devotes some time to talking about "that old and still unpaid debt" of white Americans toward African Americans.[132] There are four essential steps, according to him, that are needed for forgiveness to take place:

1) Judgment: Forgiveness begins with a remembering and a moral judgment of wrong, injustice, and injury done. There should be no readiness to forgive without repentance.
2) Forbearance: Forgiveness requires "resistance to the lures of revenge."
3) Empathy: Forgiveness entails showing empathy for the humanity of "all the agents and sufferers of evil." Empathy may cause the offender to perform an action of restorative justice. "Nonetheless, empathy towards evildoers must combine with moral judgment, or it collapses into excuse."[133]
4) Renewed community: Forgiveness requires real intent on the part of the victims to live alongside the evildoers or their political successors.

(e) Psychic Conversion

The culture of the United States, unfortunately, is resistant to talking about the evils of the past. The lure of the American dream motivates as well as deludes people into wanting to talk only of the future. But victims of evil and their descendants remember the past and cannot just start talking about the future without looking into the past.[134] Racism has unquantifiable social, political, and economic effects on the victim. More disturbingly, targets of racism are harmed psychologically from the stress and trauma of racism.[135] Oftentimes the psychological trauma goes unnoticed. Mental health experts in psychology and psychiatry conducting meta-analyses of the effect of discrimination on victims' mental health are discovering how both the physical and mental health of victims are negatively impacted by racism, whether the racial acts are intentional or unintentional, overt or covert, and fringe or systemic. In one meta-analysis geared towards understanding the extent to which racial discrimination affects the mental health of its victims, researchers compared the mental health of expectant mothers who are Black to the mental health of expectant mothers who are white. They not only found some deeply troubling disparities, they also found a high mortality rate for Black mothers and their babies. They concluded from it that race-related stress is a key health risk for expectant mothers who are Black.[136] More recently, some behavioural scientists have started speaking more forcefully about microaggressive trauma. Microaggressive trauma is a term that captures "the excessive and continuous exposure to subtle discrimination (both interpersonal and systemic) and the subsequent symptoms that develop or persist as a result."[137] Although not all micro-aggressions are life threatening, some microaggressions "can certainly be pervasive and compromise one's sense of psychological and emotional safety, resulting in typical symptoms associated with trauma."[138] Individuals with past history of microaggressive trauma can have daily life stressors and mental health issues. When they are not fully healed of past traumas, "they may internalize an array of negative emotions – including anger, sadness, worry, resentment, hopelessness, regret, and self-doubt. These emotions may then affect one's self-esteem, one's susceptibility to develop mental health problems, and even one's ability to succeed or function."[139] In addition, people's encounters with overt discrimination or microaggressions might trigger for them some past memories of discrimination. When past memories of discrimination are triggered, the person might experience re-traumatization. Re-traumatization causes psychological distress that may also be inimical to the physical health of the victim.[140] In other words, people with microaggression trauma not only react to the situations that are occurring in the moment, "but also might be reliving and reacting to unresolved, emotionally intense microaggressions of the past."[141]

Numerous studies show that some of the emotional and psychological effects of racism require mental health interventions and treatment.[142] What Robert Doran has aptly called psychic conversion has a theological role to play in these interventions. Psychic conversion is a logical development of Lonergan's description of conversion. Lonergan writes, "Conversion, as lived, affects all of a man's conscious and intentional operations. It directs his gaze, pervades his imagination, releases the symbols that penetrate to the depths of his psyche. It enriches his understanding, guides his judgments, reinforces his decisions."[143] To be clear, psychic conversion is not the same as affective conversion.[144] "It is not the achievement of an affectivity that is of a single piece because one loves God with all of one's heart and soul and mind and strength."[145] Doran developed the notion of psychic conversion as a way of relating some of the basic elements of Lonergan's analysis of the subject to depth psychology. Depth psychology, as Doran understands it, "is a theory in aid of a praxis, and the praxis is the self-knowledge and self-constitution of the person."[146] He thinks that developing psychic conversion will make accessible to us the resources of depth psychology, which can help illuminate the dimensions of consciousness. He is convinced that the notion of psychic conversion is needed as a complement to Lonergan's thought on the subject and his account of the theological foundations.[147] The resources of depth psychology will also support "the emergence and clarification of the subject in Christ Jesus, that subject who, as theologian, is also the radical foundational reality in theology."[148]

Doran's notion of psychic conversion is informed by Lonergan's remarks on the psyche in chapter 6 of *Insight* where Lonergan relates the psychic process to the subject's development of insight, and in his *Method in Theology* where he discusses dreams in relation to symbols. A similar idea is addressed in chapter 17 of *Insight* where "symbolic productions are understood in relation to the differentiation of intelligence and rationality from the sensitive stream."[149] Adopting an approach that grounds depth-psychology theories and practices in Lonergan's intentionality analysis, Doran suggests that "moments of insight, judgment, and choice, and the dynamic state of being in love with another person, being in love in the community, and being in love with God, are higher integrations of psychic process."[150] Human feelings are not static. Although fundamentally feelings are spontaneous, Lonergan notes that they also go through a process of development, as well as aberration.[151] Some spontaneous feelings are easily aroused and easy to dispense with, however "there are in full consciousness feelings so deep and strong, especially when deliberately reinforced that they channel attention, shape one's horizon, [and] direct one's life."[152] A properly developed feeling produces affective integrity. Lonergan thinks the act of loving is a supreme example of this affective integrity. "A man or woman that falls in love is engaged in loving not only when attending to the beloved but at all times. Besides particular acts of loving, there is the prior state of being in love, and that prior state is, as it were, the fount of all of one's actions."[153] An aberrant feeling, on the other hand, leads to psychic disorder. Psychic disorder leads to personal breakdown and social decline.[154] Doran, following Lonergan, locates a notable aberration of feeling in what Friedrich Nietzsche, and after him Max Scheler, called *ressentiment* (translated as a re-feeling):

> According to Scheler, *ressentiment* is a re-feeling of a specific clash with someone else's value qualities. The someone else is one's superior physically or intellectually or morally or spiritually. The re-feeling is not active or aggressive but extends over time, even a lifetime. It is a feeling of hostility,

> anger, indignation that is neither repudiated nor directly expressed. What it attacks is the value quality that the superior person possessed and the inferior not only lacked but also feels unequal to acquiring. The attack amounts to a continuous belittling of the value in question, and it can extend to hatred and even violence against those that possess that value quality.[155]

Doran interprets what Lonergan says about aberration of feelings and the cumulative decline that accompanies it at the personal and social level to mean not only that feelings have a special relationship to values, but also that the realm of the psyche is of particular relevance to the constitution of the self and the realm of value (fourth level of intentional consciousness) – a realm where one seeks not just what is apparently good, but what is truly good and worthwhile.[156] He suggests that this means that affective development or aberration involves a transvaluation and transformation of symbols. The symbols change and express the new affective capacities and dispositions.[157] What Doran calls psychic conversion is "a transformation of the psychic component of what Freud calls 'the censor' from a repressive to a constructive agency in a person's development."[158] On how this psychic conversion affects the first level of intentional consciousness,[159] Doran writes:

> Patterns of experience are either the distorted and alienated, or the integral and creative, embodiment of the human spirit. To the extent that our psychic sensitivity is victimized by oppression, the embodiment of the spirit is confined to an animal habitat, fastened on survival, intent on the satisfaction of its own depravation of the *humanum*. To the extent that the psyche is released from oppressive patterns, the embodiment of the spirit is released into a human world, and indeed ultimately into the universe of being. A true healing of the psyche would dissolve the affective wounds that block sustained self-transcendence; it would give the freedom required to engage in the constitution of a human world; but it would also render the psyche the medium of the embodiment of intentionality in the constitution of the person.[160]

From the perspective of Protestant and Reformed traditions, the five kinds of conversion described here can be thought of along the lines of the understanding of conversion in John Calvin and Karl Barth as the total and complete renewal of the person. For Calvin, for whom the human condition is "vitiated and perverted" by a double corruption, "we stand justly condemned and convicted before God to whom nothing is acceptable but righteousness, innocence, and purity."[161] The cures for the double corruption are, for him, justification (which is purely God's act) and sanctification (which makes sinners righteous). Both have their origin in Christ. Calvin uses the terms sanctification, regeneration, repentance, and conversion interchangeably, not only to speak of the interpenetration of these terms, but also to depict how they can lead to total transformation of the person. Barth, similarly, sees the call to Christian discipleship as a call to conversion. In the *Dogmatics*, he employs the metaphor of "awakening to conversion" to convey the idea of a double movement – the human sleeper and God who awakens the sleeper. Conversion, for Barth, is a free act a person makes in obedience. Our love for God is "always and wholly and exclusively in response to the fact that he has first loved us."[162] In Barth, the awakened sleeper makes a sudden transformation. Although the conversion is never a finished project and is always ongoing, the transformation is supposed to be total.

In sum, the 5 Dimensional Conversion Process (5D-C Process) is the beginning, not the end point, of the fight against racism. It presupposes that the perpetrator of violence needs far more conversion than the victim. But that does not suggest that the call to conversion excludes the victim. It can seem odd and may even appear like a second act of violence to urge the victim to come to repentance. But what needs to be kept in mind here is that conversion, as used here in Lonergan's technical sense, does not exclusively mean repentance. Rather than the turning away from, which is integral to repentance, conversion is also an achievement of love. Consequently, both the perpetrator and the victims need the 5D-C Process, though in different measures. The one dimension of conversion needed in equal measure by both victim and perpetrator is psychic conversion because racism does as much psychic violence to the victim as it does to the perpetrator.

In *Notes of a Native Son*, Baldwin details, from the example of his own father, how self-destructive hatred can be. He tells us that his father became embittered by racism to the point that he allowed his anger towards the white man to eat way at his mind. Baldwin describes his father as being defeated long before he died. He was defeated because at the bottom of his heart he really believed the image of himself that a racist society had crafted for him. The problem with his father, he tells us, was that he knew that he was Black but did not know that he was beautiful.[163] This speaks to the general problem of growing up or living in a racist climate. It inevitably distorts your sense of self. Racist stereotypes, in addition, make their targets lose faith in what they are capable of and force them to lose their sense of individuality. They become not just victims, but also invisible – to piggy-back on

Invisible Man (1952) by the African American novelist, Ralph Ellison (1914–94).[164] An invisible person, according to Ellison, is "a man who is wrong-headed."[165] Individual trauma aside, victims of racism also suffer a collective trauma from the experience of racism. Individual and collective trauma stemming from racism leave a lasting scar that affects how one sees the world and how one navigates it. Psychic conversion helps victims set aside hatred for the victimizer and confront the pain and trauma they experience. This is why forgiveness is indispensable in the quest for true conversion. Forgiveness is "an act that joins moral truth, forbearance, empathy, and commitment to repair a fractured human relation. Such a combination calls for a collective turning from the past that neither ignores past evil nor excuses it, that neither overlooks justice nor reduces justice to revenge, that insists on the humanity of enemies even in their commission of dehumanizing deeds."[166]

Conclusion

Cognitive psychology has a role to play in overcoming racism. Racism is one of the many forms of prejudice that cognitive psychologists tell us is primarily cognitive – that it is caused by the brain's reflexive reliance on sorting and categorizing the data it receives from the world. "Our brains, our minds, are molded and remolded by our experiences and our environments. We have the power to change our ways of thinking, to scrub away the residue of ancient demons."[167] Cognitive science also supports the idea that many of our discriminatory behaviours stem from stereotypes that operate in our brain outside of our conscious awareness. Prejudicial acts are triggered when our brain processes errors, irrespective of motive or intent. Using her own experiences of working with Silicon Valley entrepreneurs to work to eliminate incidents of racial profiling, the African American psychologist, Jennifer Eberhardt, notes how research supports the idea that "raising the issue of race and discrimination explicitly can lead people to be more open-minded and act more fairly, particularly when they have time to reflect on their choices."[168] That said, there are no easy psychological or natural solutions to the problem of racism, the same way there are no easy psychological or natural solutions to the problem of evil. While psychological or natural solutions can remedy some social, economic, and political effects of the problem, they hardly win hearts and minds and are rarely enduring and authentic. There is only a supernatural solution for the problem of racism, just as there is only a supernatural solution to the problem of evil. I have located this supernatural solution in the 5D-C Process. These are modalities of self-transcendence. They are distinct and yet related. The fact that the 5D-C Process is a supernatural solution does not mean that the starting point is not in the natural order. For example, achieving racial justice must begin with an acknowledgement of the racial disparities in all the major sectors of life that disproportionately disadvantage African Americans and a willingness to fix the systemic imbalance. The supernatural emphasis is mainly a way of showing that an achievement of love is not a thing one says or adverts to arbitrarily, but is a conscious and radical change that must be effected in one's life. It shows that conversion is essential to human living since "the converted and the unconverted have radically different horizons."[169] A person's understanding of others is affected by one's conversion or lack thereof. In Lonergan's schema of the occurrence of conversion, first there is religious conversion, followed by moral, and then by intellectual conversion. The schema may be so because Lonergan describes religious conversion as a total surrender. But he also acknowledges that religious conversion in this sense is very rare.[170] In practical terms, therefore, the order of the 5D-C Process may be different. A subject perpetrating racial acts may experience intellectual conversion before religious and moral conversion. The person may arrive at an existential moment when he or she realizes that racism hurts the perpetrator and the victim alike, though not to the same degree. Such realization may be tied theoretically to the acceptance of God's gift of love, but may come to the person first either in an affective dimension or intellectual cognition. This is why Lonergan's notion of sublation is very important. There is no one particular order for the five modalities of conversion and they need not occur in the same order in every instance. One may have one or two of the dimensions and be lacking in the others and a person may have aspects of all five and be more dominant in one or two dimensions than in the others. Just like the operations of the levels of consciousness are related and sublate each other, when all five modalities of conversion occur in a person, their relations are to be conceived in terms of sublation.[171] It is important to stress that Lonergan does not understand sublation in the Hegelian sense of the higher one destroying the lower, but in the Karl Rahner sense of "what sublates goes beyond what is sublated, introduces something new and distinct, puts everything on a new basis, yet so far from interfering with the sublated or destroying it, on the contrary needs it, includes it, preserves all its proper features and properties, and carries them forward to a fuller realization within a richer context."[172]

At the beginning of this work, I made an argument regarding why Black Theology needs to appropriate the method Lonergan introduced to theology. I insisted all through that the method will serve Black Theology well because it speaks to our native human orientation. The 5D-C Process further validates the claim that Lonergan's method will help to deepen Black Theology's call for a change of heart and a shared participation in our universal human community. The appropriation of Lonergan's method commits us all to an indeterminate range of as yet undreamed consequences that flow from that method.[173]

Notes

Preface

1 See the Kerner Commission report, https://belonging.berkeley.edu/1968-kerner-commission-report (accessed 22 September 2020).
2 See Bernard Lonergan, "Dimensions of Meaning," in *Collected Works of Bernard Lonergan*, vol.4, *Collection*, eds. Frederick E. Crowe and Robert M. Doran (Toronto: University of Toronto Press, 2005), 232–45.
3 Bernard Lonergan, *Collected Works of Bernard Lonergan*, vol. 3, *Insight*, eds. Frederick E. Crowe and Robert M. Doran (Toronto: University of Toronto Press, 1992), 196.
4 Ibid.
5 Jennifer L. Eberhardt, *Biased: Uncovering the Hidden Prejudice That Shapes What We See, Think, and Do* (New York: Penguin [e-book version], 2019), 1.
6 Zeus Leonardo, "The Color of Supremacy: Beyond the Discourse of 'White Privilege,'" *Educational Philosophy and Theory* 36 (2004): 137–52, 141.
7 Ibid., 143.
8 Ibid., 140.
9 Ruth Frankenberg, *White Women, Race Matters: The Social Construction of Whiteness* (Minneapolis: University of Minnesota Press, 1993), 228–9.
10 Leonardo, "The Color of Supremacy," 143.
11 Susan Durber, "White Daughter of Empire: A Pilgrim of Justice and Peace Owning White Privilege," *Ecumenical Review* 72 (2020): 87–97, at 96.

Introduction

1 See Dwight N. Hopkins, *Being Human: Race, Culture, and Religion* (Minneapolis: Fortress Press, 2005) and Kelly Brown Douglas, *What's Faith Got To Do With It? Black Bodies/Christian Souls* (Maryknoll: Orbis Books, 2005).

2 See Hopkins, *Being Human*, 184.
3 Dwight N. Hopkins, *Heart and Head: Black Theology – Past, Present, and Future* (New York: Palgrave, 2002), 29.
4 Bernard Lonergan, *Collected Works of Bernard Lonergan*, vol. 14, *Method in Theology*, ed. Robert M. Doran and John D. Dadosky (Toronto: University of Toronto Press, 2017), 4.
5 Ibid.
6 Hopkins, *Being Human*, 119.
7 Bernard Lonergan, "Belief: Today's Issue," in *Collected Works of Bernard Lonergan*, vol. 13, *A Second Collection*, ed. Robert M. Doran and John D. Dadosky (Toronto: University of Toronto Press, 2016), 75–85, 79.
8 Bernard Lonergan, "The Future of Christianity," in *A Second Collection*, 127–39, at 137.
9 Ibid.
10 Bernard Lonergan, *Collected Works of Bernard Lonergan*, vol. 10, *Topics in Education*, ed. Robert M. Doran and Frederick E. Crowe (Toronto: University of Toronto Press, 1993), 59.
11 Lonergan, *Method in Theology*, 55.
12 See James H. Cone, *My Soul Looks Back* (Maryknoll: Orbis Books, 1982).
13 See Alistair Kee, *The Rise and Demise of Black Theology* (Burlington: Ashgate Publishing, 2006).
14 See Anthony Bradley's review of Dwight Hopkins' *Heart and Head*, "Heart and Head: Black Theology – Past, Present, and Future," *Presbyterion* 30 (2004): 119–21, at 121.
15 Lonergan, *Method in Theology*, 303.
16 James H. Cone, *For My People: Black Theology and Black Church* (Maryknoll: Orbis Books, 1984), 3.
17 James H. Cone, *A Black Theology of Liberation*, Twentieth Anniversary Edition (Maryknoll: Orbis Books, 2006), xvi.
18 Ibid., xiii.
19 See Donald W. Shriver, *Honest Patriots: Loving a Country Enough to Remember Its Misdeeds* (New York: Oxford University Press, 2005), 153.
20 Eddie S. Glaude, Jr., *Begin Again: James Baldwin's America and Its Urgent Lessons for Our Own* (New York: Crown, 2020), 4.
21 Hopkins, *Heart and Head*, 159.

1 The Seven Horse Riders of Racial Apocalypse

1 Bernard Lonergan, *Collected Works of Bernard Lonergan*, vol.10, *Topics in Education: The Cincinnati Lectures of 1959 on the Philosophy of Education*, ed. Robert M. Doran and Frederick E. Crowe (Toronto: University of Toronto Press, 2000), 63.

2 See the story of Daryl Davis and how his encounter with racial prejudice early in life led him on a quest to understand the source of racial prejudice. His quest and remarkable meetings with some leaders of the KKK also shed light on the fact that racial reconciliation is different from racial justice. See https://www.ted.com/talks/daryl_davis_why_i_as_a_black_man_attend_kkk_rallies?language=en (accessed 4 January 2021).

3 Derald Wing Sue et al., *Microintervention Strategies: What You Can Do To Disarm and Dismantle Individual and Systemic Racism and Bias* (Hoboken: Wiley, 2021), xiii.

4 Charles R. Lawrence III, "Implicit Bias in the Age of Trump," *Harvard Law Review* 133 (2000): 2304–57, at 2356.

5 Ibid.

6 Lonergan, *Topics in Education*, 63.

7 Bernard Lonergan, "An Interview with Fr. Bernard Lonergan, S.J.," in *Collected Works of Bernard Lonergan*, vol. 13, *A Second Collection*, ed. Robert M. Doran and John D. Dadosky (Toronto: University of Toronto Press, 2016), 176–94, at 191.

8 Karen E. Fields and Barbara J. Fields, *RaceCraft: The Soul of Inequality in American Life* (New York: Verso, 2012), 11.

9 Eddie S. Glaude, Jr., *Begin Again: James Baldwin's America and Its Urgent Lessons for Our Own* (New York: Crown, 2020), 19.

10 Ibid.

11 This film, which premiered 15 January 2018, is based on a book James Baldwin had begun about race in America but never finished. The film draws upon Baldwin's notes on the lives and brutal murders of Medgar Evers, Malcolm X, and Martin Luther King, Jr, three civil rights icons Baldwin describes as "my friends." For more information on the film, see https://www.pbs.org/independentlens/videos/i-am-not-your-negro/ (accessed 6 December 2020).

12 Glaude, *Begin Again*, xxvi.

13 Alistair Kee, *The Rise and Demise of Black Theology* (Burlington: Ashgate Publishing, 2006), 79.

14 Glaude, *Begin Again*, xxiv.

15 Michael W. Apple, "Foreword," in *White Reign: Deploying Whiteness in America*, ed. Joe L. Kincheloe and Shirley R. Steinberg (New York: Palgrave, 2000), ix-xiii, at x.

16 Kee, *The Rise and Demise of Black Theology*, 84.

17 See Laurie M. Cassidy and Alex Mikulich, eds., *Interrupting White Privilege: Catholic Theologians Break the Silence* (Maryknoll: Orbis, 2007).

18 Frances V. Reins, "Is the Benign Really Harmless? Deconstructing Some 'Benign' Manifestations of Operationalized White Privilege," in *White Reign*, 77–101, at 78.

19 See Ronald E. Chennault, "Giving Whiteness a Black Eye: An Interview with Michael Eric Dyson," in *White Reign*, 299–328, at 300.
20 Reins, "Is the Benign Really Harmless?" 78.
21 Apple, "Foreword," x.
22 See George Mayberry, "George Mayberry's 1952 Review of Ralph Ellison's Invisible Man," *The New Republic* 25 September 2013), https://newrepublic.com/article/114842/george-mayberry-ralph-ellison-invisible-man#:~:text=To%20paraphrase%20Graham%20Greene's%20already,happens%20to%20be%20a%20Negro.&text=Ellison's%2C%20race (accessed 5 December 2020).
23 Reins, "Is the Benign Really Harmless?" 83.
24 Ibid., 79.
25 Derald Wing Sue, *Microaggressions In Everyday Life: Race, Gender, and Sexual Orientation* (Hoboken: Wiley, 2010), xi.
26 Ibid.
27 See Howard Ross, *Everyday Bias: Identifying and Navigating Unconscious Judgments in Our Daily Lives* (Lanham: Rowman and Littlefield, 2020), viii.
28 See Sue, *Microaggressions in Everyday Life*, xvi.
29 For some helpful essays by white academics, see *Interrupting White Privilege*.
30 Charles R. Lawrence III, "The Id, the Ego, and Equal Protection: Reckoning with Unconscious Racism" *Stanford Law Review* 39 (1987): 317–88, at 322.
31 Ibid., 323.
32 Ibid., 323.
33 Chennault, "Giving Whiteness a Black Eye," 303.
34 See Matthew Allen, "SoHo Karen Has History of Unruly Behavior, Run-Ins with Police," Yahoo News (3 January 2021), https://www.yahoo.com/news/soho-karen-history-unruly-behavior-151538651.html (accessed 4 January 2021).
35 See Roxanne Jones, "This is What it Looks Like When Toxic White Privilege is Left Unchecked," CNN (7 January 2021), https://www.cnn.com/2021/01/07/opinions/capitol-rioters-contrast-with-june-2020-black-lives-matter-jones/index.html (accessed 11 January 2021). For comparison on police show of force and arrests of protesters of other movements, see Eliott C. McLaughlin, "On These 9 Days, Police in DC Arrested More People Than They Did During the Capitol Siege," CNN (12 January 2021), https://www.cnn.com/2021/01/11/us/dc-police-previous-protests-capitol/index.html (accessed 12 January 2021).
36 See Elena Nicolaou, "Michelle Obama Reflects on 'Wreckage' at the U.S. Capitol: 'I Hurt for Our Country,'" *The Oprah Magazine* (7 January 2021), https://www.oprahmag.com/about/a35154576/michelle-obama-capitol-response/ (accessed 11 January 2021).

37 See Fredrick Douglass, *My Bondage and My Freedom* (New York: Dover Publications, 1969), http://www.gutenberg.org/files/202/202-h/202-h.htm (accessed 30 December 2020).
38 See Ralph Ellison, *Invisible Man* (New York: Random House, 1952).
39 See Clint Smith, "Ralph Ellison's 'Invisible Man' As a Parable of Our Time," *The New Yorker* (4 December 2016), https://www.newyorker.com/books/page-turner/ralph-ellisons-invisible-man-as-a-parable-of-our-time (accessed 29 December 2020).
40 Ralph Ellison and Richard Kostelanetz, "An Interview with Ralph Ellison," *The Iowa Review* 9 (1989): 1–10, at 8–9.
41 Christopher Pramuk, *Hope Sings, So Beautiful: Graced Encounters Across the Color Line* (Collegeville: Liturgical Press, 2013), xxiii.
42 David Tracy, *The Analogical Imagination: Christian Theology and the Culture of Pluralism* (New York: Crossroad, 1981), 149.
43 Adam Beyt, "Fruitful Bodies: Farely, Copeland, and Baldwin on Sacred Flesh," *Theology and Sexuality* 25 (2019): 45–61, at 45.
44 Pramuk, *Hope Sings, So Beautiful*, 124.
45 See Pope Francis, *Christus Vivit*, http://www.vatican.va/content/francesco/en/apost_exhortations/documents/papa-francesco_esortazione-ap_20190325_christus-vivit.html (accessed 17 January 2021). See n41. See also Elochukwu Uzukwu, *A Listening Church: Autonomy and Communion in African Churches* (Maryknoll: Orbis, 1996).
46 Pramuk, *Hope Sings, So Beautiful*, 129.
47 Beyt, "Fruitful Bodies," 45.
48 Glaude, *Begin Again*, 220.
49 Ibid., 220–1.
50 Ibid., 59.
51 Bill V. Mullen, *James Baldwin: Living in Fire* (London: Pluto Press, 2019), xi.
52 Ibid.
53 Ibid.
54 Ibid.
55 Ibid.
56 Ibid.
57 Ibid., 24.
58 Glaude, *Begin Again*, 33.
59 Ibid., 116.
60 Mullen, *James Baldwin*, 48.
61 Ibid., x.
62 Glaude, *Begin Again*, 34.
63 Ibid., 36.
64 See M. Shawn Copeland, "Breadth and Fire: The Spirit Moves Us Toward Racial Justice," *Commonweal* (July 2020): 16–19, at 18.

65 Glaude, *Begin Again*, 36.
66 See James Baldwin, *Go Tell It on the Mountain* (New York: Alfred A. Knopf, 1953).
67 See David Leeming, "The White Problem," *Pen America* (8 January 2007), https://pen.org/the-white-problem/ (accessed 14 December 2020). The Baldwin biographer, Eddie Glaude, has also compared Baldwin's social vision and criticism of societal evils to that of the prophet Jeremiah in the Old Testament; see Glaude, *Begin Again*, 120.
68 Glaude, *Begin Again*, 4.
69 See *Pen America*, "'James Baldwin Didn't Have to Go Out and Get Votes': Obama Reflects On Race, Dialogue, and Disinformation in *Pen America* Interview," *Pen America* (5 December 2020), https://pen.org/press-release/obama-baldwin-race-disinformation/ (accessed 14 December 2020).
70 Glaude, *Begin Again*, 65.
71 Sue, *Microaggressions in Everyday Life*, xvi.
72 Beyt, "Fruitful Bodies," 52.
73 Ibid.
74 Ibid.
75 Lawrence, "Implicit Bias in the Age of Trump," 2356.
76 Ibid.
77 Lonergan, *Topics in Education*, 60.
78 Karen Fields and Barbara Fields, "Racecraft," 264.
79 Glaude, *Begin Again*, 23.
80 Robert T. Carter and Thomas D. Scheuermann, *Confronting Racism: Integrating Mental Health Research into Legal Strategies and Reforms* (New York: Routledge, 2020), 6.
81 Wille Jennings, "Educating After Whiteness," *In Trust* (Fall 2020): 28–9, at 28; see also Willie Jennings, *After Whiteness: An Education in Belonging* (Grand Rapids: Eerdmans, 2020).
82 Jennings, "Educating After Whiteness," 28.
83 Reins, "Is the Benign Really Harmless?" 79.
84 Glaude, *Begin Again*, 57.
85 Karen Fields and Barbara Fields, *Racecraft*, 264.
86 Sue, *Microaggressions in Everyday Life*, xv.
87 Ta-Nehisi Coates, *Between the World and Me* (New York: Spiegel and Grau, 2015), 97.
88 Sue, *Microaggressions in Everyday Life*, xv.
89 Reins, "Is the Benign Really Harmless?" 83.
90 Karen Fields and Barbara Fields, *Racecraft*, 146–7.
91 Coates, *Between the World and Me*, 33.
92 Reins, "Is the Benign Really Harmless?" 83.

93 See Roger Haight, "The Dysfunctional Rhetoric of 'White Privilege' and the Need for 'Racial Solidarity,'" in *Interrupting White Privilege: Catholic Theologians Break the Silence*, ed. Laurie M. Cassidy and Alexander Mikulich (Maryknoll: Orbis Books, 2007), 85–94.
94 Ibid., 87.
95 Ibid., 89.
96 Ibid.
97 Ross, *Everyday Bias*, xii.
98 Charles E. Curran, "White Privilege: My Theological Journey," in *Interrupting White Privilege*, 77–84, at 78.
99 See also Jon Nilson, "Confessions of a White Catholic Racist Theologian," in *Interrupting White Privilege*, 15–39.
100 Ross, *Everyday Bias*, xii.
101 Haight, "The Dysfunctional Rhetoric of 'White Privilege' and the Need for 'Racial Solidarity,'" 88.
102 Ross, *Everyday Bias*, xii.
103 Curran, "White Privilege," 80.
104 See M. Shawn Copeland, "Racism and the Vocation of the Christian Theologian," *Spiritus* 2 (2002): 15–29.
105 Reins, "Is the Benign Really Harmless?" 79.
106 Glaude, *Begin Again*, 63.
107 Ibid., 6.
108 Bernard Lonergan, *Collected Works of Bernard Lonergan*, vol. 3, *Insight: A Study of Human Understanding*, ed. Frederick E. Crowe and Robert M. Doran (Toronto: University of Toronto Press, 1997), 152–3.
109 Richard M. Liddy, *Startling Strangeness: Reading Lonergan's Insight* (Lanham: University Press of America, 2007), 95.
110 Ibid.
111 Lonergan, *Insight*, 153.
112 Karen Fields and Barbara Fields, *Racecraft*, 283.
113 Curran, "White Privilege," 79.
114 James H. Cone, "Black Liberation Theology and Black Catholics: A Critical Conversation," *Theological Studies* 63 (2000): 731–48.
115 Glaude, *Begin Again*, 306.
116 See Ed Pavlic, *Who Can Afford to Improvise: James Baldwin and Black Music, the Lyric and the Listeners* (New York: Fordham University Press, 2016).
117 James Baldwin, *No Name in The Street* (New York: Dial Publishing, 1972), 179.
118 Glaude, *Begin Again*, 18.
119 Ibid.
120 Ibid.
121 Karen Fields and Barbara Fields, *Racecraft*, 279–80.
122 Lonergan, *Insight*, 650.

123 Karen Fields and Barbara Fields, *Racecraft*, 279.
124 Ibid.
125 Lonergan, *Insight*, 658.
126 Chennault, "Giving Whiteness a Black Eye," 303.
127 Carol Anderson, *White Rage: The Unspoken Truth of Our Racial Divide* (New York: Bloomsbury, 2017), 3.
128 As quoted by Glaude, *Begin Again*, 34. Baldwin is here using "revolution" in its pejorative sense to refer to what white subjects see as a threat to the social order.
129 See CNN, "Rep. Wilson Shouts, 'You Lie' To Obama During Speech," https://www.cnn.com/2009/POLITICS/09/09/joe.wilson/ (accessed 5 December 2020).
130 Glaude, *Begin Again*, 44.
131 Anderson, *White Rage*, 3–4.
132 Glaude, *Begin Again*, 50.
133 See Sue, *Microaggressions in Everyday Life*, 37–9.
134 Nearly one-fifth of the U.S. Congress (82 Representatives and 19 senators), all from the south, signed a manifesto of defiance (1956) titled, "The Declaration of Constitutional Principles" to declare their non-conformance with the Court decision. See "The Southern Manifesto of 1956," https://history.house.gov/Historical-Highlights/1951-2000/The-Southern-Manifesto-of-1956/ (accessed 11 November 2020).
135 "The term 'busing' is a race-neutral euphemism that allows people to pretend white opposition was not about integration but simply about a desire for their children to attend neighborhood schools." See Nikole Hannah-Jones, "It Was Never About Busing: Court-Ordered Desegregation Worked. But White Racism Made It Hard to Accept," *New York Times* (12 July 2019), https://www.nytimes.com/2019/07/12/opinion/sunday/it-was-never-about-busing.html (accessed 11 November 2020).
136 Lonergan, *Method in Theology*, 281.
137 Lonergan, "An Interview with Fr. Bernard Lonergan, S.J.," 190.
138 Coates, *Between the World and Me*, 33.
139 Lonergan, *Topics in Education*, 60.
140 The 13th Amendment, according to James A. Garfield, a congressman at the time, was designed to do more than "confer the bare privilege of not being chained." See Anderson, *White Rage*, 9.
141 I am paraphrasing the historian Frederick Maitland who said, "The slave law of the South may have been dead, but it ruled us from the grave," cited in Anderson, *White Rage*, 38.
142 Coates, *Between the World and Me*, 7.
143 Jennifer L. Eberhardt, *Biased: Uncovering the Hidden Prejudice That Shapes What We See, Think, and Do* (New York: Penguin [e-book version], 2019), 27.

144 Ibid., 29.

145 Ibid., 30.

146 Coates, *Between the World and Me*, 7.

147 Karen Fields and Barbara Fields, *Racecraft*, 19.

148 Ibid., 18.

149 Ibid., 19; quoting the British scholar, W.E.H. Lecky, who tried to make sense of how seemingly smart people for a long time believed in things that do not make sense. See W.E.H. Lecky, *History of the Rise and Influence of the Spirit of Rationalism in Europe*, with an Introduction by C. Wright Mills (New York: George Braziller, 1982), 38.

150 Glaude, *Begin Again*, 70.

151 See W.E.B. Dubois, *Black Reconstruction* (New York: Harcourt Press, 1935); see particularly the final chapter titled, "The Propaganda of History." See also Charles Lemert, "The Race of Time: Dubois and Reconstruction," *Boundary* 27 (October 2000): 215–48; Claire Parfait, "Rewriting History: The Publication of W.E.B. Dubois' *Black Reconstruction in America* (1935)," *Book History* 12 (2009): 266–94.

152 King drew extensively on Dubois when he uttered the following to debunk the lie of the reconstruction: "White historians had for a century crudely distorted the Negro's role in the Reconstruction years. It was a conscious and deliberate manipulation of history, and the stakes were high. The Reconstruction was a period in which black men had a small measure of freedom of action. If, as white historians tell, Negroes wallowed in corruption, opportunism, displayed spectacular stupidity, were wanton and evil, and ignorant, their cause was made. They would have proved that freedom was dangerous in the hands of inferior beings. One generation after another of Americans were assiduously taught these falsehoods, and the collective mind of America became poisoned with racism and stunted with myths." See Glaude, *Begin Again*, 73.

153 Glaude, *Begin Again*, 28.

154 Ibid., 7.

155 Ibid., 54.

156 Ibid., 15.

157 James Baldwin, "Letter from a Region in My Mind," in *The 60s: The Story of a Decade*, ed. Henry Finder (New York: Random House, 2016), 22–32, at 30.

158 Glaude, *Begin Again*, 28.

159 See Martin Luther King Jr., "I Have A Dream," Address Delivered at the at the March on Washington for Jobs and Freedom" (23 August 1963), https://kinginstitute.stanford.edu/king-papers/documents/i-have-dream-address-delivered-march-washington-jobs-and-freedom (accessed 26 October 2020).

160 For a rare critique of MLK's speech, see Nathan W. Schlueter, *One Dream or Two: Justice in America and in the Thought of Martin Luther King, Jr.* (Lanham: Lexington Books, 2002).
161 Glaude, *Beginning Again*, xxv.
162 Ibid., 23.
163 Lonergan, *Method in Theology*, 87.
164 Karen Fields and Barbara Fields, *Racecraft*, 268.
165 Ibid., 261.
166 Ibid., 266.
167 Reins, "Is the Benign Really Harmless?" 79.
168 Coates, *Between the World and Me*, 17–18.
169 See Bernard Lonergan, "Theology and Man's Future," in *A Second Collection*, 114–26.
170 Ibid., 120.
171 Lonergan, *Method in Theology*, 80.
172 Frances E. Kendall, *Understanding White Privilege: Creating Pathways to Authentic Relationships Across Race*, 2nd ed. (New York: Routledge, 2013), 84.
173 As quoted by Reins, "Is the Benign Really Harmless?" 78.
174 Ibid., 79.
175 Bernard Lonergan, *Collected Works of Bernard Lonergan*, vol. 14, *Method in Theology*, ed. Robert M. Doran and John D. Dadosky (Toronto: University of Toronto Press, 2017), 152.
176 Ibid., 237.
177 Glaude, *Begin Again*, 307.
178 Ibid., 111.
179 Ross, *Everyday Bias*, xviii.
180 Lonergan, *Insight*, 651.
181 Lonergan, *Method in Theology*, 394.
182 See Frederick E. Crowe, *Appropriating the Lonergan Idea*, ed. Michael Vertin (Toronto: University of Toronto, 2006), 153.
183 See Daniel P. Horan, "The Bishop's Letter Fails to Recognize that Racism Is a White Problem," *Faith Seeking Understanding* (20 February 2019), https://www.ncronline.org/news/opinion/faith-seeking-understanding/bishops-letter-fails-recognize-racism-white-problem (accessed 14 January 2021).
184 See USCCB, "Open Wide Our Hearts: The Enduring Call to Love, A Pastoral Letter Against Racism" (November 2018), p. 5, https://www.usccb.org/issues-and-action/human-life-and-dignity/racism/upload/open-wide-our-hearts.pdf (accessed 9 October 2020). The pastoral letter describes racism as a part of human sinfulness that eats up the fabric of society, and challenges Catholic Christians to acknowledge their own sinfulness, especially their complicity in the evil of racism.

185 See U.S. Bishops' Pastoral Letter on Racism, "Brothers and Sisters to Us" (1979), https://www.usccb.org/committees/african-american-affairs/brothers-and-sisters-us (accessed 14 January 2021).

186 Glaude, *Begin Again*, 6–7.

187 Mullen, *James Baldwin*, x.

188 See George Weigel, "What 'Peace' Means Today," https://www.nationalreview.com/2016/10/what-peace-means-moral-truth-starting-point/ (accessed 7 October 2020).

189 Ibid.

190 Weigel, "What 'Peace' Means Today."

191 Ibid.

192 Ibid.

193 See John C. Campbell, review of George Weigel's *Tranquillitas Ordinis: The Present Failure and Future Promise of American Catholic Thought on War and Peace*, https://www.foreignaffairs.com/reviews/capsule-review/1987-06-01/tranquillitas-ordinis-present-failure-and-future-promise-american (accessed 7 October 2020).

2 The Perplexing Matter of Black Theology

1 See Kim Parker, Juliana Menasce, and Monica Anderson, "Amid Protests, Majorities Across Racial and Ethnic Groups Express Support for the Black Lives Matter Movement," *Pew Research Center* (12 June 2020); https://www.pewresearch.org/social-trends/2020/06/12/amid-protests-majorities-across-racial-and-ethnic-groups-express-support-for-the-black-lives-matter-movement/#most-americans-say-theyve-had-conversations-about-race-or-racial-equality-in-the-last-month (accessed 22 September 2021).

2 Donald W. Shriver, *Honest Patriots: Loving a Country Enough to Remember Its Misdeeds* (New York: Oxford University Press, 2005), 128.

3 Bernard Lonergan, "Questionnaire on Philosophy: Response," in *Collected Works of Bernard Lonergan*, vol. 17, *Philosophical and Theological Papers, 1965–1980*, ed. Robert Croken and Robert M. Doran, SJ (Toronto: University of Toronto Press, 2004), 357.

4 See Michelle Alexander, *The New Jim Crow: Mass Incarceration in the Age of Colorblindness*, Tenth Anniversary Edition (New York: The New Press, 2020), ix.

5 Charles R. Lawrence III, "Implicit Bias in the Age of Trump," *Harvard Law Review* 133 (2000): 2304–57, at 2357.

6 As quoted by Eddie S. Glaude Jr., *Begin Again: James Baldwin's America and Its Urgent Lessons for Our Own* (New York: Crown, 2020), 26.

7 Michael W. Apple, "Foreword," in *White Reign: Deploying Whiteness in America*, ed. Joe L. Kincheloe et al. (New York: St. Martin's Press, 1998), ix–xiii, at x.

8 See Frantz Fanon, *Toward the African Revolution: Political Essays* (New York: Grove Press, 1967).
9 See Albert Memmi, *Ce Que Je Crois* (Paris: Grasset, 1985).
10 Alistair Kee, *The Rise and Demise of Black Theology* (Burlington: Ashgate Publishing, 2006), 77.
11 Ibid., 71.
12 Ibid., 78.
13 Ibid.
14 Ibid.
15 See Sean Blenkinsop, et al., "Shut Up and Listen: Implications and Possibilities of Albert Memmi's Characteristics of Colonization Upon the 'Natural World,'" *Studies in Philosophy and Education* 36 (2017): 349–65.
16 See Raymond F. Betts, *Assimilation and Association in French Colonial Theory, 1890–1914* (Lincoln: University of Nebraska Press, 2005).
17 Rose Arnold, *The Negro in America* (New York: Harper and Row, 1964), 42.
18 Albert Memmi, *The Colonizer and the Colonized*, trans. Howard Greenfeld (Boston: Beacon Press, 1991), 71.
19 Noel L. Erskine, *DecolonizingTheology: A Caribbean Perspective* (Maryknoll: Orbis, 1979), 3.
20 See Cyril Orji, *A Semiotic Approach to the Theology of Inculturation* (Eugene: Pickwick, 2015).
21 James H. Cone, *A Black Theology of Liberation*, Twentieth Anniversary Edition (Maryknoll: Orbis, 2006), xvii.
22 As cited in Erskine, *Decolonizing Theology*, 3.
23 Bernard Lonergan, *Collected Works of Bernard Lonergan*, vol.14, *Method in Theology*, ed. Robert M. Doran and John D. Dadosky (Toronto: University of Toronto Press, 2017), 3.
24See Bernard Lonergan, "The Absence of God in Modern Culture," in *Collected Works of Bernard Lonergan*, vol.13, *A Second Collection*, ed. Robert M. Doran and John D. Dadosky (Toronto: University of Toronto Press, 2016), 86–98.
25 See Bernard Lonergan, "Dimension of Meaning," in *Collected Works of Bernard Lonergan*, vol. 4, *Collection*, ed. Frederick E. Crowe and Robert M. Doran (Toronto: University of Toronto Press, 2005), 232–45, at 244.
26 Ibid., 238.
27 See Leopold Senghor, *The Foundations of "Africanité"* (Paris: Présence Africaine, 1971).
28 Cone, *A Black Theology of Liberation*, 4.
29 W.E.B. DuBois, "Address to the Nations of the World," in *W.E.B. DuBois Speaks: Speeches and Addresses 1890–1919*, ed. Phillip Foner (New York: Pathfinder Press, 1970), 123–7, at 125.
30 Dwight N. Hopkins, *Heart and Head: Black Theology – Past, Present, and Future* (New York: Palgrave, 2002), 30.

31 See P.L. Thomas, "Introduction," in *James Baldwin: Challenging Authors*, ed. A. Scott Henderson and P.L. Thomas (Boston: Sense Publishers, 2014), 1–7, at 1.
32 Glaude, *Begin Again*, 6.
33 Ibid.
34 Bill V. Mullen, *James Baldwin: Living in Fire* (London: Pluto Press, 2019), 1–2.
35 Ibid., 2.
36 Ibid., 3–4.
37 Ibid., 3.
38 Ibid., 3.
39 Glaude, *Begin Again*, 7.
40 Sion Dayson, "Another Country," in *James Baldwin: Challenging Authors*, 77–89, at 78.
41 Ibid.
42 McKinley E. Melton, "Conversion Calls for Confrontation: Facing the Old to Become New in the Work of James Baldwin," in *James Baldwin: Challenging Authors*, 8–27, at 8.
43 Ibid., 9.
44 Dayson, "Another Country," 79.
45 Melton, "Conversion Calls for Confrontation," 8.
46 Mullen, *James Baldwin*, 4–5.
47 Adam Beyt, "Fruitful Bodies: Farley, Copeland, and Baldwin on Sacred Flesh," *Theology and Sexuality* 25 (2019): 45–61, at 52.
48 Melton, "Conversion Calls for Confrontation," 8, 11.
49 Ibid.
50 Mullen, *James Baldwin*, xii.
51 See James Cone's interview for PBS series, "This Far by Faith" (2003), https://www.pbs.org/thisfarbyfaith/people/james_cone.html.
52 See Kelefa Sanneh, "Project Trinity: The Perilous Mission of Obama's Church," *The New Yorker* (31 March 2008), https://www.newyorker.com/magazine/2008/04/07/project-trinity (accessed 22 October 2020).
53 See James H. Cone, *Said I Wasn't Gonna Tell Nobody: The Making of a Black Theologian* (Maryknoll: Orbis Books, 2018), xv.
54 See Position Statement in Support of Black Power published by *New York Times* (07/31/1966), https://episcopalarchives.org/church-awakens/items/show/183 (accessed 8 September 2020).
55 See Black Manifesto, https://episcopalarchives.org/church-awakens/files/original/c20bd83547dd3cf92e788041d7fddfa2.pdf (accessed 8 September 2020).
56 Hans Schwarz, *Theology in a Global Context: The Last Two Hundred Years* (Grand Rapids: Eerdmans, 2005), 473.
57 Cone, *A Black Theology of Liberation*, xi.

58 See James H. Cone, *Malcolm and Martin and America: A Dream or a Nightmare?* (Maryknoll: Orbis Books, 1991), x.
59 Ibid.
60 Ibid., 296.
61 James H. Cone, *Black Theology and Black Power* (Maryknoll: Orbis, 1969), 6.
62 Cone, *A Black Theology of Liberation*, xiv.
63 Ibid., v.
64 Ibid.
65 Ibid.
66 Ibid., viii.
67 Ibid.
68 Ibid., 6.
69 Ibid.
70 Ibid.
71 Ibid., 7.
72 Ibid.
73 Robin DiAngelo, "White Fragility," *International Journal of Critical Pedagogy* 3 (2011): 54–70, at 59.
74 See James H. Cone, *Black Theology and Black Power* (Maryknoll: Orbis Books, 2019).
75 Cone, *A Black Theology of Liberation*, v.
76 James H. Cone, *The Cross and the Lynching Tree* (Maryknoll: Orbis Books, 2011), xiii.
77 Ibid.
78 Schwarz, *Theology in a Global Context*, 475.
79 J. Deotis Roberts, "Liberation Theologies: A Critical Essay," *The Journal of the Interdenominational Theological Center* 36 (2010): 45–51, at 47.
80 Ibid., 46.
81 Ibid.
82 Ibid., 47.
83 Mokgethi Motlhabi, "The Problem of Ethical Method in Black Theology," *Black Theology* 2 (2004), 57–72, at 64.
84 See J. Deotis Roberts, *A Black Political Theology* (Philadelphia: Westminster Press, 1974).
85 See David E. Goatley, ed., *Black Religion, Black Theology: The Collected Essays of J. Deotis Roberts* (Harrisburg: Trinity Press, 2003).
86 See J. Deotis Roberts, *Liberation and Reconciliation: A Black Theology* (Louisville: Westminster Press, 1971).
87 J. Deotis Roberts, *Bonhoeffer and King: Speaking Truth to Power* (Louisville: Westminster Press, 2005), ix.
88 Ibid., 33.
89 Katie G. Cannon, *Katie's Canon: Womanism and the Soul of the Black Community* (New York: Continuum, 1996), 25.

90 Katie G. Cannon, *Black Womanist Ethics* (Atlanta: Scholars Press, 1988), 4.
91 See Alice Walker, *In Search of Our Mother's Gardens* (New York: Harcourt, Brace, Jovanovich, 1983).
92 Peter J. Paris, "Katie Cannon's Non-Canonical Canon," *Interpretation: A Journal of Bible and Theology* 74 (2020): 17–22, at 17.
93 Roberts, "Liberation Theologies," 46–7.
94 Paris, "Katie Cannon's Non-Canonical Canon," 17.
95 Katie G. Cannon, *Katie's Canon: Womanism and the Soul of the Black Community* (New York: Continuum, 1995), 18.
96 Cannon, *Black Womanist Ethics*, 1; quoting Pierre L. Van Den Berghe, *Race and Racism: A Comparative Perspective* (New York: Wiley, 1967), 77.
97 Ibid.
98 See Cannon, *Katie's Canon*, 108.
99 Rosemary Radford Ruether, "Black Women and Feminism: The U.S. and South African Contexts," in Cone, *A Black Theology of Liberation*, Twentieth Anniversary Edition, 174–84, at 175.
100 Lonergan, *Method in Theology*, 82.
101 Ibid., 79.
102 Ibid.
103 Kee, *The Rise and Demise of Black Theology*, 79.
104 Roberts, *Liberation and Reconciliation: A Black Theology*, 2nd edition, 55.
105 Edward Antonio, "Black Theology as Critical Theology," *Journal of Theology for Southern Africa* 1162 (2019): 101–14, at 101.
106 Ibid., 103.
107 Ibid., 102.
108 See Sebastian Moore, "Four Steps Towards Making Sense of Theology," *The Downside Review* 3 (1993): 79–100, at 87.
109 For more on this idea, see Cyril Orji, *Unmasking the African Ghost: Theology, Politics, and the Nightmare of Failed States* (Minneapolis: Fortress Press, 2022).
110 Derald Wing Sue et al., *Microintervention Strategies: What You Can Do To Disarm and Dismantle Individual and Systemic Racism and Bias* (Hoboken: Wiley, 2021), xiii.
111 Sue, et al., *Microintervention Strategies*, xiv.
112 Kee, *The Rise and Demise of Black Theology*, 80.
113 Ibid.
114 Ibid., 79.
115 Ibid., 80.
116 Ibid.
117 Ibid., 97.
118 Ibid., 85.
119 Ibid., 97.
120 James H. Cone, *For My People: Black Theology and Black Church* (Maryknoll: Orbis Books, 1984), 1.

121 Hopkins, *Heart and Head*, 32.
122 Ibid., 31.
123 Ibid., 32.
124 Ibid., x.
125 Ibid., 160.
126 Ibid.
127 Kee, *The Rise and Demise of Black Theology*, 195.
128 Hopkins, *Heart and Head*, xi–xii.
129 See Lonergan, *Method in Theology*, chapter 3.
130 See Cyril Orji, "Are There Stages of Meaning in African Theology?" *Toronto Journal of Theology* 32 (2016): 71–93. See also John Dadosky, "Is There a Fourth Stage of Meaning?" *Heythrop* 51 (2010): 768–80.
131 Hopkins, *Heart and Head*, 37.
132 See Anthony B. Bradley, Review of *Heart and Head: Black Theology – Past, Present, and Future*, by Dwight N. Hopkins, *Presbyterion* 30 (2004): 119–21, at 121.
133 Lonergan, *Method in Theology*, 245.
134 Hopkins, *Heart and Head*, 19.
135 Robert M. Doran, *Theology and the Dialectics of History* (Toronto: University of Toronto Press, 1990), 44.
136 Ibid.
137 Bernard Lonergan, "An Interview with Fr. Bernard Lonergan, S.J.," in *Collected Works of Bernard Lonergan*, vol.13, *A Second Collection*, ed. Robert M. Doran and John D. Dadosky (Toronto: University of Toronto Press, 2016), 176–94, at 180.
138 Shawn M. Copeland, *Enfleshing Freedom: Body, Race, and Being* (Minneapolis: Fortress Press, 2010), 86.
139 See Christopher Pramuk, "'Living in the Master House': Race and Rhetoric in the Theology of M. Shawn Copeland," *Horizons* 32 (2005): 295–331, at 296.
140 M. Shawn Copeland, "Theology as Intellectually Vital Inquiry: A Black Theological Interrogation," *CTSA Proceedings* 46 (1991): 49–57, at 54.
141 M. Shawn Copeland, *The Subversive Power of Love: The Vision of Henriette Delille* (New York: Paulist Press, 2009), 4.
142 Ibid., 5.
143 M. Shawn Copeland, "Racism and the Vocation of the Christian Theologian," *Spiritus* 2 (2002): 15–29, at 25; quoting James Cone's challenge to Black Theologians.
144 Charles Curran, "White Privilege," *Horizons* 32 (2005): 361–7, at 361.
145 Ibid.
146 Ibid., 363.
147 Ibid., 367.

148 Bernard Lonergan, "Human Consciousness," in *Collected Works of Bernard Lonergan*, vol.7, *On the Ontological and Psychological Constitution of Christ*, trans. Michael G. Shields (Toronto: University of Toronto Press, 2002), 157–90, at 159–61.
149 Gordon Allport, "Attitudes," in *A Handbook of Social Psychology*, ed. C. Murchison (Worcester, MA: Clark University Press, 1935), 798–844, 798.
150 See L.L. Thurstone, "The Measurement of Attitudes," *Journal of Abnormal and Social Psychology* 26 (1931): 249–69 and L.L. Thurstone and E.J. Chave, *The Measurement of Attitude* (Chicago: University of Chicago Press, 1929).
151 Anthony G. Greenwald and Mahzarin H. Banaji, "Implicit Social Cognition: Attitudes, Self-Esteem, and Stereotypes," *Psychological Review* 102 (1995): 4–27, at 4.
152 Donald R. Kinder and Timothy J. Ryan, "Prejudice and Politics Re-Examined: The Political Significance of Implicit Bias," *Political Science Research and Methods* 5 (2017): 241–59, at 243.
153 Ibid.
154 Ibid.
155 Ibid.
156 See Bernard Lonergan, *The Way to Nicea: The Dialectical Development of Trinitarian Theology*, translated from the Latin by Conn O'Donovan (London: Daron, Longmann, and Todd, 1976).
157 Bernard Lonergan, "The Future of Thomism," in *A Second Collection*, 39–47, at 46.
158 Lonergan, "An Interview with Fr. Bernard Lonergan, S.J.," 180.
159 Doran, *Theology and the Dialectics of History*, 43.

3 The Nature of Prejudice: A Psychological and Theological Understanding

1 Michelle Alexander, *The New Jim Crow: Mass Incarceration in the Age of Colorblindness*, Tenth Anniversary Edition (New York: The New Press, 2020), xii.
2 James H. Cone, *A Black Theology of Liberation*, Twentieth Anniversary edition (Maryknoll: Orbis, 2006), 4.
3 Richard Delgado and Jean Stefancic, *Critical Race Theory: An Introduction* (New York: New York University Press, 2001), 7.
4 Ibid.
5 Ibid., 3.
6 K.W. Crenshaw et al., eds., *Critical Race theory: The key writings that formed the movement* (New York: New Press, 1995) and E. Taylor et al., eds., *Foundations of Critical Race Theory in Education* 2nd edition (New York: Routledge, 2016).

7 See Bernal D. Delgado, "Critical Race Theory, Latino Critical Theory, and Critical Raced-Gendered Epistemologies: Recognizing Students of Color as Holders and Creators of Knowledge," *Qualitative Inquiry* 8 (2002): 105–26 and Bernal D. Delgado, "Using a Chicana feminist epistemology in educational research," *Harvard Educational Review*, 68 (1988): 555–82.
8 See Robert T. Teranishi, "Asian Pacific Americans and Critical Race Theory: An Examination of School Racial Climate," *Equity and Excellence in Education* 35 (2002): 144–54 and Tracy L. Buenavista, Uma M. Jayakumar, and Kimberly Misa-Escalante, "Contextualizing Asian American Education Through Critical Race Theory: An Example of U.S. Pilipino College Student Experiences," *New Directions for Institutional Research* 142 (Summer 2009): 69–81.
9 See Nikki Sullivan, *A Critical Introduction to Queer Theory* (New York: New York University Press, 2003) and A. Javier Trevion, Michelle A. Harris, and Derron Wallace, "What's So Critical about Critical Race Theory?" *Contemporary Justice Review* 11 (2008): 7–10.
10 Delgado and Stefancic, *Critical Race Theory*, 6.
11 Ibid., 7.
12 Ibid.
13 See Faith Karimi, "What Critical Race Theory Is – and Isn't," https://www.cnn.com/2020/10/01/us/critical-race-theory-explainer-trnd/index.html (accessed 1 October 2020).
14 See Howard Ross, author of *Everyday Bias: Identifying and Navigating Unconscious Judgments in Our Daily Lives* (Lanham: Rowman and Littlefield, 2020), xviii.
15 See Gordon Allport, *The Nature of Prejudice* (New York: Addison-Wesley, 1954).
16 Irwin Katz, "Gordon Allport's *The Nature of Prejudice*," *Political Psychology* 12 (1991): 125–57, at 126.
17 Allport, *The Nature of Prejudice*, 11.
18 Allport, *The Nature of Prejudice*, 208.
19 Katz, "Gordon Allport's *The Nature of Prejudice*," 127.
20 Denis Herbstein, *White Man, We Want to Talk to You* (New York: Africana Publishing, 1979), 66.
21 Walton Johnson, "Black Consciousness, Soweto, and Revolt in South Africa," *African Studies Review* 24 (1981): 4–8, at 4.
22 Ibid., 5.
23 Ibid.
24 Lonergan, *Insight*, 28.
25 Hans-George Gadamer, *Truth and Method*, 2nd rev. ed. (New York: Continuum, 1994), 299.

26 Bernard Lonergan, *Collected Works of Bernard Lonergan*, vol. 14, *Method in Theology*, ed. Robert M. Doran and John D. Dadosky (Toronto: University of Toronto Press, 2017), 44.

27 Ibid.

28 Katz, "Gordon Allport's *The Nature of Prejudice*," 125.

29 Ibid.

30 Gadamer, *Truth and Method*, 270.

31 Ibid.

32 Ibid., 271.

33 Ibid., 277.

34 Ibid., 271.

35 Ibid., 270.

36 Ibid.

37 Ibid.

38 Ibid.

39 Allport, *The Nature of Prejudice*, 9.

40 Ibid., xviii.

41 Ibid.

42 Peter A. Bertocci, "Gordon A. Allport's *The Nature of Prejudice* and the Problem of Choice," *Pastoral Psychology* 5 (1954): 31–7, at 33.

43 See D.L. Hamilton and J.W. Sherman, "Stereotypes," in *Handbook of Social Cognition*, 2nd ed., ed. R.S. Wyer Jr. and T.K. Srulls. (Hillsdale: Erbaum, 1994), 1–68.

44 See Mahzarin R. Banaji and Anthony G. Greenwald, *Blindspot: The Hidden Biases of Good People* (New York: Bantam Books, 2016).

45 Bernard Lonergan, *Collected Works of Bernard Lonergan*, vol. 3, *Insight*, ed. Frederick E. Crowe and Robert M. Doran (Toronto: University of Toronto Press, 1992), 245.

46 Ibid., 247.

47 Ibid., 557.

48 Alexander, *The New Jim Crow*, xviii.

49 Robert T. Carter and Thomas D. Scheuermann, *Confronting Racism: Integrating Mental Health Research into Legal Strategies and Reforms* (New York: Routledge, 2020), 12.

50 Ibid., 5.

51 Ibid.

52 Ibid., 22.

53 Richard Delgado and Jean Stefancic, *Critical Race Theory: An Introduction* (New York: New York University Press, 2001), xviii.

54 Ibid., 3.

55 Lonergan, *Insight*, 199.

56 M. Shawn Copeland, *The Subversive Power of Love: The Vision of Henriette Delille* (New York: Paulist Press, 2009), 7.
57 Ibid.
58 Lonergan, *Insight*, 199.
59 See Faith Karimi, "What Critical Race Theory Is – and Isn't," https://www.cnn.com/2020/10/01/us/critical-race-theory-explainer-trnd/index.html (accessed 1 October 2020).
60 Robin DiAngelo, "White Fragility," *International Journal of Critical Pedagogy* 3 (2011): 54–70, at 55.
61 Ibid.
62Carter and Scheuermann, *Confronting Racism*, 5; quoting J. Jones and R. Carter, "Racism and Racial Identity: Merging Realities," in *Impact of Racism on White Americans*, ed. B.P. Bowser and R.G. Hunt (Newbury: Sage, 1996), 1–24, at 3.
63 Delgado and Stefancic, *Critical Race Theory*, xx.
64 Lonergan, *Insight*, 199.
65 Delgado and Stefancic, *Critical Race Theory*, 3.
66 Lonergan, *Insight*, 199.
67 Ibid.
68 Zeus Leonardo, "The Color of Supremacy: Beyond the Discourse of 'White Privilege,'" *Educational Philosophy and Theory* 36 (2004): 137–52, at 148.
69 Lonergan, *Insight*, 200.
70 Carter and Scheuermann, *Confronting Racism*, 1.
71 Delgado and Stefancic, *Critical Race Theory*, 8.
72 Ibid.
73 M. Shawn Copeland, *Enfleshing Freedom: Body, Race, and Being* (Minneapolis: Fortress Press, 2010), 1.
74 Delgado and Stefancic, *Critical Race Theory*, 3.
75 Carter and Scheuermann, *Confronting Racism*, 5.
76 Lonergan, *Method in Theology*, 217.
77 See Christopher Pramuk, *Hope Sings, So Beautiful: Graced Encounters Across the Color Line* (Collegeville: Liturgical, 2013), 37.
78 Lonergan, *Insight*, 200.
79 Ibid., 204.
80 Ibid., 202.
81 Ibid.
82 See *The Cognitive Bias Codex*, https://www.teachthought.com/critical-thinking/the-cognitive-bias-codex-a-visual-of-180-cognitive-biases/ (accessed 30 September 2021).
83 Charles R. Lawrence III, "Implicit Bias in the Age of Trump," *Harvard Law Review* 133 (2000): 2304–57, at 2356.
84 Jennifer L. Eberhardt, *Biased: Uncovering the Hidden Prejudice That Shapes What We See, Think, and Do* (New York: Penguin [e-book version], 2019), 13–14.

85 Ibid., 14.
86 Ibid., 15.
87 Ibid., 14.
88 Ibid., 15.
89 Ibid.
90 Ibid., 32.
91 Ibid., 34.
92 Copeland, *Enfleshing Freedom*, 1.
93 Lonergan, *Method in Theology*, 217.
94 Eberhardt, *Biased*, 3–4.
95 Lonergan, *Insight*, 246.
96 Eberhardt, *Biased*, 31.
97 Ibid.
98 Lonergan, *Insight*, 214.
99 Ibid.
100 Ibid.
101 Ibid., 215.
102 See Ashley Nellis, "The Color of Justice: Racial and Ethnic Disparity in State Prisons," https://www.sentencingproject.org/publications/color-of-justice-racial-and-ethnic-disparity-in-state-prisons/ (accessed 2 December 2020); The Sentencing Project Report, "Report to the United Nations on Racial Disparities in the U.S. Criminal Justice System" (19 April 2018), https://www.sentencingproject.org/publications/un-report-on-racial-disparities/ (accessed 2 December 2020).
103 Thiago J. Souza de Lima et al., "Black People are Convicted More for being Black than for being Poor: The Role of Social Norms and Cultural Prejudice on Biased Racial Judgments," *Plus One* (20 September 2019): 1–24, at 2, https://journals.plos.org/plosone/article/file?id=10.1371/journal.pone.0222874&type=printable (accessed 22 September 2020).
104 See Marc Mauer, "Addressing Racial Disparities in Incarceration," *The Prison Journal Supplement* 9 (2011): 875–1015.
105 Lonergan, *Insight*, 215.
106 Ibid., 220.
107 Ibid., 223.
108 Ibid., 226.
109 John D. Dadosky, "Lonergan, Bias, and Love: Revisiting Lonergan's Philosophical Anthropology," *Irish Theological Quarterly* 77 (2012): 244–64, at 247.
110 Ibid., 248.
111 Ibid.
112 Lonergan, *Insight*, 223.

113 See Equality and Human Rights Commission Report, "Is England Fairer? The State of Equality and Human Rights 2016," https://www.equalityhumanrights.com/sites/default/files/is-england-fairer-2016.pdf (accessed 2 September 2020).
114 Susan Durber, "White Daughter of Empire: A Pilgrim of Justice and Peace Owning White Privilege," *Ecumenical Review* 72 (2020): 87–97, at 95.
115 My transcript from a video archive.
116 Howard Ross, *Everyday Bias: Identifying and Navigating Unconscious Judgments in Our Daily Lives* (Lanham: Rowman and Littlefield, 2020), xxi.
117 Bill V. Mullen, *James Baldwin: Living in Fire* (London: Pluto Press, 2019), 3.
118 D. Katz and K. Braly, "Racial Prejudice and Racial Stereotypes," *Journal of Abnormal and Social Psychology* 30 (1935): 175–93, at 181.
119 Anthony G. Greenwald and Mahzarin H. Banaji, "Implicit Social Cognition: Attitudes, Self-Esteem, and Stereotypes," *Psychological Review* 102 (1995): 4–27, at 14.
120 Lonergan, *Insight*, 244.
121 Lonergan, *Method in Theology*, 52.
122 Lonergan, *Insight*, 246.
123 Ross, *Everyday Bias*, xxi.
124 Lonergan, *Insight*, 246.
125 See study by Daniel L. Ames, Susan T. Fiske, and Alexander T. Todorov, "Impression Formation: A Focus On Other's Intent," in *The Oxford Handbook of Social Neuroscience*, ed. Jean Decety and John T. Cacioppo, https://www.oxfordhandbooks.com/view/10.1093/oxfordhb/9780195342161.001.0001/oxfordhb-9780195342161.
126 See Michael I. Norton et al., "Color Blindness and Interracial Interaction: Playing the Political Correctness Game," *Perspectives on Psychological Science* 17 (2006): 949–53.
127 Gadamer, *Truth and Method*, 276–7.
128 Ibid., 280.
129 Mullen, *Baldwin*, 4.
130 Lonergan, *Method in Theology*, 53.
131 Gadamer, *Truth and Method*, 276.
132 For more, see Jim Sidanius and Felicia Pratto, *Social Dominance: An Intergroup Theory of Social Hierarchy and Oppression* (Cambridge: Cambridge University Press, 2001).
133 Lonergan, *Insight*, 247.
134 Ibid.
135 Ibid., 248.
136 Felicia Pratto et al., "Social Dominance Orientation: A Personality Variable Predicting Social and Political Attitudes," *Journal of Personality and Social Psychology* 67 (1994): 741–63, at 741.
137 Ibid.

138 Lonergan, *Method in Theology*, 53.
139 Felicia Pratto et al., "Social Dominance Orientation," 741.
140 Dadosky, "Lonergan, Bias, and Love," 248.
141 Copeland, *The Subversive Power of Love*, 46–7.
142 Pratto, "Social Dominance Orientation," 742.
143 Ibid.
144 Maria Krysan, "Prejudice, Politics, and Public Opinion: Understanding the Sources of Racial Policy Attitudes," *Annual Review of Sociology* 26 (2000): 135–68, at 151.
145 Ibid.
146 Ibid.
147 Lonergan, *Insight*, 249.
148 Pratto, "Social Dominance Orientation," 742.
149 Lonergan, *Insight*, 249.
150 Pratto, "Social Dominance Orientation," 758.
151 Lonergan, *Insight*, 250.
152 My transcript of library archive video.
153 Lonergan, *Insight*, 250.
154 See Angela Saini, *Superior: The Return of Race Science* (Boston: Beacon Press, 2019).
155 Lonergan, *Insight*, 251.
156 Dadosky, "Lonergan, Bias, and Love," 248.
157 Ibid.
158 Jim Wallis, "America's Original Sin: The Legacy of White Racism," *Cross Currents* 57 (2000): 197–202, at 199.
159 Alexander, *The New Jim Crow*, ix.
160 Michael I. Norton and Samuel R. Sommers, "Whites See Racism as a Zero-Sum Game that They are Now Losing," *Perspectives on Psychological Science* 6 (2011): 215–18, at 215.
161 Lonergan, *Insight*, 251.
162 Richard Rothstein, *The Color of Law: A Forgotten History of How Our Government Segregated America* (New York: Liveright Publishing, 2017), vii.
163 Ibid., viii.
164 Ibid.
165 Lonergan, *Method in Theology*, 40.
166 Ibid., 41.
167 Lonergan, *Insight*, 255.
168 Ibid.
169 Ibid.
170 See Peggy McIntosh, "White Privilege: Unpacking the Invisible Knapsack," in *White Privilege: Essential Readings on the Other Side of Racism*, ed. Paula S. Rothenberg (New York: Worth Publishers, 2016): 151–5, at 154.

171 Carter and Scheuermann, *Confronting Racism*, 4; quoting D.R. Williams and S.A. Mohammed, "Racism and Health I: Pathways and Scientific Evidence," *American Behavioral Scientist* (2013): 1–22.
172 Lonergan, *Insight*, 251.
173 Ibid., 253.
174 Wallis, "America's Original Sin," 198.
175 See Mark Ellingsen, *Blessed Are the Cynical: How Original Sin Can Make America a Better Place* (Grand Rapids: Brazos Press, 2003).
176 Wallis, "America's Original Sin," 198.
177 See Bradford E. Hinze, "Ecclesial Repentance and the Demands of Dialogue," *Theological Studies* 61 (2020): 207–38, at 222; referencing John Paul II, *Reconciliatio et Paenitentia* (4 December 1984) no. 16, http://www.vatican.va/content/john-paul-ii/en/apost_exhortations/documents/hf_jp-ii_exh_02121984_reconciliatio-et-paenitentia.html (accessed 10 February 2021) and *Sollicitudo rei Socialis* (30 December 1987) no. 36, http://www.vatican.va/content/john-paul-ii/en/encyclicals/documents/hf_jp-ii_enc_30121987_sollicitudo-rei-socialis.html (accessed 10 February 2021).
178 Hinze, "Ecclesial Repentance and the Demands of Dialogue," 36.
179 Ibid.
180 See John Paul II, "Post-Synodal Apostolic Exhortation, *Reconciliatio et Paenitentia*," https://w2.vatican.va/content/john-paul-ii/en/apost_exhortations/documents/hf_jp-ii_exh_02121984_reconciliatio-et-paenitentia.html (accessed 8 October 2020).
181 See John Paul II, *Sollicitudo rei Socialis*, http://www.vatican.va/content/john-paul-ii/en/encyclicals/documents/hf_jp-ii_enc_30121987_sollicitudo-rei-socialis.html (accessed 8 October 2020).
182 Jason Morgan, "The New Structure of Sin: Mankind in the Age of Surveillance Capitalism," *The Human Life Review* 42 (2020): 42–9, at 42.
183 Wallis, "America's Original Sin," 198.
184 Charles Curran, "White Privilege," *Horizons* 32 (2005): 361–7, at 364.
185 Carter and Scheuermann, *Confronting Racism*, 1.
186 Wallis, "America's Original Sin," 199.
187 Lonergan, *Method in Theology*, 245.
188 Ross, *Everyday Bias*, xii.
189 Ibid.
190 Ibid., xi.
191 Ibid.
192 See Lawrence, "Implicit Bias in the Age of Trump," 2356–7.
193 Jennifer Eberhardt, *Biased: Uncovering the Hidden Prejudice That Shapes What We See, Think, and Do* (New York: Viking, 2019), 152.
194 Lawrence, "Implicit Bias in the Age of Trump," 2308.
195 See Moira Warburton, "Canadian Catholic Bishops Apologize for Role in Indigenous Residential Schools," *Yahoo News* (Friday, 24 September 2021),

https://www.yahoo.com/news/canadian-catholic-bishops-apologize-role-002418531.html (accessed 1 October 2021).

196 Copeland, *The Subversive Power of Love*, 5.

197 Ibid., 6.

198 See Joy Deruy Leary, *Post Traumatic Slave Syndrome: America's Legacy of Enduring Injury and Healing* (Portland: Joy DeGruy Publications, 2005).

199 Hinze, "Ecclesial Repentance and the Demands of Dialogue," 207–8.

200 See Pope Eugene IV, *Sicut Dudum*, https://www.papalencyclicals.net/eugene04/eugene04sicut.htm (accessed 8 October 2020).

201 See "Brief of the High Pontiff Gregory XVI," http://www.vatican.va/content/gregorius-xvi/it/documents/breve-in-supremo-apostolatus-fastigio-3-dicembre-1839.html (accessed 8 October 2020).

202 Copeland, *The Subversive Power of Love*, 16.

203 Ibid.

204 See Bernard Lonergan, "Questionnaire on Philosophy: Response," in *Collected Works of Bernard Lonergan, Philosophical and Theological Papers: 1965–1980*, vol. 17, ed. Robert C. Croken and Robert M. Doran (Toronto: University of Toronto Press, 2004), 352–83.

205 See Tad Dunn, "Bernard Lonergan (1904–1984)," in *Internet Encyclopedia of Philosophy*, https://iep.utm.edu/lonergan/ (accessed 8 October 2020).

206 See Rachel L. Swarns, "272 Slaves were Sold to Save Georgetown: What Does It Owe Their Descendants?" *New York Times* (16 April 2016); https://www.nytimes.com/2016/04/17/us/georgetown-university-search-for-slave-descendants.html (accessed 24 September 2021).

207 See Donald Shriver, *Honest Patriots: Loving a Country Enough to Remember Its Misdeeds* (New York: Oxford, 2005), 195–205.

4 The Karen Phenomenon and the Conceptualist Problem of White Privilege Discourse

1 Bernard Lonergan, *Collected Works of Bernard Lonergan*, vol.7, *The Ontological and Psychological Constitution of Christ* [De Constitutione Christi Ontologica et Psychologica], trans. Michael G. Shield (Toronto: University of Toronto Press, 2002), 157–69, at 157.

2 Bernard Lonergan, *Collected Works of Bernard Lonergan*, vol. 14, *Method in Theology*, ed. Robert M. Doran and John D. Dadosky (Toronto: University of Toronto Press, 2017), 245.

3 Ibid., 18.

4 Bernard Lonergan, "The Role of the Catholic University in the Modern World," in *Collected Works of Bernard Lonergan*, vol.4, *Collection*, ed. Frederick E. Crowe and Robert M. Doran (Toronto: University of Toronto Press, 2005), 108–13, at 108.

5 Bernard Lonergan, "The Subject," in *Collected Works of Bernard Lonergan*, vol. 13, *A Second Collection*, ed. Robert M. Doran and John D. Dadosky (Toronto: University of Toronto Press, 2016), 60–74, at 64. For more on conceptualism, see also Patrick Byrne, "The Fabric of Lonergan's Thought," *Lonergan Workshop* 6 (1986): 1–84.

6 Peggy McIntosh, "White Privilege: Unpacking the invisible Knapsack," *Peace and Freedom* (July–August, 1989). The same essay is republished in *White Privilege: Essential Readings on the Other Side of Racism*, ed. Paula S. Rothenberg (New York: Worth Publishers, 2016), 151–5; references are to the latter.

7 This is the problem of critical idealism that Lonergan castigates. See Bernard Lonergan, "The Origins of Christian Realism (1972)," in *A Second Collection*, 202–20, at 205.

8 Patrick Byrne, *The Ethics of Discernment: Lonergan's Foundations for Ethics* (Toronto: University of Toronto Press, 2016), 4.

9 Ibid.

10 See Frances V. Reins, "Is the Benign Really Harmless? Deconstructing Some 'Benign' Manifestations of Operationalized White Privilege," in *White Reign*, 77–101, at 80.

11 Charles R. Lawrence, "Implicit Bias in the Age of Trump," *Harvard Law Review* 133 (2020): 2303–56, at 2323.

12 Empirical residue is a notion Lonergan introduced to explore the broader significance of inverse insight. See Bernard Lonergan, *Collected Works of Bernard Lonergan*, vol. 3, *Insight*, ed. Frederick E. Crowe and Robert M. Doran (Toronto: University of Toronto Press, 1992), 50ff.

13 See Jim Wallis, *America's Original Sin: Racism, White Privilege, and the Bridge to a New America* (Grand Rapids: Brazos Press, 2016).

14 Lonergan, "The Subject," 60.

15 See the 1968 Kerner Commission Report, https://belonging.berkeley.edu/1968-kerner-commission-report (accessed 18 September 2020).

16 See Bernard Lonergan, "The Dehellenization of Dogma," in *A Second Collection*, 11–30, at 12.

17 Lonergan, "The Subject," 64.

18 McIntosh, "White Privilege," 151.

19 Teresa A. Fowler, "How 'Studying Up' Reveals the Tensions in Accessing Whiteness in Educational Research," *Taboo* (2020): 22–37, at 24.

20 R. Frankenberg, *White Women, Race Matters: The Social Construction of Whiteness* (Minneapolis: University of Minnesota Press, 1993), 6.

21 Fowler, "How 'Studying Up' Reveals the Tensions in Accessing Whiteness in Educational Research," 24.

22 See McIntosh, "White Privilege," 151–5.

23 See David J. Leonard, *Playing While White: Privilege and Power on and Off the Field* (Seattle: University of Washington Press, 2017), 14.

24 See James H. Cone, *A Black Theology of Liberation*, Twentieth Anniversary Edition (Maryknoll: Orbis, 2006), 65.
25 See Leonard, *Playing While White*.
26 Lonergan, *Insight*, 198.
27 Matthew J. Mowry, "How White Privilege is Holding Back NH," *Business NH Magazine* (October 2017): 57–60, at 57.
28 Lonergan, "The Subject," 64.
29 Zeus Leonardo, "The Color of Supremacy: Beyond the Discourse of 'White Privilege,'" *Educational Philosophy and Theory* 36 (2004): 137–52, at 141.
30 Bernard Lonergan, *Collected Works of Bernard Lonergan*, vol. 4, *Collection*, ed. Frederick E. Crowe and Robert M. Doran (Toronto: University of Toronto Press, 2005), 108.
31 See Bernard Lonergan, "Theology and Man's Future," in *A Second Collection*, 114–26, at 122.
32 See Brenda Lett, "Melanin, White Privilege and the Damage Wrought by the Lie," *Business NH Magazine* (October 2017), 61.
33 Lonergan, *Method in Theology*, 41 (see footnote 25).
34 Lonergan, "The Subject," 64.
35 John Dadosky has offered an analysis of how Bernard Lonergan's *Insight* is a philosophical tome that seeks to articulate a post-Kantian philosophy of knowledge and consciousness that counters all "wrong turns" as well as all lack of reflexive turn to the subject. See John D. Dadosky, "Desire, Bias, and Love: Revisiting Lonergan's Philosophical Anthropology," *Irish Theological Quarterly* 77 (2012): 244–64.
36 Lonergan, "The Subject," 64.
37 Ibid.
38 Robin DiAngelo, *White Fragility: Why It's So Hard for White People to Talk about Racism* (London: Allen Lane, 2019), 55.
39 Lonergan, "The Subject," 65.
40 Leonardo, "The Color of Supremacy," 148.
41 Lonergan, "The Subject," 65.
42 See some useful analogies in M.T. Blakemore, *White Privilege* (Minneapolis: Abdo Publishing, 2018), 6–10.
43 Lonergan, *Insight*, 578.
44 Blakemore, *White Privilege*, 10.
45 Ibid.
46 Leonardo, "The Color of Supremacy," 139.
47 Ibid.
48 Ibid., 138.
49 Ibid.
50 Ibid.
51 Ibid.

52 Peggy McIntosh, "White Privilege," 151.
53 Ibid., 152. See also Khiara M. Bridges, "Race, Pregnancy, and the Opioid Epidemic: White Privilege and the Criminalization of Opioid Use During Pregnancy," *Harvard Law Review* 133 (2020): 770–851, at 779.
54 Leonardo, "The Color of Supremacy," 137.
55 Bridges, "Race, Pregnancy and Opioid Epidemic," 779.
56 Leonardo, "The Color of Supremacy," 137.
57 Ibid.
58 Ibid.
59 Ibid.
60 Ibid.
61 See Howard Ross, *Everyday Bias: Identifying and Navigating Unconscious Judgments in Our Daily Lives* (Lanham: Rowman and Littlefield, 2020).
62 Erich Fromm, *To Have or to Be?* (New York: Continuum, 2008), xii–xiii.
63 See "Karen" in Slang Dictionary, https://www.dictionary.com/e/slang/karen/ (accessed 31 August 2020).
64 See *The Urban Dictionary*, https://www.urbandictionary.com/define.php?term=Karen (accessed 31 August 2020).
65 Rachel E. Greenspan, "How the Name 'Karen" became a Stand-In for Problematic White Women and a Hugely Popular Meme," *Insider* (26 June 2020), https://www.insider.com/karen-meme-origin-the-history-of-calling-women-karen-white-2020-5 (accessed 31 August 2020).
66 See Lorraine Ali, "Commentary: 'Karen' is an Easy Target. The Truth About White Nationalism is Much Worse," *Los Angeles Times* (9 July 2020), https://www.latimes.com/entertainment-arts/tv/story/2020-07-09/the-karen-video-what-it-means-commentary (accessed 31 August 2020).
67 Leonardo, "The Color of Supremacy," 137.
68 Dadosky, "Desire, Bias, and Love," 248.
69 See S.O. Sears, "Symbolic Racism," in *Eliminating Racism: Profiles in Controversy*, ed. P.A. Katz and D.A. Taylor (New York: Plenum), 53–84.
70 See J.B. McConohay, "Modern Racism, Ambivalence, and the Modern Racism Scale," in *Prejudice, Discrimination, and Racism*, ed. J.F. Dovidio and S.L. Gaertner (Orlando: Academic Press, 1986), 91–126.
71 See M.R. Banaji, C. Hardin, and A.J. Rothman, "Implicit Stereotyping in Person Judgment," *Journal of Personality and Social Psychology* 65 (1993): 272–81; M.R. Banaji and A.G. Greenwald, "Implicit Gender Stereotyping in Judgments of Fame," *Journal of Personality and Social Psychology* 68 (1995): 181–98; M.R. Banaji, "Implicit Attitudes Can Be Measured," in *The Nature of Remembering: Essays in Honor of Robert G. Crowder*, ed. H.L. Roedinger III et al. (Washington: American Psychological Association, 2001), 117–50.
72 See J.F. Dovidio and S.L. Gaertner, "Affirmative Action, Unintentional Biases, and Intergroup Relations," *Journal of Social Issues* 52 (1996): 51–75;

J.F. Dovidio and S.L. Gaertner, "Aversive Racism and Selective Decisions 1989–1999," *Psychological Science* 11 (2000): 315–19.

73 See Derald Wing Sue, *Microaggressions in Everyday Life: Race, Gender, and Sexual Orientation* (Hoboken: Wiley, 2010).

74 Katie G. Cannon, *Katie's Canon: Womanism and the Soul of the Black Community* (New York: Continuum, 1995), 101.

75 Delores S. Williams, *Sisters in the Wilderness: The Challenge of Womanist God-Talk* (Maryknoll: Orbis, 1993), xiv.

76 Leonardo, "The Color of Supremacy," 148.

77 See Cyril Orji, "A Reappropriation of the Joseph Story in Genesis 39 and Surah 12 for Contemporary Race-Discourse," *Horizons* 51 (2024): 1–32.

78 See Ali, "Karen is an Easy Target."

79 See W.E.B. Dubois, "The Souls of White Folk," in *Darkwater: Voices from Within the Veil* (New York: Harcourt Brace, 1920), https://www.gutenberg.org/files/15210/15210-h/15210-h.htm (accessed 5 September 2020).

80 Byrne, *The Ethics of Discernment*, 8.

81 Elizabeth S. Fiorenza, *Wisdom Ways: Introducing Feminist Biblical Interpretation* (Maryknoll: Orbis Books, 2006), 210.

82 Nichi Hodgson, "The Patriarchy Is Dead … But The Kyriarchy Lives On," *The Guardian* (10 September 2010), https://www.theguardian.com/commentisfree/2010/sep/10/kyriarchy-and-patriarchy (accessed 2 October 2021).

83 Lonergan, "The Subject," 69.

84 See the Kerner Report.

85 Lonergan, "The Subject," 72.

86 See Lonergan's discussion of sublation of degrees of consciousness, "The Subject," 69.

87 Lonergan, *Insight*, 198.

88 Ibid., 199.

89 Robert T. Carter and Thomas D. Scheuermann, *Confronting Racism: Integrating Mental Health Research into Legal Strategies and Reforms* (New York: Routledge, 2020), 42.

90 See Robert P. Jones, "Racism Among White Christians is Higher than Among the Non-Religious. That's No Coincidence," *Think*, https://www.nbcnews.com/think/opinion/racism-among-white-christians-higher-among-nonreligious-s-no-coincidence-ncna1235045 (accessed 23 September 2020). See also *White Too Long: The Legacy of White Supremacy in American Christianity* (New York: Simon and Schuster, 2020).

91 Bernard Lonergan, "The Transition from a Classicist Worldview to Historical Mindedness," in *A Second Collection*, 3–10, at 4.

92 See Lonergan, *Insight*, 568.

93 McIntosh, "White Privilege," in *White Privilege*, 152.

94 Jones, "Racism Among White Christians is Higher than Among the Non-Religious."

95 Ibid.

96 Ibid.

97 Lonergan, *Insight*, 568.

98 Ibid., 567.

99 Bernard Lonergan, "An Interview with Fr. Bernard Lonergan, S.J.," in *A Second Collection*, 176–94, at 190.

100 John Heileman and Mark Halperin, *Game Change* (New York: HarperCollins, 2010), 218.

101 Lonergan, *Insight*, 561.

102 Ali, "Karen Is an Easy Target."

103 Ibid.

104 Ibid.

105 Ibid.

106 Leonardo, "The Color of Supremacy," 143.

107 Frances Reins has provided five "benign" ways white privilege is maintained in the academy. For more, see Reins, "Is the Benign Really Harmless?" 84–94.

108 See Susan Durber, "White Daughter of Empire: A Pilgrim of Justice and Peace Owning White Privilege," *Ecumenical Review* 72 (2020): 87–97, at 89.

109 Derald Wing Sue, *Microaggressions and Marginality: Manifestation, Dynamics, and impact* (Hoboken: Wiley, 2010), 10.

110 Ibid.

111 Ibid.

112 Ibid., 11.

113 Lonergan, *Insight*, 556.

114 Carter and Scheuermann, *Confronting Racism*, 45.

115 I transcribed this speech from library video of the debate.

116 J. Gordon, "White on White: Researcher Reflexivity and the Logics of Privilege in White Schools Undertaking Reform," *Urban Review* 37 (2005): 279–302, at 281.

117 See Eduardo Bonilla-Silva, *Racism without Racists: Color-blind Racism and Persistence of Racial Inequality in the United States*, 4th ed. (Lanham: Rowman and Littlefield, 2013); Amanda E. Lewis, "There is No 'Race' in the Schoolyard: Color-blind Ideology in an (Almost) All white School," *American Educational Research Journal* 38 (2001): 781–811; and Charles Gallagher, "Color-blind Privilege: The Social and Political Functions of Erasing the Color Line in Post-Race America," *Race, Gender and Class* 104 (2003): 1–17.

118 Vanessa Gonlin and Mary E. Campbell, "Is Blindness Contagious? Examining Racial Attitudes among People of Color with Close Interracial Relationships," *Sociological Perspectives* 60 (2017): 937–55, at 951–2.

119 See Kalwant Bhopal, *White Privilege: The Myth of a Post-Racial Society* (Bristol: Policy Press, 2018), xiii.
120 Durber, "White Daughter of Empire," 90.
121 Richard Dyer, "The Matter of Whiteness," in *White Privilege*, 9–13, at 10.
122 bell hooks, "'Madonna: Plantation Mistress or Soul Sister?' and 'Representations of Whiteness in the Black Imagination,'" in *Black Looks: Race and Representation* (Boston: South End Press, 1992), 157–78, at 167.
123 Dyer, "The Matter of Whiteness," 10.
124 Ibid., 11.
125 Harlon Dalton, "Failing to See," in *White Privilege*, 15–18, at 16.
126 Dyer, "The Matter of Whiteness," 12.
127 Ibid.
128 Derald W. Sue, "The Invisible Whiteness of Being: Whiteness, White Supremacy, White Privilege, and Racism," in *White Privilege*, 19–28, at 19.
129 Dyer, "The Matter of Whiteness," 12.
130 Jennifer L. Eberhardt, *Biased: Uncovering the Hidden Prejudice That Shapes What We See, Think, and Do* (New York: Viking, 2019), 185.
131 Karl Barth, *Church Dogmatics* (Edinburgh: T&T Clark, 1968), 386.
132 Dwight Hopkins, *Heart and Head: Black Theology – Past, Present, and Future* (New York: Palgrave, 2002), 161.
133 Barth, *Church Dogmatics*, 386.
134 See Bernard Lonergan, *Verbum: Word and Idea in Aquinas*, ed. Frederick E. Crowe and Robert M. Doran (Toronto: University of Toronto Press, 1997).
135 Lonergan, *Insight*, 540.
136 Ibid.
137 Bernard Lonergan, *The Triune God: Systematics* (Toronto: University of Toronto Press, 2007), 205.
138 See R. Lanier Anderson, "Truth and Objectivity in Perspectivism," *Synthese* 115 (1998): 1–32.
139 See also Richard E. Palmer, *Hermeneutics: Interpretation Theory in Schleiermacher, Dilthey, Heidegger, and Gadamer* (Evanston: Northwestern University Press, 1969).
140 See Leslie Paul Thiele, "Reading Nietzsche and Foucault: A Hermeneutic of Suspicion," *The American Political Science Review* 85 (1991): 581–92.
141 See Paul Ricoeur, *The Conflict of Interpretations: Essays in Hermeneutics*, edited by Don Ihde (Evanston: Northwestern University Press, 1974).
142 Ross, *Everyday Bias*, 4.
143 See Mahzarin R. Banaji and Anthony G. Greenwald, *Blindspot: The Hidden Biases of Good People* (New York: Bantam Books, 2016).
144 Hodgson, "The Patriarchy Is Dead."
145 Richard Barbieri, "It's Complicated," *Independent School* (Summer 2014): 96–101, at 101.

146 Ibid., 96.
147 Lonergan, *Triune God*, 205.
148 Charles R. Lawrence III, "The Id, the Ego, and Equal Protection: Reckoning with Unconscious Racism," *Stanford Law Review* 39 (1987): 317–88, at 321.
149 Ibid., 322.
150 Linda Hamilton Krieger, "The Content of Our Categories: A Cognitive Bias Approach to Discrimination and Equal Employment Opportunity," *Stanford Law Review* 47 (1995): 1161–1248, at 1216.
151 Fromm, *To Have or to Be?* xii.
152 Lawrence, "Implicit Bias in the Age of Trump," 2323.
153 Lawrence, "The Id, the Ego, and Equal Protection," 326.
154 Ibid.
155 Ibid.

5 Implicit Bias and the Zero-Sum Game Problem

1 J. Deotis Roberts, *Liberation and Reconciliation: A Black Theology*, 2nd ed. (Louisville: Westminster John Knox Press, 2005), 90.
2 Bernard Lonergan, "The Absence of God in Modern Culture," in *Collected Works of Bernard Lonergan*, vol. 13, *A Second Collection*, ed. Robert M. Doran and John D. Dadosky (Toronto: University of Toronto Press, 2016), 86–98, at 96.
3 Ibid.
4 See Cyprian Davis, *The History of Black Catholics in the United States* (New York: Crossroad, 1990).
5 See Derald Wing Sue, *Microaggressions in Everyday Life: Race, Gender, and Sexual Orientation* (Hoboken: Wiley, 2010) and Derald Wing Sue, *Microaggressions and Marginality: Manifestation, Dynamics, and Impact* (New York: Wiley, 2010).
6 Bernard Lonergan, *Collected Works of Bernard Lonergan*, vol. 3, *Insight: A Study of Human Understanding*, ed. Frederick E. Crowe and Robert M. Doran (Toronto: University of Toronto Press, 1992), 255.
7 Peggy McIntosh, "White Privilege," in *White Privilege: Essential Readings on the Other Side of Racism*, ed. Paula S. Rothenberg (New York: Worth Publishers, 2016), 151–5, at 154.
8 Robin DiAngelo, "White Fragility," *International Journal of Critical Pedagogy* 3 (2011): 54–70, at 55.
9 McIntosh, "White Privilege," 154.
10 Frances E. Kendall, *Understanding White Privilege: Creating Pathways to Authentic Relationships Across Race*, 2nd ed. (New York: Routledge, 2013), 80.

11 Ibid., 84.
12 See Donald R. Kinder and Timothy J. Ryan, "Prejudice and Politics Re-Examined: The Political Significance of Implicit Bias," *Political Science Research and Methods* 5 (2017): 241–59, at 254.
13 Kendall, *Understanding White Privilege*, 83.
14 Robert M. Doran, *Theology and the Dialectics of History* (Toronto: University of Toronto Press, 1990), 34.
15 See Charles M. Blow, "White Male Victimization Anxiety," *The New York Times* (10 October 2018), https://www.nytimes.com/2018/10/10/opinion/trump-white-male-victimization.html (accessed 12 October 2020).
16 Bernard Lonergan, "Theology and Man's Future," in *A Second Collection*, 114–26, at 126.
17 Donald R. Kinder and David O. Sears, "Prejudice and Politics: Symbolic Racism Versus Racial Threats to the Good Life," *Journal of Personality and Social Psychology* 40 (1981): 414–31, at 414.
18 Erich Fromm, *To Have or to Be?* (New York: Continuum, 2008), 80.
19 Hans-Georg Gadamer, *Truth and Method*, 2nd rev. ed. (New York: Continuum, 1994), 360.
20 See Maria Konnikova, "How Norms Change," *The New Yorker* (11 October 2017), https://www.newyorker.com/science/maria-konnikova/how-norms-change (accessed 12 October 2020).
21 Maria Krysan, "Prejudice, Politics, and Public Opinion: Understanding the Sources of Racial Policy Attitudes," *Annual Review of Sociology* 26 (2000): 135–68, at 162.
22 Ibid., 135.
23 Kinder and Sears, "Prejudice and Politics," 415.
24 Ibid.
25 Ibid.
26 Ibid.
27 Ibid.
28 Ibid., 416.
29 Ibid.
30 Ibid.
31 Megan J. Shen and Jordan P. Labouff, "More Than Political Ideology: Subtle Racial Prejudice as a Predictor of Opposition to Universal Health Care Among U.S. Citizens," *Journal of Social and Political Psychology* 4 (2016): 493–520, at 495.
32 Krysan, "Prejudice, Politics, and Public Opinion," 159.
33 Ibid.
34 Kinder and Sears, "Prejudice and Politics," 416.
35 Kendall, *Understanding White Privilege*, 84.

36 Michael W. Apple, "Foreword," in *White Reign: Deploying Whiteness in America*, ed. Joe L. Kincheloe et al. (New York: St. Martin's Press, 1998), ix–xiii, at ix.
37 Ibid.
38 DiAngelo, "White Fragility," 64.
39 Robert T. Carter and Thomas D. Scheuermann, *Confronting Racism: Integrating Mental Health Research into Legal Strategies and Reforms* (New York: Routledge, 2020), 11.
40 DiAngelo, "White Fragility," 63.
41 Kinder and Ryan, "Prejudice and Politics Re-Examined," 241.
42 Ibid.
43 Ibid.
44 Ibid.
45 Ibid., 243.
46 Bernard Lonergan, *Collected Works of Bernard Lonergan*, vol. 14, *Method in Theology*, ed. Robert M. Doran and John D. Dadosky (Toronto: University of Toronto Press, 2016), 52.
47 Kinder and Ryan, "Prejudice and Politics Re-Examined," 243.
48 Lonergan, *Method in Theology*, 52.
49 Ibid., 226; see footnote 10.
50 Kinder and Ryan, "Prejudice and Politics Re-Examined," 243.
51 Lonergan, *Method in Theology*, 52.
52 Robert M. Doran, *Theology and the Dialectics of History* (Toronto: University of Toronto Press, 1990), 34.
53 See A.G. Greenwald et al., "Measuring Individual Differences in Implicit Cognition: The Implicit Association Test," *Perspectives in Social Psychology* 74 (1998): 1464–80.
54 Russell H. Fazio and Michael A. Olson, "Implicit Measures in Social Cognition Research: Their Meaning and Use," *Annual Review of Psychology* 54 (2003): 297–327, at 299.
55 Rae Alexandra, "BLM Allies: It's Time to Take This Harvard Test About Subconscious Bias," *KQED* (9 June 2020), https://www.kqed.org/arts/13881489/blm-allies-its-time-to-take-this-harvard-test-about-subconscious-bias (accessed 12 October 2020).
56 See Kathleen Osta and Hugh Vasquez, "Don't Talk About Implicit Bias Without Talking about Structural Racism," *National Equity Project* (13 June 2019), https://medium.com/national-equity-project/implicit-bias-structural-racism-6c52cf0f4a92 (accessed 12 October 2020).
57 Doran, *Theology and the Dialectics of History*, 34.
58 Markus Brauer, Wolfgang Wasel, and Paula Niedenthal, "Implicit and Explicit components of Prejudice," *Review of General Psychology* 4 (2000): 79–101, at 88–9.

59 Kevin L. Nadal, *Microaggressions and Traumatic Stress* (Philadelphia: American Philosophical Association, 2018), 10.

60 Ibid.

61 Ibid., 11.

62 Lonergan, *Method in Theology*, 52.

63 See Derald Wing Sue, "Racial Microaggressions in Everyday Life: Is Subtle Bias Harmless?" *Psychology Today* (5 October 2010), https://www.psychologytoday.com/us/blog/microaggressions-in-everyday-life/201010/racial-microaggressions-in-everyday-life (accessed 4 October 2021).

64 See Derald Sue, *Microaggressions in Everyday Life: Race, Gender, and Sexual Orientation* and Derald Sue, *Microaggressions and Marginality: Manifestation, Dynamics, and Impact*.

65 Derald Sue, *Microaggressions in Everyday Life*, 52. See also, D.W. Sue and C.M. Capodilupo, "Racial, gender, and sexual orientation microaggressions: Implication for counseling and psychotherapy," in *Counseling the culturally diverse: Theory and practice*, 5th ed., ed. D.W. Sue and D. Sue (Hoboken: Wiley, 2008), 105–30; D.W. Sue et al., "Racial microaggressions in everyday life: Implications for clinical practice," *American Psychologist* 62 (2007): 271–86.

66 Nadal, *Microaggressions and Traumatic Stress*, 11.

67 Derald Sue, "Racial Microaggressions in Everyday Life."

68 See R.T. Carter, "Racism and Psychological and Emotional Injury: Recognizing and Assessing Race-Based Traumatic Stress," *The Counselling Psychologist* 35 (2007): 13–105.

69 Derald Sue, "Racial Microaggressions in Everyday Life."

70 Derald Sue, *Microaggressions in Everyday Life*, 125.

71 Derald Sue, "Racial Microaggressions in Everyday Life."

72 Ibid.

73 Lonergan, *Method in Theology*, 52.

74 See M. Sullaway and E. Dunbar, "Clinical Manifestations of Prejudice in Psychotherapy: Toward a Strategy of Assessment and Treatment," *Clinical Psychology: Science and Practice* 3 (1996): 296–309.

75 Sue, *Microaggressions in Everyday Life*, 238.

76 Stephanie Howard, "The Black Perspective in Clinical Social Work," *Clinical Social Work Journal* 48 (2020): 335–42, at 339.

77 Limbong, "Microaggressions Are a Big Deal." See Andrew Limbong, "Microaggressions Are a Big Deal: How to Talk Them Out and When to Walk Away" (9 June 2020), https://www.npr.org/2020/06/08/872371063/microaggressions-are-a-big-deal-how-to-talk-them-out-and-when-to-walk-away (accessed 10 October 2020).

78 Nadal, *Microaggressions and Traumatic Stress*, 4.

79 DiAngelo, "White Fragility," 56.

80 Ibid.

81 See D. Solorzano, M. Ceja, and T. Yosso, "Critical Race Theory, Racial Microaggressions, and Campus Racial Climate: The Experiences of African American College Students," *The Journal of Negro Education* 69 (2000): 60–73, and D. Solorzano and T. Yosso, "Conceptualizing a Critical Race Theory in Sociology," *The Blackwell Companion to Social Inequalities* (2005): 117–46.

82 Richard Delgado and Jean Stefancic, *Critical Race Theory: An Introduction* (New York: New York University Press, 2001), 2.

83 Ibid.

84 Kimber Shelton and Edward A. Delgado-Romero, "Sexual Orientation Microaggressions: The Experience of Lesbian, Gay, Bisexual, and Queer Clients in Psychotherapy," *Journal of Counseling Psychology* 58 (2011): 210–21, at 211.

85 Jim Wallis, *The Call to Conversion: Why Faith Is Always Personal But Never Private* (San Francisco: Harper and Row, 1981), 88.

86 Ibid., 106.

87 Limbong, "Microaggressions Are a Big Deal."

88 DiAngelo, "White Fragility," 55.

89 See PRRI 2018 Survey, https://www.prri.org/research/partisan-polarization-dominates-trump-era-findings-from-the-2018-american-values-survey/ (accessed 23 September 2020).

90 See Robert P. Jones, "Racism Among White Christians is Higher than Among the Non-Religious. That's No Coincidence," *Think*, https://www.nbcnews.com/think/opinion/racism-among-white-christians-higher-among-nonreligious-s-no-coincidence-ncna1235045 (accessed 23 September 2020).

91 Ibid.

92 Lonergan, "The Absence of God in Modern Culture," 98.

93 Derald Wing Sue et al., "Disarming Racial Microaggressions: Microintervention Strategies for Targets, White Allies, and Bystanders," *American Psychologist* 74 (2019): 128–42.

94 See Derald Wing Sue et al., *Microintervention Strategies: What You Can Do to Disarm and Dismantle Individual and Systemic Racism and Bias* (New York: Wiley, 2020), 169–90.

95 Ibid., 185.

96 Doran, *Theology and the Dialectics of History*, 181.

97 For more on microaggression, see Kevin L. Nadal, *Queering Law and Order: LGBTQ Communities and the Criminal Justice System* (Lanham: Lexington Books, 2020) and *That's So Gay! Microaggressions and the Lesbian, Gay, Bisexual, and Transgender Community* (Philadelphia: American Psychological Association, 2013); Gina C. Torino et al., *Microaggression Theory: Influence and Implications* (Hoboken: John Wiley and Sons, 2019); Paula Lundberg-Love, Kevil L. Nadal, and Michele Paludi, *Women and Mental Disorders* (Westport: Praeger Publishing, 2011).

98 Doran, *Theology and the Dialectics of History*, 182.
99 Lonergan, *Method in Theology*, 381.
100 Ibid., 36.
101 Delgado and Stefancic, *Critical Race Theory*, 2.
102 Ibid.
103 Kendall, *Understanding White Privilege*, 83.
104 Osta and Vasquez, "Don't Talk about Implicit Bias Without Talking about Structural Racism."
105 Robert T. Carter and Thomas D. Scheuermann, *Confronting Racism: Integrating Mental Health Research into Legal Strategies and Reforms* (New York: Routledge, 2020), 26.
106 Ibid., 22.
107 Ibid., 31.
108 Ibid.
109 Kendall, *Understanding White Privilege*, 84.
110 Ibid.
111 See P.L. Thomas, "Introduction," in *James Baldwin: Challenging Authors*, ed. A. Scott Henderson and P.L. Thomas (Boston: Sense Publishers, 2014), 1–7, at 1.
112 Ibid.
113 Rainier Harris, "This is the Casual Racism That I Face at My Elite High School," *The New York Times* (24 September 2020), https://www.nytimes.com/2020/09/24/nyregion/regis-catholic-school-racism.html?smid=em-share (accessed 7 October 2020).
114 DiAngelo, "White Fragility," 65.
115 See Charles M. Blow, "Call A Thing A Thing," *The New York Times* (9 July 2020), https://www.baltimoresun.com/featured/sns-nyt-op-call-a-thing-a-thing-20200709-ujpppesbujd75lo7xxt5qjv5si-story.html (accessed 12 October 2020).
116 DiAngelo, "White Fragility," 61.
117 Kinder and Ryan, "Prejudice and Politics Re-Examined," 256.
118 Kendall, *Understanding White Privilege*, 82.
119 DiAngelo, "White Fragility," 61.
120 Kendall, *Understanding White Privilege*, 82.
121 Ibid., 84.
122 Ibid., 82.
123 Ibid., 83.
124 See Frances V. Reins, "Is the Benign Really Harmless?: Deconstructing Some 'Benign' Manifestations of Operationalized White Privilege," in *White Reign*, 77–102.
125 Carter and Scheuermann, *Confronting Racism*, 30.
126 See Janice G. Asare, "Your Unconscious Bias Trainings Keep Failing Because You're Not Addressing Systemic Bias" (29 December 2019),

https://www.forbes.com/sites/janicegassam/2020/12/29/your-unconscious-bias-trainings-keep-failing-because-youre-not-addressing-systemic-bias/?utm_source=FACEBOOK&utm_medium=social&utm_term=Valerie%2F#35cf6b4c1e9d (accessed 12 October 2020).

127 Nadal, *Microaggression and Traumatic Stress*, 8.

128 Ibid.

129 Bernard Lonergan, *Collected Works of Bernard Lonergan*, vol. 3, *Insight: A Study of Human Understanding*, ed. Frederick E. Crowe and Robert M. Doran (Toronto: University of Toronto Press, 1997), 250.

130 DiAngelo, "White Fragility," 61.

131 Ibid., 58.

132 Kendall, *Understanding White Privilege*, 80.

133 DiAngelo, "White Fragility," 61.

134 Lonergan, *Method in Theology*, 53.

135 See Jone E. Urrestarazu, "The Other Pandemic: Systemic Racism and Its Consequences," *European Network of Quality Bodies* (8 June 2020), https://equineteurope.org/2020/the-other-pandemic-systemic-racism-and-its-consequences/ (accessed 13 October 2020).

136 Lonergan, *Method in Theology*, 53.

137 Lonergan, *Insight*, 224.

138 Jim Wallis, "America's Original Sin: The Legacy of White Racism," *Cross Currents* 57 (200): 197–202, at 198.

139 Ibid., 199.

140 DiAngelo, "White Fragility," 58.

141 Carter and Scheuermann, *Confronting Racism*, 11.

142 See Pope Francis, Apostolic Exhortation, *Evangelii Gaudium* (24 Nov. 2013), 59, http://w2.vatican.va/content/francesco/en/apost_exhortations/documents/papa-francesco_esortazione-ap_20131124_evangelii-gaudium.html (accessed 13 October 2020).

143 Ibid.

144 Lonergan, *Insight*, 254.

145 Lonergan, *Method in Theology*, 53.

146 Kirwan Institute for the Study of Race and Ethnicity, "Understanding Implicit Bias," http://kirwaninstitute.osu.edu/research/understanding-implicit-bias/ (accessed 26 September 2020).

147 Ibid.

148 Ibid.

149 Lonergan, *Method in Theology*, 52.

150 Lonergan, *Insight*, 250.

151 Charles Curran, "White Privilege," *Horizons* 32 (2005): 361–7, at 363.

152 James H. Cone, *A Black Theology of Liberation*, Twentieth Anniversary Edition (Maryknoll: Orbis Books, 2006), 18.
153 Ibid.
154 M. Shawn Copeland, "Anti-Blackness and White Supremacy in the Making of American Catholicism," *American Catholic Studies* 5 (2016): 6–8, at 7.
155 Ibid.
156 Ibid.
157 Ibid., 8.
158 Lonergan, "The Absence of God in Modern Culture," 97.
159 DiAngelo, "White Fragility," 56.
160 Ibid., 64.
161 Ibid., 56.
162 Ibid., 66.
163 Ibid., 56.
164 Ibid., 54.
165 Ibid., 66.
166 Lonergan, *Insight*, 246.
167 Kinder and Ryan, "Prejudice and Politics Re-Examined," 257.
168 Fromm, *To Have or to Be*? x.
169 Lonergan, "The Absence of God in Modern Culture," 98.
170 Lonergan, *Method in Theology*, 381.
171 Lonergan, "Theology and Man's Future," 124.
172 Ibid., 125.
173 Ibid.
174 Fromm, *To Have or to Be*? x.

6 Overcoming Racism and Conversion

1 Erich Fromm, *To Have or to Be?* (New York: Continuum, 2008), xi.
2 Bernard Lonergan, *Collected Works of Bernard Lonergan*, vol. 14, *Method in Theology*, ed. Robert M. Doran and John D. Dadosky (Toronto: University of Toronto Press, 2017), 257.
3 Ibid.
4 Richard Rothstein, *The Color of Law: A Forgotten History of How Our Government Segregated America* (New York: Liveright Publishing, 2017), xvii.
5 Robert T. Carter and Thomas D. Scheuermann, *Confronting Racism: Integrating Mental Health Research into Legal Strategies and Reforms* (New York: Routledge, 2020), 2.
6 S.E. Taylor, *Health Psychology* 9th ed. (Boston, MA: McGraw Hill, 2015), 113.

7 See Lonergan's distinction between common-sense knowledge and scientific knowledge. Bernard Lonergan, "Belief: Today's Issue," in *Collected Works of Bernard Lonergan*, vol. 13, *A Second Collection*, ed. Robert M. Doran and John D. Dadosky (Toronto: University of Toronto Press, 2016), 75–85, at 76.

8 Lonergan, *Method in Theology*, 259.

9 Carter and Scheuermann, *Confronting Racism*, 41.

10 See Charles M. Blow, "Call A Thing A Thing," *The New York Times* (9 July 2020), https://www.baltimoresun.com/featured/sns-nyt-op-call-a-thing-a-thing-20200709-ujpppesbujd75lo7xxt5qjv5si-story.html (accessed 12 October 2020).

11 Ibid.

12 M. Shawn Copeland, "Breadth and Fire: The Spirit Moves Us Toward Racial Justice," *Commonweal* (July 2020): 16–19, at 18.

13 Carter and Scheuermann, *Confronting Racism*, 100.

14 Kevin L. Nadal, *Microaggressions and Traumatic Stress* (Philadelphia: American Philosophical Association, 2018), 13.

15 Ibid., ix.

16 Bernard Lonergan, *Collected Works of Bernard Lonergan*, vol.10, *Topics in Education: The Cincinnati Lectures of 1959 on the Philosophy of Education*, ed. Robert M. Doran and Frederick E. Crowe (Toronto: University of Toronto Press, 2000), 170.

17 Ibid.

18 Ibid.

19 Bernard Lonergan, "Unity and Plurality: The Coherence of Christian Truth," in *A Third Collection: Papers by Bernard J.F. Lonergan, S.J.*, ed. Frederick E. Crowe, SJ (New York: Paulist Press, 1985), 239–50, at 247.

20 Ibid.

21 See F. Laubach, J. Goetzmann, and U. Becker, "Conversion, Penitence, Repentance, Proselyte," in *The New International Dictionary of New Testament Theology*, vol. 1, ed. C. Brown (Exeter: Paternoster, 1975) 353–62.

22 R.T. France, "Conversion in the Bible," *Evangelical Quarterly* 65 (1993): 291–310, at 293.

23 Ibid., 294.

24 Ibid., 295. See also George Bertram, "Strepho" in *The Theological Dictionary of the New Testament*, ed. Gerhard Friedrich, trans. and ed. Geoffrey W. Bromiley, 10 vols. (Grand Rapids: Eerdmans, 1964–76); see vol. 7: 714–29.

25 See Gabriel Fackre, *Word in Deed: Theological Themes in Evangelism* (Grand Rapids: Eerdmans, 1975), 84–94.

26 Ibid., 85.

27 See John Wesley, *The New Birth John Wesley Sermons* [The Bicentennial Edition] vols. 1–4, ed. Albert C. Outler (Nashville: Abingdon Press, 1984), see particularly vol.2, p. 187.

28 See The Heidelberg Catechism, https://www.crcna.org/welcome/beliefs/confessions/heidelberg-catechism (accessed 6 October 2021). See also http://www.heidelberg-catechism.com/en/topics/conversion.html (accessed 6 October 2021).

29 See Steven Lawson, "What Is True Conversion?" https://www.ligonier.org/learn/articles/what-true-conversion (accessed 6 October 2021).

30 Jim Wallis, *The Call to Conversion: Why Faith Is Always Personal But Never Private* (San Francisco: Harper and Row, 1981), xviii.

31 Ibid., 22.

32 Ibid., xviii.

33 Ibid., xvii.

34 Bernard Lonergan, *Collected Works of Bernard Lonergan*, vol. 3, *Insight: A Study of Human Understanding*, ed. Frederick E. Crowe and Robert M. Doran (Toronto: University of Toronto Press, 1997), 689.

35 Ibid.

36 Lonergan, *Method in Theology*, 225.

37 Robert M. Doran, *Theology and the Dialectics of History* (Toronto: University of Toronto Press, 1990), 52.

38 John Dadosky has fleshed this out as the fourth stage of meaning. See John D. Dadosky, "Furthering Along the Fourth Stage of Meaning: Lonergan, Alterity, and Genuine Religion," *Irish Theological Quarterly* 85 (2019): 64–79.

39 Lonergan, *Method in Theology*, 251.

40 Ibid., 270.

41 Ibid.

42 Ibid., 391.

43 Lonergan, *Topics in Education*, 66–7.

44 Lonergan, *Method in Theology*, 391.

45 I am indebted to Prof. John Dadosky for pointing me to Michael Stoeber who distinguished destructive suffering from redemptive suffering. Stoeber writes, "So there is a distinction here between (1) destructive suffering, which diminishes and hinders the person in some way or another and for which there is no transformative impetus or response in the person (but there will, we hope, be healing or recovery) and (2) transformative suffering – that which contributes positively to personal growth – what we might call redemptive suffering." See Michael Stoeber, *Reclaiming Theodicy: Reflections on Suffering, Compassion and Spiritual Transformation* (New York: Palgrave McMillan, 2002), 61.

46 See John D. Dadosky, "The Transformation of Suffering in Paul of the Cross, Lonergan and Buddhism," *New Blackfriars* 96 (2015): 542–63, at 549.

47 Lonergan, *Method in Theology*, 221.

48 Ibid., 221–2.

49 Ibid., 222.

50 Ibid., 223.
51 Ibid.
52 Ibid.
53 Ibid.
54 Ibid.
55 Ibid., 51.
56 Ibid., 126.
57 Ibid.
58 Ibid., 252.
59 Ibid., 126.
60 Robin DiAngelo, "White Fragility," *International Journal of Critical Pedagogy* 3 (2011): 54–70, at 66–7.
61 Lonergan, *Method in Theology*, 252.
62 France, "Conversion in the Bible," 292.
63 See Gerald Manley Hopkins, "As Kingfishers Catch Fire," https://www.poetryfoundation.org/poems/44389/as-kingfishers-catch-fire (accessed 6 October 2021).
64 Lonergan, *Method in Theology*, 251.
65 Ibid., 226.
66 Ibid., 228.
67 Ibid.
68 Ibid., 126.
69 Richard M. Liddy, *Startling Strangeness: Reading Lonergan's Insight* (Lanham: University Press of America, 2007), 212, referencing Peter Berger, *The Social Construction of Reality* (New York: Doubleday, 1966), 158.
70 Berger, *The Social Construction of Reality*, 158.
71 Ibid.
72 Lonergan, *Method in Theology*, 228–9.
73 Doran, *Theology and the Dialectics of History*, 59.
74 Wallis, *The Call to Conversion*, xv.
75 Ibid.
76 Ibid.
77 Ibid., 6.
78 Ibid.
79 See Lawrence Kohlberg, *Essays on Moral Development*, vol.1: *The Philosophy of Moral Development: Moral Stages and the Idea of Justice* (San Francisco: Harper and Row, 1981) and Lawrence Kohlberg, "The Claim to Moral Adequacy of a Highest Stage of Moral Judgment," *Journal of Philosophy* 70 (1973): 630–46.
80 See Abraham Maslow, *Towards a Psychology of Being* (Princeton: D. Van Nostrand, 1962).
81 Carter and Scheuermann, *Confronting Racism*, 5.
82 Rothstein, *The Color of Law*, vii.

83 See Amy E. Hillier, "Redlining and the Home Owners' Loan Corporation," *Journal of Urban History* 29 (2003): 394–420.
84 Lonergan, *Insight*, 248.
85 Michelle Alexander, *The New Jim Crow: Mass Incarceration in the Age of Colorblindness*, Tenth Anniversary Edition (New York: The New Press, 2020), xxx.
86 Lonergan, *Insight*, 650.
87 Walter Conn, "Bernard Lonergan's Analysis of Conversion," *Angelicum* 53 (1976): 362–404, at 380.
88 Lonergan, *Method in Theology*, 40.
89 Conn, "Bernard Lonergan's Analysis of Conversion," 374.
90 Lonergan, *Method in Theology*, 225.
91 Ibid., 251.
92 Ibid., 225.
93 Ibid.
94 Wallis, *The Call to Conversion*, 129.
95 Lonergan, *Method in Theology*, 226.
96 See "This is the Casual Racism that I Face at My Elite High School," *New York Times* (24 September 2020), https://www.nytimes.com/2020/09/24/nyregion/regis-catholic-school-racism.html?smid=em-share (accessed 7 October 2020).
97 Conn, "Bernard Lonergan's Analysis of Conversion," 374.
98 Lonergan, *Method in Theology*, 270.
99 Doran, *Theology and the Dialectics of History*, 59.
100 Lonergan, *Method in Theology*, 227.
101 Ibid., 228.
102 Conn, "Bernard Lonergan's Analysis of Conversion," 380.
103 See Nelson Mandela, *The Struggle is My Life* (International Defense and Aid Fund for Southern Africa, 1978), 155–75.
104 See Richard J. Herrnstein and Charles Murray, *The Bell Curve* (New York: Free Press, 1996).
105 See Jim Naureckas, "Racism Resurgent: How Media Let the Bell Curve's Pseudo-Science Define the Agenda on Race," *Fairness and Accuracy in Reporting* (1 January 1995).
106 See Eric Siegel, "The Real Problem with Charles Murray and the Bell Curve," *Scientific American* (12 April 2017), https://blogs.scientificamerican.com/voices/the-real-problem-with-charles-murray-and-the-bell-curve/ (accessed 7 December 2020).
107 Glaude, *Begin Again*, 5.
108 Ibid., 7.
109 Lonergan, *Method in Theology*, 223.
110 Ibid., 270.

111 Ibid., 224.
112 Ibid.
113 Richard Rothstein has not only debunked the myth that the presence of African Americans causes property value to fall, he also provides good statistical evidence to show how racial integration causes property value to increase. See Rothstein, *The Color of Law*, 94–9.
114 See Institute for Healthcare Improvement Multimedia Team, "How to Reduce Implicit Bias," http://www.ihi.org/communities/blogs/how-to-reduce-implicit-bias (accessed 24 November 2020).
115 Doran, *Theology and the Dialectics of History*, 59.
116 Lonergan, *Method in Theology*, 251.
117 Doran, *Theology and the Dialectics of History*, 9.
118 Lonergan, *Method in Theology*, 118.
119 Ibid., 40.
120 Ibid., 270.
121 Carter and Scheuermann, *Confronting Racism*, 7.
122 Doran, *Theology and the Dialectics of History*, 51.
123 Lonergan, *Method in Theology*, 40.
124 Ibid., 52.
125 Ibid., 54.
126 See David S. Crystal, Melanie Killen, and Martin Ruck, "It is Who You Know that Counts: Intergroup Contacts and Judgments about Race-Based Exclusion," *British Journal of Development Psychology* 26 (2008): 51–70.
127 Ibid., 66.
128 Dietrich Bonhoeffer, *The Cost of Discipleship* (New York: McMillan, 1937), 47.
129 Lonergan, *Topics in Education*, 67.
130 Ibid., 67–8.
131 Ibid., 68.
132 Donald Shriver, *An Ethic for Enemies: Forgiveness in Politics* (New York: Oxford University Press, 1995), 213–14.
133 Ibid., 128.
134 See Donald Shriver, *Honest Patriots: Loving a Country Enough to Remember Its Misdeeds* (New York: Oxford, 2005).
135 Robert T. Carter, "Racism and Psychological and Emotional Injury: Recognizing and Assessing Race-Based Traumatic Stress," *The Counselling Psychologist* 35 (2007): 13–105, at 14.
136 Carter and Scheuermann, *Confronting Racism*, 10.
137 Nadal, *Microaggression and Traumatic Stress*, 13.
138 Ibid.
139 Ibid., 14.
140 Ibid.

141 Ibid.
142 Carter and Scheuermann, *Confronting Racism*, 96.
143 Lonergan, *Method in Theology*, 126.
144 Doran, *Theology and the Dialectics of History*, 59.
145 Ibid.
146 Ibid., 43.
147 Ibid., 42.
148 Ibid.
149 Ibid., 45.
150 Ibid., 44.
151 Lonergan, *Method in Theology*, 33.
152 Ibid.
153 Ibid.
154 Ibid., 55.
155 Ibid., 34.
156 Doran, *Theology and the Dialectics of History*, 56.
157 Ibid., 59.
158 Ibid.
159 Ibid.
160 Ibid., 62.
161 John Calvin, *Institutes of the Christian Religion*, vol. 20, ed. J.T. McNeill, The Library of Christian Classics, vol. XX (Philadelphia: Westminster, 1960), 8.
162 Karl Barth, *Church Dogmatics* IV, trans. and ed. G.W. Bromiley (Edinburgh: T&T Clark, 1958), 584.
163 See James Baldwin, *Notes of a Native Son* (Boston: Beacon Press, 1955).
164 See Ralph Ellison, *Invisible Man* (New York: Random House, 1952).
165 Ralph Ellison and Richard Kostelanetz, "An Interview with Ralph Ellison," *The Iowa Review* 9 (1989): 1–10, at 9.
166 Shriver, *An Ethic for Enemies*, 7.
167 Jennifer L. Eberhardt, *Biased: Uncovering the Hidden Prejudice That Shapes What We See, Think, and Do* (New York: Viking, 2019), 152.
168 Ibid., 185.
169 Lonergan, *Method in Theology*, 254.
170 Conn, "Bernard Lonergan's Analysis of Conversion," 393.
171 Lonergan, *Method in Theology*, 227.
172 Ibid.
173 See Fromm, *To Have or to Be?* x.

Bibliography

Alexander, Michelle. *The New Jim Crow: Mass Incarceration in the Age of Colorblindness*, Tenth Anniversary Edition. New York: The New Press, 2020.

Alexandra, Rae. "BLM Allies: It's Time to Take This Harvard Test About Subconscious Bias." *KQED* (9 June 2020). https://www.kqed.org/arts/13881489/blm-allies-its-time-to-take-this-harvard-test-about-subconscious-bias (accessed 12 October 2020).

Ali, Lorraine. "Commentary: 'Karen' Is an Easy Target. The Truth About White Nationalism Is Much Worse." *Los Angeles Times* (9 July 2020). https://www.latimes.com/entertainment-arts/tv/story/2020-07-09/the-karen-video-what-it-means-commentary (accessed 31 August 2020).

Allen, Matthew. "SoHo Karen Has History of Unruly Behavior, Run-Ins with Police." Yahoo News (3 January 2021). https://www.yahoo.com/news/soho-karen-history-unruly-behavior-151538651.html (accessed 4 January 2021).

Allport, Gordon. "Attitudes." In *A Handbook of Social Psychology*, edited by C. Murchison, 798–844. Worcester, MA: Clark University Press, 1935.

– *The Nature of Prejudice*. New York: Addison-Wesley, 1954.

Ames, Daniel L, Susan T. Fiske, and Alexander T. Todorov. "Impression Formation: A Focus On Other's Intent." In *The Oxford Handbook of Social Neuroscience*, edited by Jean Decety and John T. Cacioppo. https://www.oxfordhandbooks.com/view/10.1093/oxfordhb/9780195342161.001.0001/oxfordhb-9780195342161.

Anderson, Carol. *White Rage: The Unspoken Truth of Our Racial Divide*. New York: Bloomsbury, 2017.

Anderson, R. Lanier. "Truth and Objectivity in Perspectivism." *Synthese* 115 (1998): 1–32.

Antonio, Edward. "Black Theology as Critical Theology." *Journal of Theology for Southern Africa* 1162 (2019): 101–14.

Apple, Michael W. "Foreword." In *White Reign: Deploying Whiteness in America*, edited by Joe L. Kincheloe and Shirley R. Steinberg, ix–xiii. New York: Palgrave, 2000.

Arnold, Rose. *The Negro in America*. New York: Harper and Row, 1964.

Asare, Janice G. "Your Unconscious Bias Trainings Keep Failing Because You're Not Addressing Systemic Bias." (29 December 2019). https://www.forbes.com/sites/janicegassam/2020/12/29/ your-unconscious-bias-trainings-keep-failing-because-youre-not-addressing-systemic-bias/?utm_source=FACEBOOK& utm_medium=social&utm_term=Valerie%2F#35cf6b4c1e9d (accessed 12 October 2020).

Baldwin, James. *Go Tell It on the Mountain*. New York: Alfred A. Knopf, 1953.

– "Letter from a Region in My Mind." In *The 60s: The Story of a Decade*, edited by Henry Finder, 22–32. New York: Random House, 2016.

– *No Name in The Street*. New York: Dial Publishing, 1972.

– *Notes of a Native Son*. Boston: Beacon Press, 1955.

Banaji, Mahzarin. R. "Implicit Attitudes Can Be Measured." In *The Nature of Remembering: Essays in Honor of Robert G. Crowder*, edited by H.L. Roedinger III et al., 117–50. Washington: American Psychological Association, 2001.

Banaji, Mahzarin R., and Anthony G. Greenwald. *Blindspot: The Hidden Biases of Good People*. New York: Bantam Books, 2016.

– "Implicit Gender Stereotyping in Judgments of Fame." *Journal of Personality and Social Psychology* 68 (1995): 181–98.

Banaji, Mahzarin R., C. Hardin, and A.J. Rothman. "Implicit Stereotyping in Person Judgment." *Journal of Personality and Social Psychology* 65 (1993): 272–81.

Barbieri, Richard. "It's Complicated." *Independent School* (Summer 2014): 96–101.

Barth, Karl. "The Awakening to Conversion." In *Church Dogmatics*, translated by G.W. Bromiley. Edinburgh: T&T Clark, 1958.

– *Church Dogmatics* IV, edited and translated by G.W. Bromiley. Edinburgh: T&T Clark, 1958.

Berger, Peter. *The Social Construction of Reality*. New York: Doubleday, 1966.

Bertocci, Peter A. "Gordon A. Allport's *The Nature of Prejudice* and the Problem of Choice." *Pastoral Psychology* 5 (1954): 31–7.

Betts, Raymond F. *Assimilation and Association in French Colonial Theory, 1890–1914*. Lincoln: University of Nebraska Press, 2005.

Beyt, Adam. "Fruitful Bodies: Farely, Copeland, and Baldwin on Sacred Flesh." *Theology and Sexuality* 25 (2019): 45–61.

Bhopal, Kalwant. *White Privilege: The Myth of a Post-Racial Society*. Bristol: Policy Press, 2018.

Black Manifesto. https://episcopalarchives.org/church-awakens/files/original/c20bd83547dd3cf92e788041d7fddfa2.pdf (accessed 8 September 2020).

Black Power. "Position Statement in Support of Black Power." *New York Times* (07/31/1966). https://episcopalarchives.org/church-awakens/items/show/183 (accessed 8 September 2020).

Blakemore, M.T. *White Privilege*. Minneapolis: Abdo Publishing, 2018.

Blenkinsop, Sean, et al. "Shut Up and Listen: Implications and Possibilities of Albert Memmi's Characteristics of Colonization Upon the 'Natural World.'" *Studies in Philosophy and Education* 36 (2017): 349–65.

Blow, Charles M. "Call A Thing A Thing." *The New York Times* (9 July 2020). https://www.baltimoresun.com/featured/sns-nyt-op-call-a-thing-a-thing-20200709-ujpppesbujd75lo7xxt5qjv5si-story.html (accessed 12 October 2020).

– "White Male Victimization Anxiety." *The New York Times* (10 October 2018). https://www.nytimes.com/2018/10/10/opinion/trump-white-male-victimization.html (accessed 12 October 2020).

Bonhoeffer, Dietrich. *The Cost of Discipleship*. New York: McMillan, 1937.

Bonilla-Silva, Eduardo. *Racism without Racists: Color-blind Racism and Persistence of Racial Inequality in the United States*, 4th ed. Lanham: Rowman and Littlefield, 2013.

Bradley, Anthony B. Review of *Heart and Head: Black Theology – Past, Present, and Future*, by Dwight N. Hopkins. *Presbyterion* 30 (2004): 119–21.

Brauer, Markus, Wolfgang Wasel, and Paula Niedenthal. "Implicit and Explicit components of Prejudice." *Review of General Psychology* 4 (2000): 79–101.

Bridges, Khiara M. "Race, Pregnancy, and the Opioid Epidemic: White Privilege and the Criminalization of Opioid Use During Pregnancy." *Harvard Law Review* 133 (2020): 770–851.

Buenavista, Tracy L., Uma M. Jayakumar, and Kimberly Misa-Escalante. "Contextualizing Asian American Education Through Critical Race Theory: An Example of U.S. Pilipino College Student Experiences." *New Directions for Institutional Research* 142 (Summer 2009): 69–81.

Byrne, Patrick. *The Ethics of Discernment: Lonergan's Foundations for Ethics*. Toronto: University of Toronto Press, 2016.

– "The Fabric of Lonergan's Thought." *Lonergan Workshop* 6 (1986): 1–84.

Calvin, John. *Institutes of the Christian Religion*, vol. 20, edited by J.T. McNeill. The Library of Christian Classics. Philadelphia: Westminster, 1960.

Campbell, John C. Review of George Weigel's *Tranquillitas Ordinis: The Present Failure and Future Promise of American Catholic Thought on War and Peace*. https://www.foreignaffairs.com/reviews/capsule-review/1987-06-01/tranquillitas-ordinis-present-failure-and-future-promise-american (accessed 7 October 2020).

Cannon, Katie G. *Black Womanist Ethics*. Atlanta: Scholars Press, 1988.

– *Katie's Canon: Womanism and the Soul of the Black Community*. New York: Continuum, 1995.

Carter, Robert T. "Racism and Psychological and Emotional Injury: Recognizing and Assessing Race-Based Traumatic Stress. *The Counselling Psychologist* 35 (2007): 13–105.

Carter, Robert T., and Thomas D. Scheuermann. *Confronting Racism: Integrating Mental Health Research into Legal Strategies and Reforms*. New York: Routledge, 2020.

Cassidy, Laurie M., and Alex Mikulich, eds. *Interrupting White Privilege: Catholic Theologians Break the Silence*. Maryknoll: Orbis, 2007.

Chennault, Ronald E. "Giving Whiteness a Black Eye: An Interview with Michael Eric Dyson." In *White Reign: Deploying Whiteness in America*, edited by Joe L. Kincheloe and Shirley R. Steinberg, 299–328. New York: Palgrave, 2000.

CNN. "Rep. Wilson Shouts, 'You Lie' To Obama During Speech." 9 September 2009. https://www.cnn.com/2009/POLITICS/09/09/joe.wilson/ (accessed 5 December 2020).

Coates, Ta-Nehisi. *Between the World and Me*. New York: Spiegel and Grau, 2015.

Cognitive Bias Codex, The. https://www.teachthought.com/critical-thinking/the-cognitive-bias-codex-a-visual-of-180-cognitive-biases/ (accessed 30 September 2021).

Cone, James H. "Black Liberation Theology and Black Catholics: A Critical Conversation." *Theological Studies* 63 (2000): 731–48.

– *Black Theology and Black Power*. Maryknoll: Orbis, 1969.

– *A Black Theology of Liberation*, Twentieth Anniversary Edition. Maryknoll: Orbis Books, 2006.

– *The Cross and the Lynching Tree*. Maryknoll: Orbis Books, 2011.

– *For My People: Black Theology and Black Church*. Maryknoll: Orbis Books, 1984.

– Interview for PBS series, "This Far by Faith" (2003). https://www.pbs.org/thisfarbyfaith/people/james_cone.html.

– *Malcolm and Martin and America: A Dream or a Nightmare*. Maryknoll: Orbis Books, 1991.

– *My Soul Looks Back*. Maryknoll: Orbis Books, 1982.

– *Said I Wasn't Gonna Tell Nobody: The Making of a Black Theologian*. Maryknoll: Orbis Books, 2018.

Conn, Walter. "Bernard Lonergan's Analysis of Conversion." *Angelicum* 53 (1976): 362–404.

Copeland, Shawn M. "Anti-Blackness and White Supremacy in the Making of American Catholicism." *American Catholic Studies* 5 (2016): 6–8.

– "Breadth and Fire: The Spirit Moves Us Toward Racial Justice." *Commonweal* (July 2020): 16–19.

– *Enfleshing Freedom: Body, Race, and Being*. Minneapolis: Fortress Press, 2010.

– "Racism and the Vocation of the Christian Theologian." *Spiritus* 2 (2002): 15–29.

– *The Subversive Power of Love: The Vision of Henriette Delille*. New York: Paulist Press, 2009.

– "Theology as Intellectually Vital Inquiry: A Black Theological Interrogation." *CTSA Proceedings* 46 (1991): 49–57.

Crenshaw, K.W., et al., eds. *Critical Race theory: The key writings that formed the movement*. New York: New Press, 1995.

Crowe, Frederick E. *Appropriating the Lonergan Idea*, edited by Michael Vertin. Toronto: University of Toronto Press, 2006.

Crystal, David S., Melanie Killen, and Martin Ruck. "It is Who You Know that Counts: Intergroup Contacts and Judgments about Race-Based Exclusion." *British Journal of Development Psychology* 26 (2008): 51–70.

Curran, Charles. "White Privilege." *Horizons* 32 (2005): 361–7.

– "White Privilege: My Theological Journey." In *Interrupting White Privilege: Catholic Theologians Break the Silence*, edited by Laurie M. Cassidy and Alexander Mikulich, 77–84. Maryknoll: Orbis Books, 2007.

Dadosky, John D. "Furthering Along the Fourth Stage of Meaning: Lonergan, Alterity, and Genuine Religion." *Irish Theological Quarterly* 85 (2019): 64–79.

– "Is There a Fourth Stage of Meaning?" *Heythrop* 51 (2010): 768–80.

– "Lonergan, Bias, and Love: Revisiting Lonergan's Philosophical Anthropology." *Irish Theological Quarterly* 77 (2012): 244–64.

– "The Transformation of Suffering in Paul of the Cross, Lonergan and Buddhism." *New Blackfriars* 96 (2015): 542–63.

Dalton, Harlon. "Failing to See." In *White Privilege: Essential Readings on the Other Side of Racism*, edited by Paula S. Rothenberg, 15–18. New York: Worth Publishers, 2016.

Davis, Cyprian. *The History of Black Catholics in the United States*. New York: Crossroad, 1990.

Davis, Daryl. TED Talk. https://www.ted.com/talks/daryl_davis_why_i_as_a_black_man_attend_kkk_rallies?language=en (accessed 4 January 2021).

Dayson, Sion. "Another Country." In *James Baldwin: Challenging Authors*, edited by A. Scott Henderson and P.L. Thomas, 77–89. Boston: Sense Publishers, 2014.

Delgado, Bernal D. "Critical Race Theory, Latino Critical Theory, and Critical Raced-Gendered Epistemologies: Recognizing Students of Color as Holders and Creators of Knowledge." *Qualitative Inquiry* 8 (2002): 105–26.

– "Using a Chicana feminist epistemology in educational research." *Harvard Educational Review* 68 (1988): 555–82.

Delgado, Richard, and Jean Stefancic. *Critical Race Theory: An Introduction*. New York: New York University Press, 2001.

DiAngelo, Robin. "White Fragility." *International Journal of Critical Pedagogy* 3 (2011): 54–70.

– *White Fragility: Why It's So Hard for White People to Talk about Racism*. London: Allen Lane, 2019.

Doran, Robert M. *Theology and the Dialectics of History*. Toronto: University of Toronto Press, 1990.

Douglas, Kelly Brown. *What's Faith Got To Do With It? Black Bodies/Christian Souls*. Maryknoll: Orbis Books, 2005.

Douglass, Fredrick. *My Bondage and My Freedom*. New York: Dover Publications, 1969. http://www.gutenberg.org/files/202/202-h/202-h.htm (accessed 30 December 2020).

Dovidio, J.F., and S.I. Gaertner. "Affirmative Action, Unintentional Biases, and Intergroup Relations." *Journal of Social Issues* 52 (1996): 51–75.

– "Aversive Racism and Selective Decisions 1989–1999." *Psychological Science* 11 (2000): 315–19.

Dubois, W.E.B. "Address to the Nations of the World." In *W.E.B. DuBois Speaks: Speeches and Addresses 1890–1919*, edited by Phillip Foner, 123–7. New York: Pathfinder Press, 1970.

– *Black Reconstruction*. New York: Harcourt Press, 1935.

– "The Souls of White Folk." In *Darkwater: Voices from Within the Veil*. New York: Harcourt Brace, 1920. https://www.gutenberg.org/files/15210/15210-h/ 15210-h.htm (accessed 5 September 2020).

Dunn, Tad. "Bernard Lonergan (1904–1984)." In *Internet Encyclopedia of Philosophy*. https://iep.utm.edu/lonergan/ (accessed 8 October 2020).

Durber, Susan. "White Daughter of Empire: A Pilgrim of Justice and Peace Owning White Privilege." *Ecumenical Review* 72 (2020): 87–97.

Dyer, Richard. "The Matter of Whiteness." In *White Privilege: Essential Readings on the Other Side of Racism*, edited by Paula S. Rothenberg, 9–13. New York: Worth Publishers, 2016.

Eberhardt, Jennifer L. *Biased: Uncovering the Hidden Prejudice That Shapes What We See, Think, and Do*. New York: Viking, 2019; Penguin [e-book version], 2019.

Ellingsen, Mark. *Blessed Are the Cynical: How Original Sin Can Make America a Better Place*. Grand Rapids: Brazos Press, 2003.

Ellison, Ralph. *Invisible Man*. New York: Random House, 1952.

Ellison, Ralph, and Richard Kostelanetz. "An Interview with Ralph Ellison." *The Iowa Review* 9 (1989): 1–10.

Equality and Human Rights Commission Report. "Is England Fairer? The State of Equality and Human Rights 2016." https://www.equalityhumanrights.com/sites/default/files/is-england-fairer-2016.pdf (accessed 2 September 2020).

Erskine, Noel L. *Decolonizing Theology: A Caribbean Perspective*. Maryknoll: Orbis, 1979.

Eugene IV (Pope). *Sicut Dudum*. https://www.papalencyclicals.net/eugene04/eugene04sicut.htm (accessed 8 October 2020).

Fackre, Gabriel. *Word in Deed: Theological Themes in Evangelism*. Grand Rapids: Eerdmans, 1975.

Fanon, Frantz. *Toward the African Revolution: Political Essays*. New York: Grove Press, 1967.

Fazio, Russell H., and Michael A. Olson. "Implicit Measures in Social Cognition Research: Their Meaning and Use." *Annual Review of Psychology* 54 (2003): 297–327.

Fields, Karen E., and Barbara J. Fields. *RaceCraft: The Soul of Inequality in American Life*. New York: Verso, 2012.

Fowler, Teresa A. "How 'Studying Up' Reveals the Tensions in Accessing Whiteness in Educational Research." *Taboo* (2020): 22–37.

France, R.T. "Conversion in the Bible." *Evangelical Quarterly* 65 (1993): 291–310.

Francis (Pope). Apostolic Exhortation, *Evangelii Gaudium* (24 Nov. 2013). http://w2.vatican.va/content/francesco/en/apost_exhortations/documents/papa-francesco_esortazione-ap_20131124_evangelii-gaudium.html (accessed 13 October 2020).

– *Christus Vivit*. http://www.vatican.va/content/francesco/en/apost_exhortations/documents/papa-francesco_esortazione-ap_20190325_christus-vivit.html (accessed 17 January 2021).

Frankenberg, Ruth. *White Women, Race Matters: The Social Construction of Whiteness*. Minneapolis: University of Minnesota Press, 1993.

Fromm, Erich. *To Have or to Be?* New York: Continuum, 2008.

Gadamer, Hans-Georg. *Truth and Method*, Second Revised Edition. New York: Continuum, 1994.

Gallagher, Charles. "Color-blind Privilege: The Social and Political Functions of Erasing the Color Line in Post-Race America." *Race, Gender and Class* 104 (2003): 1–17.

Glaude, Eddie S., Jr. *Begin Again: James Baldwin's America and Its Urgent Lessons for Our Own*. New York: Crown, 2020.

Goatley, David E., ed. *Black Religion, Black Theology: The Collected Essays of J. Deotis Roberts*. Harrisburg: Trinity Press, 2003.

Gonlin, Vanessa, and Mary E. Campbell. "Is Blindness Contagious? Examining Racial Attitudes among People of Color with Close Interracial Relationships." *Sociological Perspectives* 60 (2017)" 937–55.

Gordon, J. "White on White: Researcher Reflexivity and the Logics of Privilege in White Schools Undertaking Reform." *Urban Review* 37 (2005): 279–302.

Greenspan, Rachel E. "How the Name 'Karen" became a Stand-In for Problematic White Women and a Hugely Popular Meme." *Insider* (26 June 2020). https://www.insider.com/karen-meme-origin-the-history-of-calling-women-karen-white-2020-5 (accessed 31 August 2020).

Greenwald, Anthony G., and Mahzarin H. Banaji. "Implicit Social Cognition: Attitudes, Self-Esteem, and Stereotypes." *Psychological Review* 102 (1995): 4–27.

Greenwald, A.G., et al. "Measuring Individual Differences in Implicit Cognition: The Implicit Association Test." *Perspectives in Social Psychology* 74 (1998): 1464–80.

Haight, Roger. "The Dysfunctional Rhetoric of 'White Privilege' and the Need for 'Racial Solidarity'." In *Interrupting White Privilege: Catholic Theologians Break the Silence*, edited by Laurie M. Cassidy and Alexander Mikulich, 85–94. Maryknoll: Orbis Books, 2007.

Hamilton, D.L., and J.W. Sherman. "Stereotypes." In *Handbook of Social Cognition*, 2nd ed., edited by R.S. Wyer Jr. and T.K. Srull, 1–68. Hillsdale: Erbaum, 1994.

Hannah-Jones, Nikole. "It Was Never About Busing: Court-Ordered Desegregation Worked. But White Racism Made It Hard to Accept." *New York Times* (12 July 2019). https://www.nytimes.com/2019/07/12/opinion/sunday/it-was-never-about-busing.html (accessed 11 November 2020).

Harris, Rainier. "This is the Casual Racism That I Face at My Elite High School." *The New York Times* (24 September 2020). https://www.nytimes.com/2020/09/24/nyregion/regis-catholic-school-racism.html?smid=em-share (accessed 7 October 2020).

The Heidelberg Catechism. https://www.crcna.org/welcome/beliefs/confessions/heidelberg-catechism (accessed 6 October 2021).

– http://www.heidelberg-catechism.com/en/topics/conversion.html (accessed 6 October 2021).

Herbstein, Denis. *White Man, We Want to Talk to You*. New York: Africana Publishing, 1979.

Herrnstein, Richard J., and Charles Murray. *The Bell Curve*. New York: Free Press, 1996.

Hillier, Amy E. "Redlining and the Home Owners' Loan Corporation." *Journal of Urban History* 29 (2003): 394–420.

Hinze, Bradford E. "Ecclesial Repentance and the Demands of Dialogue." *Theological Studies* 61 (2020): 207–38.

hooks, bell. "'Madonna: Plantation Mistress or Soul Sister?' and 'Representations of Whiteness in the Black Imagination.'" In *Black Looks: Race and Representation*, 157–78. Boston: South End Press, 1992.

Hopkins, Dwight N. *Being Human: Race, Culture, and Religion*. Minneapolis: Fortress Press, 2005.

– *Heart and Head: Black Theology – Past, Present, and Future*. New York: Palgrave, 2002.

Hopkins, Gerald Manley. "As Kingfishers Catch Fire." https://www.poetryfoundation.org/poems/44389/as-kingfishers-catch-fire (accessed 6 October 2021).

Horan, Daniel P. "The Bishop's Letter Fails to Recognize that Racism Is a White Problem." *Faith Seeking Understanding* (20 February 2019). https://www.ncronline.org/news/opinion/faith-seeking-understanding/bishops-letter-fails-recognize-racism-white-problem (accessed 14 January 2021).

Howard, Stephanie. "The Black Perspective in Clinical Social Work." *Clinical Social Work Journal* 48 (2020): 435–42.

Institute for Healthcare Improvement Multimedia Team. "How to Reduce Implicit Bias." http://www.ihi.org/communities/blogs/how-to-reduce-implicit-bias (accessed 24 November 2020).

Jennings, Wille. *After Whiteness: An Education in Belonging*. Grand Rapids: Eerdmans, 2020.

– "Educating After Whiteness." *In Trust* (Fall 2020): 28–9.

Jeremias, Joachim. *New Testament Theology*. New York: Scribner's, 1971.

John Paul II (Pope). Post-Synodal Apostolic Exhortation, *Reconciliatio et Paenitentia* [Reconciliation and Penance] (4 December 1984). http://www.vatican.va/content/john-paul-ii/en/apost_exhortations/documents/hf_jp-ii_exh_02121984_reconciliatio-et-paenitentia.html (accessed 10 February 2021).

– *Sollicitudo rei Socialis* (30 December 1987). http://www.vatican.va/content/john-paul-ii/en/encyclicals/documents/hf_jp-ii_enc_30121987_sollicitudo-rei-socialis.html (accessed 10 February 2021).

Johnson, Walton. "Black Consciousness, Soweto, and Revolt in South Africa." *African Studies Review* 24 (1981): 4–8.

Jones, J., and R. Carter. "Racism and Racial Identity: Merging Realities." In *Impact of Racism on White Americans*, edited by B.P. Bowser and R.G. Hunt, 1–24. Newbury: Sage, 1996.

Jones, Robert P. "Racism Among White Christians is Higher than Among the Non-Religious. That's No Coincidence." *Think*. 27 July 2020. https://www.nbcnews.com/think/opinion/racism-among-white-christians-higher-among-nonreligious-s-no-coincidence-ncna1235045 (accessed 23 September 2020).

– *White Too Long: The Legacy of White Supremacy in American Christianity*. New York: Simon and Schuster, 2020.

Jones, Roxanne. "This is What it Looks Like When Toxic White Privilege is Left Unchecked." CNN (7 January 2021). https://www.cnn.com/2021/01/07/opinions/capitol-rioters-contrast-with-june-2020-black-lives-matter-jones/index.html (accessed 11 January 2021).

Karimi, Faith. "What Critical Race Theory Is – and Isn't." https://www.cnn.com/2020/10/01/us/critical-race-theory-explainer-trnd/index.html (accessed 1 October 2020).

Katz, D., and K. Braly. "Racial Prejudice and Racial Stereotypes." *Journal of Abnormal and Social Psychology* 30 (1935): 175–93.

Katz, Irwin. "Gordon Allport's *The Nature of Prejudice*." *Political Psychology* 12 (1991): 125–57.

Kee, Alistair. *The Rise and Demise of Black Theology*. Burlington, VT: Ashgate Publishing, 2006.

Kendall, Frances E. *Understanding White Privilege: Creating Pathways to Authentic Relationships Across Race*, 2nd ed. New York: Routledge, 2013.

Kerner Commission Report. https://belonging.berkeley.edu/1968-kerner-commission-report (accessed 18 September 2020).

Kinder, Donald R., and Timothy J. Ryan. "Prejudice and Politics Re-Examined: The Political Significance of Implicit Bias." *Political Science Research and Methods* 5 (2017): 241–59.

Kinder, Donald R., and David O. Sears. "Prejudice and Politics: Symbolic Racism Versus Racial Threats to the Good Life." *Journal of Personality and Social Psychology* 40 (1981): 414–31.

King, Martin Luther, Jr. "I Have A Dream." Address Delivered at the at the March on Washington for Jobs and Freedom" (23 August 1963). https://kinginstitute.stanford.edu/king-papers/documents/i-have-dream-address-delivered-march-washington-jobs-and-freedom (accessed 26 October 2020).

Kirwan Institute for the Study of Race and Ethnicity. "Understanding Implicit Bias." http://kirwaninstitute.osu.edu/research/understanding-implicit-bias/ (accessed 26 September 2020).

Kohlberg, Lawrence. "The Claim to Moral Adequacy of a Highest Stage of Moral Judgment." *Journal of Philosophy* 70 (1973): 630–46.

– *Essays on Moral Development*. Vol. 1, *The Philosophy of Moral Development: Moral Stages and the Idea of Justice*. San Francisco: Harper and Row, 1981.

Konnikova, Maria. "How Norms Change." *The New Yorker* (11 October 2017). https://www.newyorker.com/science/maria-konnikova/how-norms-change (accessed 12 October 2020).

Krysan, Maria. "Prejudice, Politics, and Public Opinion: Understanding the Sources of Racial Policy Attitudes." *Annual Review of Sociology* 26 (2000): 135–68.

Laubach, F., J. Goetzmann, and U. Becker. "Conversion, Penitence, Repentance, Proselyte." In *The New International Dictionary of New Testament Theology*, vol. 1, edited by C. Brown, 353–62. Exeter: Paternoster, 1975.

Lawrence, Charles R., III. "The Id, the Ego, and Equal Protection: Reckoning with Unconscious Racism." *Stanford Law Review* 39 (1987): 317–88.

– "Implicit Bias in the Age of Trump." *Harvard Law Review* 133 (2000): 2304–57.

Lawson, Steven. "What Is True Conversion?" https://www.ligonier.org/learn/articles/what-true-conversion (accessed 6 October 2022).

Leary, Joy Deruy. *Post Traumatic Slave Syndrome: America's Legacy of Enduring Injury and Healing*. Portland: Joy DeGruy Publications, 2005.

Lecky, W.E.H. *History of the Rise and Influence of the Spirit of Rationalism in Europe*, with an introduction by C. Wright Mills. New York: Georgie Braziller, 1982.

Leeming, David. "The White Problem." *Pen America* (8 January 2007). https://pen.org/the-white-problem/ (accessed 14 December 2020).

Lemert, Charles. "The Race of Time: Dubois and Reconstruction." *Boundary* 27 (October 2000): 215–48.

Leonard, David J. *Playing While White: Privilege and Power on and off the Field*. Seattle: University of Washington Press, 2017.

Leonardo, Zeus. "The Color of Supremacy: Beyond the Discourse of 'White Privilege.'" *Educational Philosophy and Theory* 36 (2004): 137–52.

Lett, Brenda. "Melanin, White Privilege and the Damage Wrought by the Lie." *Business NH Magazine* (28 December 2017). https://www.businessnhmagazine.com/article/melaninampcomma-white-privilege-and-the-damage-wrought-by-the-lie.

Lewis, Amanda E. "There is No 'Race' in the Schoolyard: Color-blind Ideology in an (Almost) All white School." *American Educational Research Journal* 38 (2001): 781–811.

Liddy, Richard M. *Startling Strangeness: Reading Lonergan's Insight*. Lanham: University Press of America, 2007.

Limbong, Andrew. "Microaggressions Are a Big Deal: How to Talk Them Out and When to Walk Away" (9 June 2020). https://www.npr.org/2020/06/08/872371063/microaggressions-are-a-big-deal-how-to-talk-them-out-and-when-to-walk-away (accessed 10 October 2020).

Lonergan, Bernard. "The Absence of God in Modern Culture." In *Collected Works of Bernard Lonergan*. Vol. 13, *A Second Collection*, edited by Robert M. Doran and John D. Dadosky, 86–98. Toronto: University of Toronto Press, 2016.

– "Belief: Today's Issue." In *Collected Works of Bernard Lonergan*. Vol. 13, *A Second Collection*, edited by Robert M. Doran and John D. Dadosky, 75–85. Toronto: University of Toronto Press, 2016.

– *Collected Works of Bernard Lonergan*. Vol. 4, *Collection*, edited by Frederick E. Crowe and Robert M. Doran. Toronto: University of Toronto Press, 2005.

– *Collected Works of Bernard Lonergan*. Vol. 3, *Insight: A Study of Human Understanding*, edited by Frederick E. Crowe and Robert M. Doran. Toronto: University of Toronto Press, 1997.

– *Collected Works of Bernard Lonergan*. Vol. 14, *Method in Theology*, edited by Robert M. Doran and John D. Dadosky. Toronto: University of Toronto Press, 2017.

– *Collected Works of Bernard Lonergan*. Vol. 7, *On the Ontological and Psychological Constitution of Christ* [De Constitutione Christi Ontologica et Psychologica], translated by Michael G. Shield. Toronto: University of Toronto Press, 2002.

– *Collected Works of Bernard Lonergan*. Vol.10, *Topics in Education: The Cincinnati Lectures of 1959 on the Philosophy of Education*, edited by Robert M. Doran and Frederick E. Crowe. Toronto: University of Toronto Press, 2000.

– *Collected Works of Bernard Lonergan*. Vol.2, *Verbum: Word and Idea in Aquinas*. Edited by Frederick E. Crowe and Robert M. Doran. Toronto: University of Toronto Press, 1997.

– "The Dehellenization of Dogma," In *Collected Works of Bernard Lonergan*. Vol. 13, *A Second Collection*, edited by Robert M. Doran and John D. Dadosky, 11–30. Toronto: University of Toronto Press, 2016.
– "Dimension of Meaning." In *Collected Works of Bernard Lonergan*. Vol. 4, *Collection*, edited by Frederick E. Crowe and Robert M. Doran, 232–45. Toronto: University of Toronto Press, 2005.
– "Human Consciousness." In *Collected Works of Bernard Lonergan*. Vol.7, *On the Ontological and Psychological Constitution of Christ*, translated by Michael G. Shields, 157–90. Toronto: University of Toronto Press, 2002.
– "An Interview with Fr. Bernard Lonergan, S.J." In *Collected Works of Bernard Lonergan*. Vol. 13, *A Second Collection*, edited by Robert M. Doran and John D. Dadosky, 176–94. Toronto: University of Toronto Press, 2016.
– "The Origins of Christian Realism (1972)." In *Collected Works of Bernard Lonergan*. Vol. 13, *A Second Collection*, edited by Robert M. Doran and John D. Dadosky, 202–20. Toronto: University of Toronto Press, 2016.
– "Questionnaire on Philosophy: Response." In *Collected Works of Bernard Lonergan*. Vol. 17, *Philosophical and Theological Papers: 1965–1980*, edited by Robert C. Croken and Robert M. Doran, 352–83. Toronto: University of Toronto Press, 2004.
– "The Role of the Catholic University in the Modern World." In *Collected Works of Bernard Lonergan*. Vol.4, *Collection*, edited by Frederick E. Crowe and Robert M. Doran, 108–13. Toronto: University of Toronto Press, 2005.
– "The Subject." In *Collected Works of Bernard Lonergan*. Vol. 13, *A Second Collection*, edited by Robert M. Doran and John D. Dadosky, 60–74. Toronto: University of Toronto Press, 2016.
– "Theology and Man's Future." In *Collected Works of Bernard Lonergan*. Vol. 13, *A Second Collection*, edited by Robert M. Doran and John D. Dadosky, 114–26. Toronto: University of Toronto Press, 2016.
– "The Transition from a Classicist Worldview to Historical Mindedness." In *Collected Works of Bernard Lonergan*. Vol. 13, *A Second Collection*, edited by Robert M. Doran and John D. Dadosky, 3–10. Toronto: University of Toronto Press, 2016.
– *The Triune God: Systematics*. Toronto: University of Toronto Press, 2007.
– "Unity and Plurality: The Coherence of Christian Truth." In *A Third Collection: Papers by Bernard J.F. Lonergan, S.J.*, edited by Frederick E. Crowe, SJ, 239–50. New York: Paulist Press, 1985.
– *The Way to Nicea: The Dialectical Development of Trinitarian Theology*. Translated from the Latin by Conn O'Donovan. London: Darton, Longman, and Todd, 1976.
Lundberg-Love, Paula, Kevin L. Nadal, and Michele Paludi. *Women and Mental Disorders*. Westport: Praeger Publishing, 2011.
Maslow, Abraham. *Towards a Psychology of Being*. Princeton: D. Van Nostrand Company, 1962.

Mauer, Marc. "Addressing Racial Disparities in Incarceration." *The Prison Journal Supplement* 9 (2011): 875–1015.

Mayberry, George. "George Mayberry's 1952 Review of Ralph Ellison's *Invisible Man*." *The New Republic* (25 September 2013). https://newrepublic.com/article/114842/george-mayberry-ralph-ellison-invisible-man#:~:text=To%20paraphrase%20Graham%20Greene's%20already,happens%20to%20be%20a%20Negro.&text=Ellison's%2C%20race (accessed 5 December 2020).

McConohay, J.B. "Modern Racism, Ambivalence, and the Modern Racism Scale." In *Prejudice, Discrimination, and Racism*, edited by J.F. Dovidio and S.L. Gaertner, 91–126. Orlando: Academic Press, 1986.

McIntosh, Peggy. "White Privilege." In *White Privilege: Essential Readings on the Other Side of Racism*, edited by Paula S. Rothenberg, 151–5. New York: Worth Publishers, 2016.

– "White Privilege: Unpacking the Invisible Knapsack." *Peace and Freedom* (July–August, 1989), 10-12.

McLaughlin, Eliott C. "On These 9 Days, Police in DC Arrested More People Than They Did During the Capitol Siege." CNN (12 January 2021). https://www.cnn.com/2021/01/11/us/dc-police-previous-protests-capitol/index.html (accessed 12 January 2021).

Melton, McKinley E. "Conversion Calls for Confrontation: Facing the Old to Become New in the Work of James Baldwin." In *James Baldwin: Challenging Authors*, edited by A. Scott Henderson and P.L. Thomas, 8–27. Boston: Sense Publishers, 2014.

Memmi, Albert. *Ce Que Je Crois*. Paris: Grasset, 1985.

– *The Colonizer and the Colonized*. Translated by Howard Greenfeld. Boston: Beacon Press, 1991.

Moore, Sebastian. "Four Steps Towards Making Sense of Theology." *The Downside Review* 3 (1993): 79–100.

Morgan, Jason. "The New Structure of Sin: Mankind in the Age of Surveillance Capitalism." *The Human Life Review* 42 (2020): 42–9.

Motlhabi, Mokgethi. "The Problem of Ethical Method in Black Theology." *Black Theology* 2 (2004): 57–72.

Mowry, Matthew J. "How White Privilege is Holding Back NH." *Business NH Magazine* (October 2017): 57–60.

Mullen, Bill V. *James Baldwin: Living in Fire*. London: Pluto Press, 2019.

Nadal, Kevin L. *Microaggressions and Traumatic Stress*. Philadelphia: American Philosophical Association, 2018.

– *Queering Law and Order: LGBTQ Communities and the Criminal Justice System*. Lanham: Lexington Books, 2020.

– *That's So Gay! Microaggressions and the Lesbian, Gay, Bisexual, and Transgender Community*. Philadelphia: American Psychological Association, 2013.

Naureckas, Jim. "Racism Resurgent: How Media Let the Bell Curve's Pseudo-Science Define the Agenda on Race." *Fairness and Accuracy in Reporting* (1 January 1995).

Nellis, Ashley. "The Color of Justice: Racial and Ethnic Disparity in State Prisons." https://www.sentencingproject.org/publications/color-of-justice-racial-and-ethnic-disparity-in-state-prisons/ (accessed 2 December 2020).

Nicolaou, Elena. "Michelle Obama Reflects on 'Wreckage' at the U.S. Capitol: 'I Hurt for Our Country.'" *The Oprah Magazine* (7 January 2021). https://www.oprahmag.com/about/a35154576/michelle-obama-capitol-response/ (accessed 11 January 2021).

Nilson, Jon. "Confessions of a White Catholic Racist Theologian." In *Interrupting White Privilege: Catholic Theologians Break the Silence*, edited by Laurie M. Cassidy and Alexander Mikulich, 15–39. Maryknoll: Orbis Books, 2007.

Norton, Michael I., and Samuel R. Sommers. "Whites See Racism as a Zero-Sum Game that They are Now Losing." *Perspectives on Psychological Science* 6 (2011): 215–18.

Norton, Michael I., et al. "Color Blindness and Interracial Interaction: Playing the Political Correctness Game." *Perspectives on Psychological Science* 17 (2006): 949–53.

Orji, Cyril. "Are There Stages of Meaning in African Theology?" *Toronto Journal of Theology* 32 (2016): 71–93.

– "A Reappropriation of the Joesph Story in Genesis 39 and Surah 12 for Contemporary Race-Discourse." *Horizons* 51 (2024), 1–32.

– *A Semiotic Approach to the Theology of Inculturation*. Eugene: Pickwick, 2015.

– *Unmasking the African Ghost: Theology, Politics, and the Nightmare of Failed States*. Minneapolis: Fortress Press, 2022.

Osta, Kathleen, and Hugh Vasquez. "Don't Talk About Implicit Bias Without Talking about Structural Racism." *National Equity Project* (13 June 2019). https://medium.com/national-equity-project/implicit-bias-structural-racism-6c52cf0f4a92 (accessed 12 October 2020).

Palmer, Richard E. *Hermeneutics: Interpretation Theory in Schleiermacher, Dilthey, Heidegger, and Gadamer*. Evanston: Northwestern University Press, 1969.

Parfait, Claire. "Rewriting History: The Publication of W.E.B. Dubois' *Black Reconstruction in America* (1935)." *Book History* 12 (2009): 266–94.

Paris, Peter J. "Katie Canon's Non-Canonical Canon." *Interpretation: A Journal of Bible and Theology* 74 (2020): 17–22.

Parker, Kim, Juliana Menasce, and Monica Anderson. "Amid Protests, Majorities Across Racial and Ethnic Groups Express Support for the Black Lives Matter Movement." *Pew Research Center* (12 June 2020). https://www.pewresearch.org/social-trends/2020/06/12/amid-protests-majorities-across-racial-and-ethnic-groups-express-support-for-the-black-lives-matter

-movement/#most-americans-say-theyve-had-conversations-about-race-or-racial-equality-in-the-last-month (accessed 22 September 2021).

Pavlic, Ed. *Who Can Afford to Improvise: James Baldwin and Black Music, the Lyric and the Listeners*. New York: Fordham University Press, 2016.

PBS Video. https://www.pbs.org/independentlens/videos/i-am-not-your-negro/ (accessed 6 December 2020).

Pen America. "'James Baldwin Didn't Have to Go Out and Get Votes': Obama Reflects On Race, Dialogue, and Disinformation in Pen America Interview." *Pen America* (5 December 2020). https://pen.org/press-release/obama-baldwin-race-disinformation/ (accessed 14 December 2020).

Pramuk, Christopher. *Hope Sings, So Beautiful: Graced Encounters Across the Color Line*. Collegeville: Liturgical Press, 2013.

Pratto, Felicia, et. al. "Social Dominance Orientation: A Personality Variable Predicting Social and Political Attitudes." *Journal of Personality and Social Psychology* 67 (1994): 741–63.

PRRI 2018 Survey. https://www.prri.org/research/partisan-polarization-dominates-trump-era-findings-from-the-2018-american-values-survey/ (accessed 23 September 2020).

Reins, Frances V. "Is the Benign Really Harmless? Deconstructing Some 'Benign' Manifestations of Operationalized White Privilege." In *White Reign: Deploying Whiteness in America*, edited by Joe L. Kincheloe and Shirley R. Steinberg, 77–101. New York: Palgrave, 2000.

Ricoeur, Paul. *The Conflict of Interpretations: Essays in Hermeneutics*. Edited by Don Ihde. Evanston: Northwestern University Press, 1974.

Roberts, Deotis J. *A Black Political Theology*. Philadelphia: Westminster Press, 1974.

– *Bonhoeffer and King: Speaking Truth to Power*. Louisville: Westminster Press, 2005.

– *Liberation and Reconciliation: A Black Theology*. Louisville: Westminster Press, 1971.

– *Liberation and Reconciliation: A Black Theology*, Second Edition. Louisville: Westminster John Knox Press, 2005.

– "Liberation Theologies: A Critical Essay." *The Journal of the Interdenominational Theological Center* 36 (2010): 45–51.

Ross, Howard. *Everyday Bias: Identifying and Navigating Unconscious Judgments in Our Daily Lives*. Lanham: Rowman and Littlefield, 2020.

Rothstein, Richard. *The Color of Law: A Forgotten History of How Our Government Segregated America*. New York: Liveright Publishing, 2017.

Ruether, Rosemary Radford. "Black Women and Feminism: The U.S. and South African Contexts." In James Cone, *A Black Theology of Liberation*, Twentieth Anniversary Edition, 174–84.

Saini, Angela. *Superior: The Return of Race Science*. Boston: Beacon Press, 2019.

Sanneh, Kelefa. "Project Trinity: The Perilous Mission of Obama's Church." *The New Yorker* (31 March 2008). https://www.newyorker.com/magazine/2008/04/07/project-trinity (accessed 22 October 2020).

Schlueter, Nathan W. *One Dream or Two: Justice in America and in the Thought of Martin Luther King, Jr.* Lanham: Lexington Books, 2002.

Schwarz, Hans. *Theology in a Global Context: The Last Two Hundred Years*. Grand Rapids: Eerdmans, 2005.

Sears. S.O. "Symbolic Racism." In *Eliminating Racism: Profiles in Controversy*, edited by P.A. Katz and D.A. Taylor, 53–84. New York: Plenum. 1988.

Senghor, Leopold. *The Foundations of "Africanité."* Paris: Présence Africaine, 1971.

The Sentencing Project Report. "Report to the United Nations on Racial Disparities in the U.S. Criminal Justice System" (19 April 2018). https://www.sentencingproject.org/publications/un-report-on-racial-disparities/ (accessed 2 December 2020).

Shelton, Kimber, and Edward A. Delgado-Romero. "Sexual Orientation Microaggressions: The Experience of Lesbian, Gay, Bisexual, and Queer Clients in Psychotherapy." *Journal of Counseling Psychology* 58 (2011): 210–21.

Shen, Megan J., and Jordan P. Labouff. "More Than Political Ideology: Subtle Racial Prejudice as a Predictor of Opposition to Universal Health Care Among U.S. Citizens." *Journal of Social and Political Psychology* 4 (2016): 493–520.

Shriver, Donald. *Honest Patriots: Loving a Country Enough to Remember Its Misdeeds*. New York: Oxford, 2005.

– *An Ethic for Enemies: Forgiveness in Politics*. New York: Oxford University Press, 1995.

Sidanius, Jim, and Felicia Pratto. *Social Dominance: An Intergroup Theory of Social Hierarchy and Oppression*. Cambridge: Cambridge University Press, 2001.

Siegel, Eric. "The Real Problem with Charles Murray and the Bell Curve." *Scientific American* (12 April 2017). https://blogs.scientificamerican.com/voices/the-real-problem-with-charles-murray-and-the-bell-curve/ (accessed 7 December 2020).

Slang Dictionary. https://www.dictionary.com/e/slang/karen/ (accessed 31 August 2020).

Smith, Clint. "Ralph Ellison's 'Invisible Man' As a Parable of Our Time." *The New Yorker* (4 December 2016). https://www.newyorker.com/books/page-turner/ralph-ellisons-invisible-man-as-a-parable-of-our-time (accessed 29 December 2020).

Solorzano, D., M. Ceja, and T. Yosso. "Critical Race Theory, Racial Microaggressions, and Campus Racial Climate: The Experiences of African American College Students." *The Journal of Negro Education* 69 (2000): 60–73

Solorzano, D., and T. Yosso. "Conceptualizing a Critical Race Theory in Sociology." *The Blackwell Companion to Social Inequalities* (2005): 117–46.

The Southern Manifesto of 1956. https://history.house.gov/Historical-Highlights/1951-2000/The-Southern-Manifesto-of-1956/ (accessed 11 November 2020).

Souza de Lima, Thiago J., et al. "Black People are Convicted More for being Black than for being Poor: The Role of Social Norms and Cultural Prejudice on Biased Racial Judgments." *Plus One* (20 September 2019), 1–24. https://journals.plos.org/plosone/article/file?id=10.1371/journal.pone.0222874&type=printable (accessed 22 September 2020).

Stoeber, Michael. *Reclaiming Theodicy: Reflections on Suffering, Compassion and Spiritual Transformation*. New York: Palgrave McMillan, 2002.

Sue, Derald W. "The Invisible Whiteness of Being: Whiteness, White Supremacy, White Privilege, and Racism." In *White Privilege: Essential Readings on the Other Side of Racism*, edited by Paula S. Rothenberg, 19–28. New York: Worth Publishers, 2016.

– *Microaggressions and Marginality: Manifestation, Dynamics, and Impact*. New York: Wiley, 2010.

– *Microaggressions in Everyday Life: Race, Gender, and Sexual Orientation*. Hoboken: Wiley, 2010.

– "Racial Microaggressions in Everyday Life: Is Subtle Bias Harmless?" *Psychology Today* (5 October 2010). https://www.psychologytoday.com/us/blog/microaggressions-in-everyday-life/201010/racial-microaggressions-in-everyday-life (accessed 4 October 2021).

Sue, Derald Wing, et al. "Disarming Racial Microaggressions: Microintervention Strategies for Targets, White Allies, and Bystanders." *American Psychologist* 74 (2019): 128–42.

Sue, Derald Wing, et al. *Microintervention Strategies: What You Can Do To Disarm and Dismantle Individual and Systemic Racism and Bias*. Hoboken: Wiley, 2021.

Sue, D.W., and C.M. Capodilupo. "Racial, Gender, and Sexual Orientation Microaggressions: Implication for Counseling and Psychotherapy." In *Counseling the culturally diverse: Theory and practice*, 5th edition, edited by D.W. Sue and D. Sue, 105–30. Hoboken: Wiley, 2008.

Sue, D.W., et al. "Racial microaggressions in Everyday Life: Implications for Clinical Practice." *American Psychologist* 62 (2007): 271–86.

Sullaway, M., and E. Dunbar. "Clinical Manifestations of Prejudice in Psychotherapy: Toward a Strategy of Assessment and Treatment." *Clinical Psychology: Science and Practice* 3 (1996): 296–309.

Sullivan, Nikki. *A Critical Introduction to Queer Theory*. New York: New York University Press, 2003.

Taylor, E., et al., eds. *Foundations of Critical Race Theory in Education*, 2nd edition. New York: Routledge, 2016.

Taylor, S.E. *Health Psychology*, 9th edition. Boston: McGraw Hill, 2015.

Teranishi, Robert T. "Asian Pacific Americans and Critical Race Theory: An Examination of School Racial Climate." *Equity and Excellence in Education* 35 (2002): 144–54.

Thiele, Leslie Paul. "Reading Nietzsche and Foucault: A Hermeneutic of Suspicion." *The American Political Science Review* 85 (1991): 581–92.

Thomas, P.L. "Introduction." In *James Baldwin: Challenging Authors*, edited by A. Scott Henderson and P.L. Thomas, 1–7. Boston: Sense Publishers, 2014.

Thurstone, L.L. "The Measurement of Attitudes." *Journal of Abnormal and Social Psychology* 26 (1931): 249–69.

Thurstone, L.L., and E.J. Chave. *The Measurement of Attitude*. Chicago: University of Chicago Press, 1929.

Torino, Gina C., et al. *Microaggression Theory: Influence and Implications*. Hoboken: John Wiley and Sons, 2019.

Tracy, David. *The Analogical Imagination: Christian Theology and the Culture of Pluralism*. New York: Crossroad, 1981.

Trevion, Javier A., Michelle A. Harris, and Derron Wallace. "What's So Critical about Critical Race Theory?" *Contemporary Justice Review* 11 (2008): 7–10.

The Urban Dictionary. https://www.urbandictionary.com/define.php?term=Karen (accessed 31 August 2020).

Urrestarazu, Jones E. "The Other Pandemic: Systemic Racism and Its Consequences." *European Network of Quality Bodies* (8 June 2020). https://equineteurope.org/2020/the-other-pandemic-systemic-racism-and-its-consequences/ (accessed 13 October 2020).

USCCB. "Open Wide Our Hearts: The Enduring Call to Love, A Pastoral Letter Against Racism" (November 2018). https://www.usccb.org/issues-and-action/human-life-and-dignity/racism/upload/open-wide-our-hearts.pdf (accessed 9 October 2020).

– "Brothers and Sisters to Us" (1979). https://www.usccb.org/committees/african-american-affairs/brothers-and-sisters-us (accessed 14 January 2021).

Uzukwu, Elochukwu. *A Listening Church: Autonomy and Communion in African Churches*. Maryknoll: Orbis, 1996.

van den Berghe, Pierre L. *Race and Racism: A Comparative Perspective*. New York: Wiley, 1967.

Vatican. "Brief of the High Pontiff Gregory XVI." http://www.vatican.va/content/gregorius-xvi/it/documents/breve-in-supremo-apostolatus-fastigio-3-dicembre-1839.html (accessed 8 October 2020).

Walker, Alice. *In Search of Our Mother's Gardens*. New York: Harcourt, Brace, Jovanovich, 1983.

Wallis, Jim. "America's Original Sin: The Legacy of White Racism." *Cross Currents* 57 (2000): 197–202.

– *America's Original Sin: Racism, White Privilege, and the Bridge to a New America*. Grand Rapids: Brazos Press, 2016.

– *The Call to Conversion: Why Faith Is Always Personal But Never Private*. San Francisco: Harper and Row, 1981.

Warburton, Moira. "Canadian Catholic Bishops Apologize for Role in Indigenous Residential Schools." *Yahoo News* (Friday 24 September 2021). https://www.yahoo.com/news/canadian-catholic-bishops-apologize-role-002418531.html (accessed 1 October 2021).

Weigel, George. "What 'Peace' Means Today." https://www.nationalreview.com/2016/10/what-peace-means-moral-truth-starting-point/ (accessed 7 October 2020).

Wesley, John. *The New Birth John Wesley Sermons* [The Bicentennial Edition] vols. 1–4. Edited by Albert C. Outler. Nashville: Abingdon Press, 1984.

Williams, Delores S. *Sisters in the Wilderness: The Challenge of Womanist God-Talk*. Maryknoll: Orbis, 1993.

Williams, D.R., and S.A. Mohammed. "Racism and Health I: Pathways and Scientific Evidence." *American Behavioral Scientist* (2013): 1–22.

Index